W9-DEO-030

TEACHERS AND TEACHER EDUCATION IN DEVELOPING COUNTRIES
Issues in Planning, Management and Training

Teachers and Teacher Education in Developing Countries

LINDA A. DOVE

CROOM HELM
London • Sydney • Dover, New Hampshire

© 1986 Linda Dove
Croom Helm Ltd, Provident House, Burrell Row,
Beckenham, Kent, BR3 1AT
Croom Helm Australia Pty Ltd, Suite 4, 6th Floor,
64-76 Kippax Street, Surry Hills, NSW 2010, Australia

British Library Cataloguing in Publication Data

Dove, Linda
    Teachers and teacher education in
    developing countries.
    1. Teachers, Training of — Developing
    countries
    I. Title
    370'.7'1091724   LB1727.D44
    ISBN 0-7099-0886-5

Croom Helm, 27 South Main Street,
Wolfeboro, New Hampshire 03894-2069, USA

Library of Congress Cataloging in Publication Data

Dove, Linda A.
    Teachers and teacher education in developing
countries.

    Bibliography: p.
    Includes index.
    1. Teachers–developing countries–history.
2. Teachers–training of–developing countries–history.
3. Teachers and community–developing countries–
history. I. Title.
LB2832.4.D44D68   1986   370'.7'1091724   86-6334
ISBN 0-7099-0886-5

Printed and bound in Great Britain by Mackays of Chatham Ltd, Kent

CONTENTS

TABLES AND FIGURES

ACKNOWLEDGEMENTS

The theme of this book was inspired mainly by my student colleagues from Africa, Asia and Latin America who have studied in the Department of Education in Developing Countries at the University of London Institute of Education. Over the last decade they have kept me alive to the issues of educational development and teacher training with which they grapple in their daily working lives in ministries of education, universities, colleges and schools. It would be impossible to mention by name all the ministry officials and educators in the many countries where I have had the privilege of working but I thank them all for helping me gain experience of their countries' education systems. In particular, I wish to record the invaluable experience which my colleagues in Bangladesh afforded me during our efforts together to launch the universal primary education UPE programme in the 1980s. My thanks are due also to my colleagues at the University of London Institute of Education for their patience with me during the preparation of this study. In particular, my gratitude goes to Siti Ahmed, Mark Bray, Boniface Chivore, Trevor Coombe, Usman Kagbo, John Lauglo, Fazlur Moorad, Tony Somerset and Carew Treffgarne for their helpful comments on sections of the draft. I owe many insights to them but responsibility for the final version is, of course, mine. Without the aid of the Institute of Education Library staff, the bibliography would not have been compiled. I thank, in particular, Diana Guthrie, Peter Moss, and Anne Peters. Finally, and above all, I record my appreciation to my husband, Raymond, without whose friendship and support this study would not have been completed.

INTRODUCTION

This book draws together much of the experience, thinking and research which has accumulated in recent years about the lives and work of schoolteachers in developing countries. Many millions of words have been written about contemporary educational planning and management for the age of mass education, but very few, relatively speaking, about the roles of teachers in schools and society. Compared with planners and managers in ministries of education, schoolteachers, who spend their working days in classrooms with young learners, do jobs which are almost invisible to the community at large. This invisibility may partly explain the lack of serious study and research into their work and relationships with society, despite the fact that, in contemporary societies, they are arguably the most numerous and widely dispersed occupational group paid largely from the public purse.

The intention in the following pages is to make the teachers more visible. Readers are invited to explore the theme from a variety of perspectives. In Part One, those interested in the historical, sociological and professional context of schoolteaching may discover who the teachers are, where they come from, what society expects from them, and what problems they face as members of the community. In Part Two, readers interested in planning and management issues are invited to concentrate on the implications of planning and management practices for the development of national teaching professions. They are asked to consider, for instance, what are the implications of plans to build more schools for the training and supply of teachers and what factors must be considered in determining sound policies for teacher recruitment and posting. Part Three turns to the vitally important area of teacher education and training. This should interest those who wish to reflect on how contemporary training systems evolved historically and those who are, perhaps, critical of many current training programmes. Part Three also attempts a survey of some of the more recent innovations in teacher training in a variety of countries where the expanding and changing needs of school systems make conventional approaches inappropriate.

But the reader should not be misled into thinking that this is a 'how to do it' volume of tips and techniques for planning, administration or teacher training. Rather, it is addressed to all those who are concerned that youth should have the very best teachers that society can produce. Hopefully, it is a book to which policy makers, planners, managers, teacher trainers and, indeed, teachers themselves, will turn when they wish to stand aside from technical tasks to reflect on the whys and wherefores of what they are doing.

The focus of the book is on issues and problems common, particularly, to developing countries in Africa, Asia and Latin America, which are attempting to expand and upgrade their schools. These are countries where population growth and illiteracy are high and educational needs urgent. Though a high proportion of their national budgets is devoted to education, planning and management structures are relatively weak and many of their teachers are under-educated or untrained. They are, generally speaking, countries which have few or unexploited natural resources, low levels of industrialisation and human resource development or have only recently become independent; national incomes are relatively low and they are dependent for much of their educational development on external aid in one form or another.

The book takes examples and case studies from all over the developing world to illustrate general points. However, for every general point there is always the exceptional situation. No one is more aware than the author that the term 'developing country' is an inadequate and unsatisfactory label for all the varied contexts and conditions in which teachers operate, and that the issues discussed have relevance also in many industrialised, 'developed' countries. The only justification, then, for utilising the concept of 'developing countries' here is that many analyses of teachers, their origins, their social status, their professional concerns and their technical tasks, have been carried out in the context of the resource-rich countries of North

2

America and Europe and very few, as stated above, in countries which operate in very much more difficult, financial, administrative and physical conditions and in very different social and cultural contexts.

If we accepted at face value some of the more extravagant claims made for personal computers, a book about teachers would not be needed. For, at the press of a keyboard and with the magic of the micro-chip, we could all teach ourselves everything we wanted to know. Teachers would be dispensable. Because teachers are inevitably costly, often ill-equipped and sometimes difficult to control, planners and managers in developing and developed countries alike, have welcomed alternative technologies which promise to eliminate or reduce the need for teachers. They may be simple self-instructional programmed materials or sophisticated radio, television-satellite or computer-assisted techniques. Some of these innovations have been more successful than others but none has proved to be the panacea which had been anticipated for the inadequacies of conventional classroom teaching and learning. Significantly here, an important lesson of experience has been that human interaction between teacher and learner is invaluable for motivation in learning. In plain words, teachers are still vital elements in modern education systems.

Classroom teachers are, perhaps, all the more indispensable in the context of developing countries. In the rural areas, at least, electric points for televisions and computers are often few and far between and sophisticated machinery is costly and difficult to maintain. Skilled personnel to manage sophisticated distance teaching programmes and, importantly, to devise appropriate texts, are also scarce. All this is not to suggest that innovatory technologies in developing countries should not be attempted. Indeed, changes must come about if every child is to receive a sound education. Rather, it is to argue that, at least for the foreseeable future, teachers are not only a vital element in educational provision but possibly also the most important element in educational change. Without their support even the most promising plans for the development of schools must founder.

It is, therefore, for these reasons and others, as the reader will discover in the pages which follow, that this book concentrates on clarifying some of the factors which contribute to the contemporary status of teachers as professionals in schools and society. Unless those who plan and manage

educational development pay attention to some of the
dynamics of teachers' attitudes and behaviour and
their response to proposals for educational change,
innovations are unlikely to succeed. Similarly, this
book argues strongly for many more resources and much
more serious effort to be given to teacher education
and training. Society has high expectations of
teachers and demands of them ever more challenging
standards of performance. It is only good sense,
therefore, to invest more heavily in training them to
do their vitally important work efficiently and well.

Part One

TEACHERS, SOCIETY AND SCHOOLS

Chapter One

TEACHERS PAST AND PRESENT

Most of us have vivid memories from our schooldays of teachers who had a formative influence on us for good or bad. We recall in detail their dress and appearance, their teaching skills, their discipline and the values to which they exposed us. As parents we tend to use the standards set by the best teachers of our own schooldays to judge those who teach our children. We note the vast changes in the curriculum which teachers today have to master. We comment, with approval or disapproval, on the unfamiliar teaching methods which many teachers use and on changes which have taken place in their social status, their professional conduct and attitudes.

Our ideas about teachers tend to be limited by our experience and that of our children and grandchildren: two or three generations at the most. Yet there is no such person as the typical teacher. Teachers' roles, their status in society, the work they do and the values they represent are related in complex ways to the settings in which they operate. In this chapter we remind ourselves of some of the historical contexts in which teachers, particularly schoolteachers, have operated. This will provide a perspective from which to examine, in Chapter Two, some of the cultural, socio-economic and political factors, past and present, which affect their work and status in society.

EVERY ADULT A TEACHER

Parents, adult relatives, skilled craftspeople and community elders have always participated in the socialisation, education and training of youth. In an informal but by no means haphazard way, teaching and learning, from one generation to the next, has always gone on, even though there may have been no books, timetables or school walls. Teaching through folklore, poetry, drama and dance, by precept and example, through training, reward and punishment has continued to be the way in which societies have perpetuated their knowledge, skills and customs.

President Julius Nyerere of Tanzania describes some features of informal teaching and learning in his Education for Self Reliance (1967:2). He sets out his ideas about how the modern system of education for independent Tanzania should evolve on the basis of indigenous values.

> The fact that pre-colonial Africa did not have 'schools' - except for short periods of initiation in some tribes - did not mean that the children were not educated. They learned by living and doing. In the homes and on the farms they were taught the skills of society and the behaviour expected of its members. They learned the kind of grasses which were suitable for which purposes, the work which had to be done on the crops, or the care which had to be given to animals, by joining with their elders in this work. They learned the tribal history, and the tribe's relationship with other tribes and with the spirits, by listening to the stories of the elders. Through these means and by the custom of sharing to which young people were taught to conform, the values of society were transmitted. Education was thus 'informal'; every adult was a teacher to a greater or lesser degree.

The maxim, 'every adult is a teacher' is one which has been adopted in a number of countries in recent times. Governments, from Ethiopia and Somalia to Iran and Thailand, have set up voluntary or national service schemes in attempts to spread literacy and basic education as quickly and inexpensively as possible. Tanzania itself, in the early days of independence utilised students from the university in this way in ujamaa (self reliance) villages. 'Each one teach one' programmes rely on educated people to help others less privileged along the path to education. Such 'teachers' are playing a role in social development and change and are counted as an important educational resource by planners.

Suppose that a learned elder is describing teaching and learning in his community in the time of his grandfather. He would emphasise how adults would choose to teach those things which were useful and relevant to the daily lives of the young. He would explain that most people taught by example or by having children try out new skills. He would mention the community's concern to pass on to its children not only instrumental knowledge but also an appreciation of aesthetic, moral and spiritual dimensions of life. Such an account, emphasising relevance, learning-from-doing and a balanced, general education, has a contemporary tone. It suggests, correctly, that teachers, yesterday as today, are centrally concerned with selecting from a cultural inheritance those traditions which society sees as useful and worthwhile to pass from generation to generation.

But the reader should beware of being misled by the generalisations which exist in the literature about education in such out-of-school settings. To take just a few examples from the case of sub-Saharan Africa. Bagunwa (1975) idealises the way in which informal teaching by adults inculcated in the young a respect for service to the community and of learning through practical experience. He suggests that schoolteachers, in contrast, imported contrary values of individualism and competition into previously harmonious African societies and substituted practical knowledge by theoretical 'school knowledge'. Similarly, Dzobo (1975) claims that certain values, such as the solidarity of the family and the supremacy of the community over the individual were universally taught by one generation to the next. Blakemore and Cooksey (1980:11-13) base their explanation for the perpetuation of informal, out-of-school education in pre-Colonial African societies on the thesis that such societies were somehow static and 'simple' with undifferentiated occupational structures based on subsistence agriculture and few external relationships.

Such reasoning ignores the social realities of what were, in fact, diverse and complex societies. As we know, some communities were settled agricultural-ists, others nomadic hunters, some were traders or craftspeople. Some ruled great empires. Some had hereditary chiefs, others managed their affairs by consensus politics. This social diversity was reflected also in methods of education (Moumouni 1968; Akinpelu 1974; Yoloye 1983). Whilst all adults had a part to play in socialising youth into the customs of the community, specialists and experts had responsibility for imparting a broad generalisable education and training in occupational skills. For

9

instance, when socialising Ibo youth into their cultural inheritance, adults emphasised the values of individualism and competition (Nwa-Chil 1973). A general education amongst the Akan of Ghana included religion, magic and empirical knowledge at a level appropriate to the age-sets of the youth (Bartels 1975). Amongst the Mende of Sierra Leone, specialist teachers initiated boys and girls into adulthood through a period of training under the auspices of the secret <u>Poro</u> and <u>Bundu</u> societies (Forde 1975). In areas of the continent as far apart as Yorubaland and Sudan, skilled members of trade or craft guilds trained young people in specific occupational skills (Callaway 1965:61-88; Peil 1977:91).

A great deal more research is needed into the precise nature of teaching and learning in out-of-school settings. This would help to dispel stereotypes which suggest that, before the advent of formal school systems, education and training were somehow simple processes, fit only for 'simple societies'. It would also throw more light on just how much of what we take for granted as an intrinsic part of modern education, its teaching methods and curricula, is in fact an inheritance from earlier traditions. This again would help us to understand better how educational change comes about.

But all of this, though of great importance, would have to be the subject of another book. The point to be emphasised here is that educational planners in developing countries should, perhaps, look afresh at the idea of 'every adult a teacher'; that every adult has something of value to teach the next generation. Furthermore, society should consider every <u>educated</u> adult as a privileged person who might be expected to render a service to society by becoming a teacher, at some time or another and in one way or another, whether in the factory, on the farm, in the mosque or on the sports field.

SCHOOLTEACHERS

Teachers and schools of a type we would recognise today have existed since ancient times. Schoolteachers, or more precisely, schoolmasters, certainly existed before the emergence of modern mass school systems. In ancient China and in ancient Rome they sometimes worked in schools sponsored by the state; in ancient Athens patrons supported scholars who educated the children of the wealthy (Richardson 1963; Howie 1963; Castle 1966).

10

Perhaps a distinguishing feature of school-teachers, in contrast to adults who teach in out-of-school settings, such as the workplace, is that they are centrally concerned with book-learning, with education based on literacy. Because literacy takes time to acquire, school curricula or programmes tend to be highly organised, structured and graded. It becomes the task of schoolteachers to teach the skills of literacy and to interpret the knowledge contained in books to learners.

To illustrate this proposition, let us examine the village schools of the South Behar District of India as they were between 1835 and and 1838. The Adams Reports (Dibona 1983) are the detailed observations of a British education officer on the indigenous schools of Behar and Bengal. One remarkable fact was the multiplicity of schools at village level established well before British rule in India. But the main point of interest in our context is how each of the four types of school, Hindi, Sanskrit, Persian and Arabic, was organised around a group of teachers who were able to educate village youth in a particular, highly valued language, to introduce them to texts, sacred or secular, and, thereby, to the broader culture which the language represented.

All the schools in South Behar were one-teacher schools. Some villages had all four types. According to Adams, there were 285 Hindi schools. The teachers were mainly of the Hindu scribe caste but there were a few Muslims also. Some had school houses but many taught their pupils in the corners of shops and sugar houses, on thresholds and verandahs or even at the sides of roads. Most of their pupils were aged between 9 and 16 years and came from the Hindu lower castes. The teachers taught them reading and writing in their home language and also in Hindi. In return they sometimes received a small payment from the Hindu authorities but mostly they relied on payment in kind from the villagers.

Adams counted 27 Sanskrit schools. In some villages there were as many as six; in others, none. Amongst the teachers he discovered two renowned authors. All the teachers, however, were Brahmans. Some had built school houses at their own expense and others used temples, outhouses and the thresholds of their patrons' houses. They often took their pupils into their own homes and shared their food with them. They taught a broad general curriculum, through a wide variety of subjects, including Sanskrit grammar, literature, rhetoric, logic, medicine,

11

mythology and astrology.

The teachers in the 279 Persian schools in South Behar taught a language which had value in more than one way. They educated their pupils broadly in Persian grammar, literature and poetry. They also attracted to their classes Urdu speakers who, through learning Persian were able, Adams suggested, to acquire some skills in written Urdu, since the two languages share common features. This was important to the Urdu-speaking community at a time when the language of administration Hindi, was dominant.

Most of the teachers were Muslim but they taught secular subjects to both Muslim and Hindu boys. They existed on the goodwill of the community, sometimes receiving a small payment when a pupil began a new text. Sometimes their pupils stayed with them for ten or more years until they were young men.

The fourth category of schools which Adams enumerated were what he called the Arabic schools. They were probably akin to the Mosque schools described below. There were twelve of these schools in South Behar. The teachers were poor kalmullahs or priests supported by the mosque. Their aim was to inculcate certain prayer rituals and verses of the Koran, mainly through chanting and memory drills. Arabic was the language of the scriptures but the teachers were not so much teachers of Arabic as religious instructors. However, some of them also had a reputation for scholarship in Persian and were thus able to provide a secular education to their pupils in subjects such as law, astronomy and Euclidean geometry.

From this outline description of the village schools of India in the early nineteenth century, we can distinguish four different roles which the teachers carried out. The Hindi schoolteachers were providing home language training and training in Hindi. This would be directly useful to non-Hindi speaking children, since Hindi was the language of administration. The Persian and Sanskrit teachers were imparting a broad general education and culture through the medium of two languages in which much of both ancient and contemporary wisdom was written down. The Persian teachers were also, incidentally, fostering the community identity of Urdu-speakers whose own language was not used for official purposes. The Arabic teachers were mainly concerned with religious instruction and were perhaps the only group of teachers who may be considered religious teachers as such.

Teachers in Religious Schools

The main duty of teachers in schools supported by particular religious faiths or sects is to impart the tenets of the faith to their pupils. Such teachers may be priests, monks or laymen. Because most of the great world religions, such as Buddhism, Christianity, Hinduism and Islam, have their holy writings, their teachers are inevitably involved in teaching the skills of reading (if not always comprehension and writing) in the language of the scriptures.

We do not have statistics to tell us precisely how many schools exist, wholly or partly financed, managed and operated by particular religious communities. But they do form a significant proportion of the total school resources available in the world today, and at every level from elementary instruction to higher university studies.

The extent of provision varies. In some countries, religious schools form a small proportion of the total number of schools. In many others, religious school provision is extensive enough to form a school system in its own right. The Buddhist schools of Sri Lanka, described below, are but one example of a structured and graded religious school system serving almost all parts of a country. The state provides some subsidies to the Buddhist schools and in return their programmes include secular elements which the Ministry of Education regards as an important supplement to state provision. In other contexts, religious schools are almost entirely separated from the state system. Morocco, for example, has many Islamic schools but they do not contribute to the secular system of education regulated by the state.

The issue of religious schools deserves a special research study to find out, country by country, their precise status. We need to know much more on a global basis about the financing, management and operation of religious schools and the characteristics, qualifications and competencies of their teachers. Here, because of the actual and potential importance of religious schoolteachers in terms of both the quantity and quality of their programmes, we examine, through one or two case studies, the diversity and complexity of the situations in which they work.

Buddhist Schoolteachers in Sri Lanka.

Sri Lanka provides an example of an ancient system of religious

schooling which still flourishes today. The
Buddhists started a school system as early as the
third century AD. It began to decline from the
sixteenth century following the Portuguese, Dutch
and, later, the British, conquests of the island
(Muelder 1962:10-12). But even today there are about
300 officially recognised Buddhist schools and 2,000
teachers, according to a recent School Census (Sri
Lanka, Ministry of Education 1982).

The school system has three levels (Ruberu
1962:1-15). In the past, as today, the youngest
children, boys and girls, went to the village school
usually held in the home of the schoolmaster. He
spent most of his time teaching his pupils to read in
their own language. They also learned some writing
skills from him, mainly by tracing in sand spread on
a table, on a tray or on the ground. The
Vandakavipota, a poetry book of the sixteenth century
used in the schools, describes the strict discipline
of the village teachers (Ruberu 1962:4).

> The teacher has evoked the power of the coconut
> ekel (whip). Now my mind will not tempt me to do
> anything wrong. I will read my lessons quickly
> and without mischief. But it looks as if my
> mother has put me in a prison.

Most boys who went to the village school were
subsequently apprenticed to learn the skills
appropriate to their caste. Girls went home to learn
domestic skills. But the successful village
schoolteacher first ensured that all his pupils
became literate in their own tongue.

The village school also provided the first level
of education for the few boys who wanted to become
monks or enter a profession. They went on to the
Temple School or Monastery. The teachers were monks.
They did not charge fees but relied on support from
lay patrons of the temple. They were scholars in
their own rights. The study of Buddhism and Pali, the
language of the Buddhist scriptures, formed a very
important part of their teaching. They also taught
vocational subjects like astrology and Sanskrit, the
language of medicine. They ensured that their pupils
had a broad cultural education through poetry,
grammar, rhetoric, literature, history, arithmetic,
painting and sculpture.

At the third level of the Buddhist school system
were the Pirivenas. Today this term stands for all
levels of Buddhist schooling. But in former times
these institutions were great international centres

of Buddhist scholarship. They attracted foreigners
and encouraged contact with Hindu scholars. The
Sinhalese kings were their enthusiastic patrons. The
teacher-monk-scholars taught Buddhist philosophy,
astronomy, medicine, poetry and drama.

Islamic School Teachers. The Arabic schools on which
Adams reported were probably similar to the Koranic
schools dispersed widely today in towns and villages
throughout the Islamic world (Khan 1981). The
teachers are usually humble priests or others with a
knowledge of the sacred writings in Arabic, who can
teach young boys to recite verses from the Koran
(Bagader 1984). Islamic scholars and priests also
provide more advanced Muslim education and religious
instruction in secondary schools and the ancient
Islamic universities such as those in north Africa.
      The organisation and content of Islamic
schooling varies across the world according to the
particular historical and social context (MacEoin
and Al-shahi 1983; al-Attas 1979; Brown and Hiskett
1975). Here we cannot possibly do justice to the
richness and diversity of Islamic culture and
education. Instead, we outline briefly just three
issues with implications for teachers in Islamic
elementary schools.
      The first issue is how far Islamic school
teachers can expect to retain the loyalties of their
pupils in the modern, secular world. Islamic scholars
are currently engaged in a protracted debate about
how best their teachers can meet the challenges of
secularism (Ali 1984). Western values, and in
particular, western empiricism and science, often
appear antithetic to a life based on religious
revelation (Nasseef 1984; Saqueb 1980; Arrayed
1980). The duty of the teacher is to teach the
Islamic scriptures and way of life. But teachers face
problems in retaining pupils who are attracted by
secular values and secular schools which offer
education in an international language, scientific
and technical studies and the prospect of employment
in the modern sector. Clarke, (1978) discussing the
impact of the UPE policy in northern Nigeria,
suggests that it has aroused suspicion and fear in
both the Muslim population and the Koranic school
teachers. For the people, the main fear has been that
their religious faith and traditional values will be
corrupted (Ali 1984). So far this apprehension has
proved to be exaggerated. For the teachers, the main
anxiety has been that enrollment at Koranic schools

15

would decline. This has, in fact, turned out to be the case, as children flock to the new government schools.

Of course, this is not an entirely new challenge for the teachers. Until very recently it was the Christian mission schools in Nigeria, as elsewhere, which competed with Koranic schools (Brown and Hiskett 1975; Abu 1975). Christian school teachers have usually managed to attract pupils because they combined religious instruction with vocationally useful language and general studies. Looked at from the point of view of the Koranic school teachers, it is understandable why they continue to regard UPE schools as threats not only to their religious purposes but also to their livelihoods. We have to remember that Koranic teachers are often dependent for their subsistence on the goodwill and gifts of the faithful. They may easily maintain their influence over the very poorest and most traditional of their people, those who perceive very little to gain from sending their children to secular schools because they do not expect them to be able to continue in school long enough to have good employment prospects. But they are less able to retain their influence over the wealthier, upwardly-mobile families who are more likely to have ambitious employment aspirations for their children.

The response by the Islamic school authorities to this issue has varied. In some situations the people have been exhorted to uphold traditional values and send their children to Koranic school as a basic duty. In others, there have been attempts to introduce into the school programme elements of modern science, appropriately Islamicised so as not to conflict with Muslim beliefs. But this task of reconciliation in itself has taxed the ingenuity of the scholars. In addition, there is the enormous challenge of training the teachers to cope with unfamiliar, secular subjects. The Ismaili community, followers of the Aga Khan, is currently engaged in a sustained effort to train its teachers through the Institute of Ismaili Studies. It is searching for a means of reconciling the Muslim faith with the modern world whilst retaining valued traditions. The Ismailis perceive themselves as a 'progressive' community, willing to adapt to necessary changes in the interests of modernism. But they have a stimulating challenge ahead. The challenge is even greater for the ordinary teachers, relatively isolated from the support of Islamic scholars and reliant on traditional values.

The second issue concerns how far Islamic school teachers can be integrated into modern, secular, state school systems. Under severe financial pressures and faced with expensive development plans, governments have begun to look for additional educational resources. In particular, the expansion of primary education has encouraged some governments to look to the elementary level Islamic schools to supplement state schooling. This is, of course, not a new policy. For example, in northern India and northern Nigeria, the British colonial authorities persisted somewhat half-heartedly and unsuccessfully, over many years at the turn of the century, to bring Islamic schools under the umbrella of government educational provision (Ahmed 1974; Hubbard 1975). More recently, many governments, as we shall see below, have allowed Christian mission schools to continue to fill gaps in national school systems.

There are two main approaches to the issue of integration. The one followed in Pakistan, Bangladesh and Indonesia, for example, is for government to encourage the development of two distinct but cooperating school systems. The Islamic teachers are trained in secular subjects whilst the government teachers are trained in religious education. The other approach has been tried in northern Nigeria where Koranic school teachers or 'Arabists' have been trained to teach in the new government primary schools (Bray 1981:54–64). Whichever approach is tried, the main problems are, firstly, to allay the fears of the Muslim faithful, including the teachers, that traditional values are not under attack and, secondly, to train the teachers sufficiently well to ensure that they can teach competently in secular subjects.

Finally, we turn our attention to the vital issue of female teachers and Islamic schools. Girls from wealthier Muslim families have always been able to have an education, albeit a somewhat restricted and sheltered one at home. This excerpt from the autobiography of Begum Shaista Ikramullah (1963) paints a picture of female teachers and pupils in India at the end of the nineteenth century.

My mother's education followed the orthodox pattern. She was taught to read the Koran by one of the many distant relatives who lived in the house. In a household like my grandfather's these ladies occupied the position of super governesses or seamstresses ... They made one or two of the children their special charge and became responsible for everything pertaining to their welfare and education ... After learning to read the Koran, girls were taught to read and write in Urdu but were not encouraged to delve very deeply into the literature ... Cooking and sewing were considered the important items of a girl's education and here again one of the aunts was put in charge. Music was not taught for it unfortunately had fallen into disrepute.

Muslims differ about whether girls should go to school or be educated at home (Hussain 1984). In Turkey, for instance, which since the time of Atatwk has had a secular constitution, the education of girls is encouraged. Mixed schools are the norm and there are almost as many girls as boys in primary and lower secondary schools. In other countries girls are kept at home because this is how Muslim authorities and parents interpret the scriptures. But there is also a convention that girls, once they reach puberty, should not be educated alongside boys or male teachers. However, this custom is slowly changing. In Oman, for instance, the government has actively encouraged girls to enrol in formal school. The government has a strategy of recruiting female teachers in the expectation that parents will be more willing to send their girls to school. But in Koranic schools everywhere, female teachers are not as yet recruited. Could this possibly mean that the mothers of the future, educated exclusively in the secular school system, will prefer to send their own children, boys and girls, to secular schools to the neglect of the religious schools?

In Pakistan, another country where the government is encouraging female primary education, a different strategy has been adopted on an experimental basis. Schools are segregated. Girls' schools have female teachers, where possible. Where schools are close together, walls are built to safeguard the reputation of the girls. This policy appears to have popular appeal. But, again, unless the Islamic schools start to utilise female teachers, it is unlikely, in the opinion of the author, that they will retain their influence over the secular-educated female population growing to adulthood today.

Christian Mission Teachers. No description of teachers who have taught in schools run by some of

18

the world's great religious groups would be complete without some mention of the Christian mission schoolteachers. It would be impossible here to do justice to the complex history of Christian mission schools over the last four centuries (Bereday and Lauwerys 1966). However, we can remind ourselves of the environments in which these teachers have worked and their effect on educational development.

Roman Catholic missions were among the earliest to spread Christianity in Asia, Africa and Latin America. Their priests and missionaries taught in the schools, conducted worship and did community welfare work. Protestant missions of numerous denominations started their own evangelical work and set up their schools a century or so later.

But whether Catholic or Protestant, mission schoolteachers from abroad sometimes had to contend, not just with harsh and unaccustomed living conditions, but with indifference and outright hostility amongst those whom they wished to convert and educate in the Christian tradition. For example, Roman Catholics survived riskily in West Africa in the last years of the fifteenth century. Their first teachers arrived in Sri Lanka (Ceylon) with Portuguese support in 1505 and in Thailand in 1511. They had an uphill struggle to gain converts. In Thailand, Buddhist rulers were sometimes attracted by the benefits of western civilisation such as printing presses, medical and scientific skills which the teachers brought with them; but they were also affronted by their arrogance and insensitivity to local traditions and fearful of hostile reactions from the powerful Buddhist priesthood (Watson 1980:76-87). In Sri Lanka the missions had a similar experience and had also to meet challenges from Hindu interests (Ruberu 1962:18-29).

By the early years of the twentieth century Christian missions of a very great number of different denominations, from almost all the European countries and from North America, had spread their schools across the Caribbean, Latin America, Asia and Africa. In Zimbabwe, then Southern Rhodesia, for instance, the London Missionary Society established the first mission station in Inyathi in 1859. Sixty-five years later, there were over 1,200 schools catering for 77,000 African pupils (Chivore 1985:83-84). In Zimbabwe today the mission school influence is still strong. In many other countries schools established by the missions formed the foundation on which modern state school systems were later built.

19

But in the early days, the foreign mission
schoolteachers of various Christian persuasions
hardly saw themselves as pioneers of an integrated
school system. Indeed, they were frequently at odds
among themselves and competed for converts and pupils
in the same locality. Local populations were
sometimes the victims of the competition between
missions. For instance, in the 150 years of the
Portuguese occupation of Sri Lanka, the Franciscans,
Jesuits, Dominicans and Augustinians, among the
Roman Catholics alone, established schools.
Protestant sects arrived with the Dutch East India
Company in 1656 and yet others took over when the
British East India Company superseded the Dutch in
1798. These changes led to radical turnabouts in
ruling Christian orthodoxies and in the management of
schools (Ruberu 1962:8-26).

The main purpose of the early Christian mission
teachers was to christianise the population. Their
first duty was to teach children to read the Bible,
often in their own tongue. Health care, writing, and
simple calculation came next. Sometimes they taught
agricultural and craft skills. As colonial
governments came increasingly to support mission
schools with financial subsidies, the teachers found
themselves implementing colonial educational policy.
In Portuguese territories, for example, the policy
was one of assimilation. In British colonies the
concept of 'adapted' education found expression in a
curriculum which was intended to keep the population
in the rural areas, to impart skills promoting self-
help and to educate a few at post-elementary level in
English so that they could serve in the lower ranks
of the colonial administration and in commercial
enterprises. In the 1920's and 1930's mission
schoolteachers nurtured, wittingly or unwittingly,
the generations of western-educated elites who were
to demand freedom from colonial rule for their
people.

Many foreign mission schoolteachers were
committed to their educational work and respected by
their pupils. Thelma Awori, for instance, was a
Liberian pupil who went to the College of West
Africa, an elite mission school founded by the
Methodists. She recalls her teacher, Miss Susan
Mitchell, with respect (Awori 1975: 126).

Some called her the disciplinarian at the
College of West Africa ... She made sure
everyone was 'good'. She was never brutal and I
never saw her use the rod ... but students

respected her ... She emphasised learning about
Liberia and a maintenance of high academic
standards. We studied her textbooks in Liberian
history and geography. She not only enhanced our
spirit of nationalism but did her best to
impress upon our scattered young minds the
importance of diligence.

But foreign mission teachers were often
perceived as arrogant, racialist and hypocritical,
in the sense that their own lives did not live up to
the Christian values which they preached (Berman
1975:33). Edward W. Blyden, an eminent Sierra
Leonean, made a bitter attack on European
missionaries in 1876 when he accused them of
regarding 'the African mind ... as blank or worse
than blank, filled with everything dark and horrible
and repulsive' (Blyden 1975:32).
Local mission pupils often graduated to become
catechists or pupil teachers if they proved
themselves good Christians and intelligent students.
Some remained lowly village teachers but for others
school teaching became the route to secondary and
higher education, a means of upward social and
occupational mobility. Many experienced teachers
today are the product of mission schooling and many
successful people in other walks of life started
their careers as elementary school teachers.
Whilst a few, mainly urban, mission schools had
good facilities and teachers, the majority of small
rural schools had to make do with limited amenities
and taught a restricted range of subjects. Mwanakatwe
(1968:12) describes a typical bush school in colonial
Zambia in the early years of the twentieth century.

... there were very few, in fact hardly any,
local teachers who were capable of giving
effective instruction in the three R's and Bible
knowledge. Therefore, whereas education was
effective at mission stations where the
missionary or his wife took the basic classroom
lessons, in the village schools the level of
education was generally ineffective and
completely unsatisfactory. Before 1928 there
were few, if any, properly qualified indigenous
teachers ... Also teachers' pay was poor and
conditions of service unsatisfactory. School
equipment ... was either in short supply or
unavailable. Absenteeism was the order of the
day ... The poor quality of the village school
teachers was recognised by missionaries who

wished to improve the level of educational work.

Christian mission schools expanded over nearly four centuries (Bereday and Lauwerys 1966). They have had an enduring influence on styles of school management and the curriculum of state school systems. In many countries of Africa, Asia, Latin America and Oceania, they continue, with or without state aid, to fill gaps in state school provision. In some countries today, Papua New Guinea is just one example, their teachers are relatively poorly paid compared with government teachers. In others they receive equal or better treatment. In Sri Lanka, for example, the government has reduced the number of Christian mission schools to a handful but the few which remain are prestigious and their teachers enjoy favourable conditions of service.

ORIGINS OF GOVERNMENT SCHOOLTEACHERS

It is impossible to generalise about the origins of the government schoolteachers of today. They are as diverse as the history of educational development from country to country. However, Christian mission schools have had a big role to play.

There must be many senior government schoolteachers still working, who were once employed in Christian mission schools and were trained in mission teacher training institutions. In general, mission activity in education over the last 30 years has declined as governments began to build up national school systems under their own control. In some countries, the mission schools were taken over completely by government, as for example, in Ethiopia, Lesotho and Zaire. Perhaps more commonly, state control was extended gradually. By the 1920s, missions were increasingly having to accept grants from government to finance their activity. This financial control sometimes led to complete take-over in the years after the second world war.

By way of illustration, we trace here the origins of modern government schoolteachers in Tanzania from the foundation of a small school system by the German authorities in 1891 (Mbilinyi 1979; Cameron and Dodd 1970). These schools were specifically designed to produce teachers and clerks for the colonial administration. They were secular schools. The medium of instruction was Swahili, the language of administration. The German governor, von Soden, also utilised Islamic schools to provide clerks, soldiers and policemen but Christian missionaries, who were becoming influential, proved hostile to this policy and prevented any closer integration of Islamic schools with the state system. In the inter-war years Christian mission schools began to dominate. Under British rule, they provided increasingly the clerks, teachers and other skilled personnel needed by the administration. The authorities began to donate financial grants-in-aid. Many of Tanzania's most senior teachers today may well have started their careers as pupils in mission 'bush' schools where they would have learned Swahili. Later, they may have been able to enter one of the few 'central' schools situated in both urban and rural areas where they would have learned English.

Cameron and Dodd (1970:71) show that by 1945 there were 200 government and native authority (indirectly governed) primary schools, eight government secondary schools and eight government teacher training centres. In addition, there were 300 government-assisted Christian mission primary and 500 registered unassisted schools, ten secondary schools and 16 teacher training centres. These statistics are sufficient to indicate that older Tanzanian teachers, trained before the second world war and now retired or approaching retirement, would most likely have had at least part of their own schooling and teacher training in Christian mission schools.

Between 1945 and independence in 1961, the state took increasing control over Christian mission schools and began to develop an African school system comprising primary, middle and secondary schools and teacher training colleges (Cameron and Dodd 1970:108). Tanzanian teachers in their 20's or 30's today could well have had their own education and training in some of the urban day or rural residential primary or secondary schools or in the two teacher training colleges. These teachers were a highly privileged group relative to other Africans. In 1961 only 45 per cent of the school-age population went even to primary school. Only 4,500 African pupils entered secondary schools.

After independence in 1961, what had previously been a racially-segregated education system was integrated. There was a popular demand to nationalise the remaining Christian mission schools but President Nyerere himself resisted these pressures on the grounds that they catered to as many as 60 per cent of all children in school and at half the cost of government schools.

23

The new government embarked upon a new policy of eight years' basic education for all. Secondary and higher education were restricted. Graduate teachers were few. Primary school leavers were recruited to become village teachers on a work-study training scheme (Mrutu 1979). This was an emergency scheme to supplement the traditional pre-service teacher training college output. In 1965, a unified teaching service was created, providing uniform conditions of service, similar to those for civil servants, for all teachers in government and non-government schools. Many of the younger teachers in schools today were trained under the emergency scheme and have since participated in in-service upgrading schemes organised by the Ministry of National Education.

PRIVATE SCHOOL TEACHERS

In this book we concentrate mainly on government schools and government schoolteachers. But, finally, in this chapter, we must remember the significant numbers of teachers who work in private schools. Of course, what constitutes a private school varies from country to country. Some are government-assisted and at least partially government-controlled. Some are financed and managed by religious or other voluntary groups. Some are independent of government control and run for profit on a fee-levying basis. In a number of countries, private, fee-levying schools form a significant proportion of the total school provision (Tang 1985; Ocho 1983). This is particularly the case in countries in Latin America and in India, Kenya and the Philippines.

The status of teachers in private schools varies a great deal. Some private school teachers, particularly in those run for a profit by individual entrepreneurs and not subject to strict state control, are often poorly paid (ILO/UNESCO 1983:44). Teachers in the Kenyan 'harambee' (self-help) schools, for instance, are often unqualified and on low salaries (Moock 1974). In other private schools, particularly perhaps, those assisted and partially regulated by the state, teachers may be better paid and even enjoy conditions superior to those of government teachers. This is the case, for instance, in the elite secondary schools in Turkey and in some of the assisted (ex-Christian missionary) schools in Sri Lanka.

of the assisted (ex-Christian missionary) schools in Sri Lanka.

Table 1.1: % Teachers in Private Schools in Selected Countries

	Pre-Primary	Primary	General Secondary
AFRICA			
Cameroon	31.3	35.5	40.2
Gabon	-	39.0	40.4
Mauritius	100.0	21.5	86.6
Tanzania	-	0.3	-
ASIA			
Bangladesh	-	16.6	95.5
Indonesia	99.3	24.3	59.3
Thailand	-	-	68.0
CARIBBEAN			
Barbados	-	8.5	18.0
Jamaica (1976)	87.0	-	-
LATIN AMERICA			
Argentina (1981)	32.6	18.1	34.8
Colombia	41.8	16.4	56.8
Ecuador	-	18.4	36.1
Nicaragua	40.7	13.0	48.4
Peru	34.5	15.5	20.8
Uruguay	-	14.8	-
Venezuela	20.5	13.0	-
MIDDLE EAST			
Egypt	-	4.4	6.4
Jordan	98.6	24.5	15.6
Kuwait	21.7	13.7	11.8
Saudi Arabia	-	2.5	2.7
OCEANIA			
Papua New Guinea (1978)	55.9	-	-

Notes: 1. 'Private Schools' includes non-government, financially independent, government-aided and non-controlled.
2. Years 1979 and 1980.

Source: ILO/UNESCO (1983) Report of Joint ILO/UNESCO Committee of Experts on the Application of the Recommendation concerning the Status of Teachers (ILO, Geneva), pp.38-39.

25

Unfortunately, international statistics are weak on private schools and their teachers. This is partly because governments do not always find it easy to keep track of them. But, in view of the fact that private schooling is likely to grow, especially in countries where school-age populations are rising and budgets are tight, research directed to finding out more about the backgrounds, characteristics and qualifications of teachers in private schools is urgently needed.

CONCLUSION

In this chapter the term 'teacher' has been applied to many different people working in diverse contexts across many centuries. We have emphasised the fact that many teachers operate outside school walls and that much teaching and learning has always been informal. We have described some of the teachers past and present who work in the different types of schools, emphasising here teachers at the elementary level in village schools where language and literacy training is paramount, teachers in schools run by religious organisations, teachers in a variety of private schools and schools financed and managed through Ministries of Education. Also, we have attempted the difficult task of tracing the origins of some of the schoolteachers working in the classrooms of contemporary school systems.

In this chapter, therefore, we have painted with a broad brush a picture of teachers past and present and in many different societies. In the pages which follow, this picture will be filled out in more detail. In Chapter Two we examine further the relationships between schoolteachers and the social contexts in which they work.

Chapter Two

TEACHERS IN SOCIETY

The word 'teacher' evokes for most of us today an
image of classrooms, children and books. But in this
chapter we focus on teachers' roles in society rather
than on their work in schools. The social environment
in which teachers operate influences their
educational roles. Society's attitudes towards
teachers affect their conduct and status and, in
turn, teachers' relationships with society affect
society's expectations of them.
    In this chapter, then, we examine the role of
school teachers in social change, the part they have
played in nationalist and independence movements and
their contemporary relationships with the communities in which they work. Finally, we assess the status
of teachers in regard to the contribution they make
to community life.

TRADITION AND CHANGE

As we have seen, teachers have always played a major
role in maintaining traditions by transmitting the
culture of one generation to the next. We have also
seen how teachers have played a part in introducing
new values, ideas and skills. In the early days, for
example, Muslim and Christian mission schoolteachers
preached radically new religious values. They were
often responsible for converting whole communities.
Later, their role was to maintain these traditions
from one generation to the next.

Blunt Instruments of Change
Christian Mission schoolteachers also imported
literacy in western languages and western ideas,
values and technologies. Some communities greatly

respected them for the innovations they introduced. The Ibo people of Nigeria, for example, sent their children to school because they placed high priority on upward mobility, gaining access to salaried occupations in the modern sector of the economy and to positions of power in modern political and bureaucratic institutions (Nwa-Chil 1973).

Other communities, in contrast, did not take readily to what schoolteachers have to offer. The Muslim rulers of northern Nigeria refused to send their children to western schools throughout most of the colonial period because they already had a system of education which served their needs. Burmese villagers who were hostile to the external values purveyed by teachers, absorbed them into the life of the community in such a way that their potential as change agents was neutralised (Nash 1962; Nash 1974). Sometimes communities accepted certain aspects of change offered by the teachers and rejected others. A common example is the acceptance of academic learning and rejection of vocationally oriented knowledge and skills (Foster 1965).

Some of the factors to do with why people accept, reject or partially accept innovations introduced through schools have to do with the energy and skill of school managements and teachers in promoting change. But the social context of the school is also very important. In general, teachers are largely unsuccessful in introducing innovations if society is not ready for them and if the social conditions and social aspirations of people render the knowledge and skills which the teachers have to offer irrelevant to their situation (Dove 1980a). This may be the case for a complex variety of reasons. In some communities with strong and stable traditions, people perceive teachers as agents of an alien culture, language or political group. People who enjoy a reasonable standard of life, based on a self-sufficient local economy, sometimes prefer to ostracise the schools and teachers rather than run the risk that they will have a disruptive effect on youth by raising aspirations and tempting them to seek new opportunities away from home. However, if social attitudes or conditions change, people's respect for what schoolteachers have to offer may also change. There is evidence today, for instance, that when young people perceive that they have no chance of entering salaried white-collar occupations, and that entrepreneurial and craft skills can generate a good income, they begin to value teachers with technical skills as well as those with

traditional academic qualifications (Lauglo 1985).
In summary, this suggests that teachers are
limited, in terms of their effectiveness in
introducing innovations in schools, by society's
readiness to accept them. And society's readiness is,
in turn, determined by its perceptions of the
relevance and usefulness of the changes to its
members. From colonial times to the present day,
educational policy makers have discovered that
schools and the teachers who work in them make blunt
instruments of change. Often what are planned to be
restricted or technical changes in schools have
widespread social repercussions. One example of this
was the socially divisive effects of the introduction
of metropolitan languages in schools in the colonial
era when pupils educated in English, French, Spanish
or Portuguese often lost touch with their home
cultures and communities.

Combining Tradition and Change
Society today is ambiguous in its attitude towards
teachers. It expects them to be agents of both
tradition and change. Parents want their children to
learn to be decent, well-adjusted adults and expect
teachers to create the appropriate moral and
disciplinary climate to preserve valued traditions
of behaviour. But they also expect them to introduce
their children to new skills which they cannot
acquire at home and which they judge will enhance
their chances of gaining good jobs and social status.
Modern governments too, concerned to create
unified societies from the often fragmented
communities which emerged from colonialism to become
nation-states, look to teachers to promote both
tradition and change. For example, the preamble to
the Malaysian Moral Education syllabus which the
Ministry of Education recently introduced into
schools expresses concern about indiscipline,
truancy, disrespect for elders, vandalism and other
anti-social tendencies among youth (Mukherjee 1982).
It suggests that lifestyles are moving from rural,
agrarian ones to urban ones. 'Various influences
compete with traditional norms, principles and
values of society'.
The function of the Moral Education programme is
to maintain and improve 'moral consciousness'. The
role of teachers is to help pupils 'to identify,
clarify and internalise values which will be based on
the religious, traditions and values of multi-racial
Malaysian society' as well as universal moral values

underlined by the national philosophy of Rukunegara.
These 'five pillars of the nation' are belief in God,
loyalty to the king and country, upholding the
constitution, the rule of law, good conduct and
morality.

Malaysia's introduction of Moral Education as a
compulsory subject in schools is a serious attempt to
use the schools to marry tradition and change, to
strengthen certain traditional values and to forge a
new multi-racial society. In the light of the
foregoing discussion we can suggest that the
innovation will succeed only if the traditional
values and the principles of multi-racialism are
supported also in the wider society, in employment,
language and social welfare policies. A second
condition is that the teachers of all races, Malay,
Chinese or Indian, must be competent to teach the new
syllabus and fully behind the policy goals.

POLITICAL ROLES OF TEACHERS

The idea is sometimes put forward that education is
so valuable that it must be outside the political
arena and that teachers as purveyors of education
must stay out of politics. But this is wishful
thinking simply because teachers are inextricably
involved in political issues by the very nature of
their work. Politics concerns the procedures by which
scarce resources are allocated and distributed in
society. We often distinguish political processes
such as negotiation, consultation and voting by the
fact that they are non-violent procedures, rule-
governed activities by which decisions are made about
the allocation and distribution of social resources.
Sometimes the line between oppositional political
activity and violence is very thin, especially when
there are bitter differences between groups who
uphold and those who challenge the status quo.

Because schooling (and the improved life-
chances it offers) is generally highly valued and
because access to it is limited, there is inevitably
political competition in society about who should go
to school, to what type of school and for how long.
Teachers who work in national school systems stand at
the door of the school. They are naturally seen by
parents as agents of government policy, whether in
opening wide the door to all children or restricting
access and opportunity. Some would suggest that
teachers are agents of a capitalist ruling class
which uses the schools as instruments of domination,

creating class divisions through hierarchical school organisation and stratified curricula (Carnoy 1974:1-232; Bowles 1978).

Whether the government teachers of today see themselves as part of an organised system of domination is to say the least debatable. They do, however, have a real 'stake in the system' unlike their, frequently less well paid, counterparts in privately managed schools. Indeed, there is evidence that teachers who work for non-governmental organisations, such as religious and community groups with their own distinctive ideologies or counter-cultures, may adopt conscious political roles. They may often advocate changes in the distribution of educational benefits and challenge official orthodoxies (Dove 1982c).

Teachers in Nationalist Politics
We may distinguish the roles which teachers play as gatekeepers of the educational system from those which they sometimes play as an occupational group in the wider political arena. A survey conducted by the author highlighted the fact that school teaching provided a spring board from which many prominent participants in independence and nationalist movements launched into political careers (Dove 1979:176-191). In Africa and the Caribbean this phenomenon was particularly evident. Teachers rose to the very top of post-independence governments. For instance, at least twelve subsequent heads of state started out as schoolteachers. In ex-British colonies there were Nyerere of Tanzania, Kaunda of Zambia, Abubakar Tafawa Balewa of Nigeria, Nkrumah and Ankrah of Ghana. In ex-French West Africa there were Senghor of Senegal, Dacko of the Central African Republic, Diori of Niger, Tomalbaye of Chad, Maga of Dahomey, Kayibanda of Rwanda and El-Azhari of Sudan. More recently Daniel Arap Moi, a former teacher, became president in Kenya. In the Caribbean, Eric Williams of Trinidad is perhaps the most widely known ex-teacher politician and in Papua New Guinea schoolteacher, Michael Somare, became prime minister at independence. In South Asia teachers have been outnumbered in politics by lawyers, doctors and landowners but even so the phenomenon of school teacher-politicians has not been absent.

Some ex-teachers reached the very pinnacles of newly independent political systems but there were many more who participated in politics on legislative bodies and local political organisations which

gradually emerged as political parties. Abernethy
(1969) has documented the increasing participation
of teachers in tribal unions and other grassroots
political organisations in Nigeria during the period
before independence in 1959. In 1951 nearly a quarter
of the representatives in the new House of Assembly
in the Western Region and a third in the Eastern
Region were ex-teachers.

Before independence these ex-teachers were
involved in oppositional challenges to colonial
regimes. Because schooling was a highly valued
political resource they were often able to win
constituencies in grassroots politics in their own
communities by establishing schools in response to
popular demand. On the whole they preferred to pursue
their nationalist goals through established
political machinery. But in other parts of the world
teachers' involvement in nationalist politics took a
more radical form.

Resistance Movements

When the French took over Vietnam after many
centuries of indigenous rule they introduced a new
school system (Kelly 1978a; Kelly 1978b). They aimed
to replace the traditional Vietnamese schools which
supported the Vietnamese monarchy and purveyed
Confucian philosophy. The teachers were very
influential because they taught the pupils who were
destined for the elite civil service. They acted as
political brokers or go-betweens for the peasants in
their relations with the monarchy. They had wide
powers of patronage. They led the peasants in
rebellions against the French rule and continued
their resistance to French domination until the
second world war.

The teachers carried their resistance into the
classrooms. They defied the French by teaching
Confucianism instead of the authorised curriculum.
But such was the resentment amongst the rural
Vietnamese against what they saw as the destruction
by the French of the symbols of their culture that
they took over the schools themselves and supported
the teachers in their 'subversive' political
teachings. Teachers who attempted to keep to the
official line were often hounded out of the
community.

The French had also set up Franco-Vietnamese
schools whose teachers had been through French-style
colonial schools and teacher training. These
teachers found their expectations of a comfortable,

autonomous professional career dashed by the tight supervision exercised by the French authorities. They joined the other Vietnamese teachers in opposing official French educational policy. They taught French language for instrumental reasons but they taught the rest of the official curriculum very selectively, ignoring moral education, history and other subjects which were culturally alien. They attacked the moral education syllabus for denigrating Vietnamese values. They injected nationalist topics into their teaching.

The French authorities attempted to counter the influence of the teachers in both the traditional and the Franco-Vietnamese schools. They abolished some schools and placed the rest under supervision. They imposed a new curriculum which interpreted Vietnamese society through French eyes. They attempted to weaken the teachers by recruiting new ones who had few ties with the peasantry and by 're-training'. But they were never able to suppress completely the political influence of the teachers at classroom level.

Politics and the Classroom

It is in the classroom that teachers are most free from interference. There, they alone decide how to interpret the curriculum for the pupils. If teachers are determined to resist, it is very difficult, as we have seen in the Vietnam case study, for the authorities to close the gap between policy goals and policy implementation. This is as true today as it was when schoolteachers were in the vanguard of nationalist and independence movements. But governments often see teachers as natural propagators of official policy, partly because they are a very numerous group of educated people at grassroots level, partly because they are, in any case, often paid out of public funds and partly because they are in the business of communication.

Let us suppose that the government has launched a family planning campaign as part of a policy of population control. Teaching materials reach all the schools and principals (headteachers) go for a brief orientation during which they hear that henceforth every teacher is to utilise the family planning materials across the curriculum. But has the administration bothered to find out what the teachers themselves know or think about family planning? Have the campaign managers considered what would be the effect on teachers' relationships with parents and

33

community in localities where people were hostile to such ideas?

In circumstances where teachers are required to teach about controversial social issues but have little competence and ambiguous community support, the majority are likely to pay only lip-service to their teaching. Some may be personally hostile to the message of the new material. A few may risk their jobs by open challenge. But all that is really necessary to defeat the object of the campaign is passive resistance. The manner in which the teachers interpret curricular materials in the classroom can defeat the most imaginative of policies.

Governmental Attitudes

We have pursued the theme of the political roles of teachers because governmental authorities tend to have unrealistic views about the linkages between teaching and politics. On the one hand, there is a tendency for policy makers and planners to perceive educators as, somehow apolitical, divorced from the political life of the societies in which they work. Much rhetoric about the roles of teachers in national development paints them as, ideally, dedicated men and women for whom teaching is a vocation, requiring little sensitivity to the political cultures and contexts in which schools operate.

On the other hand, governments are very alert to the potential political strength of large teaching forces. Sometimes, especially if they are government servants, teachers have to pass inspection by political screening authorities before their appointments are confirmed. And in many countries the professional freedoms and personal liberties of teachers are circumscribed by restrictive rules concerning professional association, freedom of expression and political participation (WCTOP 1975; Morris 1977; ILO/UNESCO 1983:21).

For the reader interested in this theme, the history of teachers' involvement in political movements in Latin America provides rich material (Aguilar and Retamal 1982). Christian mission teachers have traditionally played a reconstruction-ist role in Latin American society. But in the early days of state school systems, government teachers were of lowly social origins, poor and oppressed by bureaucratic controls. They played a prominent part in the nationalist and independence movements of the 1920s. In many countries, Argentina, Bolivia, Chile, Columbia, Mexico, Peru and Venezuela among them, teachers' aspirations for radical professional and social reform supported the aims of emerging national governments (Burroughs 1974). Teachers formed unions to improve the educational conditions of the peasants. In Chile, for example, the Union of Teachers, formed in the early 1920s and claiming membership of 6,000 maestros, cooperated with the government to reduce illiteracy from 50 per cent to 25 per cent. However, in the case of El Salvador, teachers' professionalism was sometimes restricted by government (Moran 1942:203).

For the past thirty years teachers have not been able to organise their own associations independent of offical control. They have not made a single demand nor have they been able to express their views as a group on professional or administrative questions in the field.

Government Servants
Presumably, wherever teachers feel strongly enough about controversial social and political issues, they will continue to take part in political activity of one sort or another. But it is unlikely that we will see more examples of schoolteacher politicians of the type who rose to the top of national level politics after independence in Africa and the Caribbean. Conditions have changed. In those days teachers, even primary school teachers, were among the most educated in their societies and, in rural areas at least, could identify closely with their potential "constituency". As teachers they had little chance of promotion within the profession. But teaching gave them opportunity to pursue political ambitions. And in many cases, colonial rule gave them a cause against which they could fight for their own people.
Today, in many countries which achieved political autonomy over the last two or three generations, political power of one sort or another has consolidated. There is very little recruitment of outsiders into the 'political class'. In any case, the majority of teachers are government employees or enjoy certain benefits as teachers in government-recognised schools. In Algeria, for instance, in 1976, 121,000 out of 268,000 (45 per cent) civil servants were teachers (Cameron and Hurst 1983:600). In such circumstances they are often restricted in political voice and activity under their conditions of service. As teachers they can look forward to a

certain amount of security in financial terms. They have a stake in the system. They are no longer the sole source of assistance to the community since there are many other educated people and social welfare agencies to which to turn. Many teachers are posted away from their own homes and are strangers amongst people of different cultures, languages and aspirations, with whom they may find it hard to identify. More women are entering teaching and are traditionally less inclined to participate in politics and public affairs than men. For all these reasons the days of the entrepreneurial teacher-politician are probably gone.

TEACHER-COMMUNITY RELATIONS

Nowadays teachers rarely take part in formal political activity but they are still inextricably involved in informal political relations with the communities which their schools serve. This is because they are involved in distributing the scarce educational goods which schools have at their disposal. The problem is that governments, parents and communities often hold differing and over-ambitious expectations of the schools. Teachers stand in the middle of the arena. Here we discuss the challenges which this poses for teachers and examine why it is important for policy makers, educational administrators and teacher educators to take into account the community context in which teachers work.

Colonial governments of the past and national governments of today have always tried to use schools as agents of economic and political development. Schools have been used to produce the educated human capital required for economic and manpower development. Such policies require teachers to inculcate in youth an achievement motivation, a meritocratic ethic and positive attitudes towards innovation and service to the nation (Harber 1984).

But because access to schooling has been unequally distributed, between urban and rural areas, between social classes and ethnic groups, schools have contributed to division and class differentiation in society. At the community level this means that teachers, as local representatives of the school system, find themselves in an ambiguous situation. Parents whose children succeed in school see the teachers as 'one of us' and parents whose children are left out or left behind in the competition for success in school tend to regard

36

teachers as indifferent, if not hostile, to their interests.

Government has often tended to look to the schools to promote national values and integration. In the 1950s and 1960s there was a great deal of centrally planned curriculum development activity which went some way towards ridding school syllabuses of metropolitan bias and introducing national goals and concerns (Dove 1983a:149-157). There was progress also in revising textbooks and examinations. Governments introduced language policies for schools which were intended to enhance national unity. Sometimes the language chosen as the medium of instruction was a 'neutral' international language, sometimes a language used by a dominant group in the country, such as Hindi in India, Swahili in Tanzania or Urdu in Pakistan, would become the national language to serve as a link between all citizens (Treffgarne 1981:198-208).

Today efforts still continue to promote national integration through the curriculum. For example, recent recommendations for Singapore's schools, suggest that teachers should inculcate Loyalty to the Country (Ong and Moral Education Committee 1979:9). The syllabus includes,

i.   Love of the Country:
     Sense of national identity and commitment, Protection and upholding of the democratic system, Defence of our Country, Patriotism, Loyalty, Justice and Equality
ii. Spirit of Nation Building:
     Appreciation of the efforts made by our forefathers in building the nation and their contributions to national development; Understanding the progress of Singapore and the pioneer spirit, Understanding the internal and external threats to Singapore's survival and Prosperity.

Another way in which governments have tried to use schools as tools of social policy is by requiring teachers to recognise and promote local, community cultures (Bacchus 1982). Such policies are, of course, by no means new. Colonial regimes tried to 'adapt' metropolitan curricula to meet local conditions and to instil a local sense of identity with the community (Lewis 1962; Bude 1983a; Barrington 1982). In varying degrees, such community-oriented policies had three aims: to promote community development; to cultivate pride in local communities and to prevent the drift away to urban centres by youth searching for white-collar employment.

Attempts to implement such policies have concentrated on decentralisation of curriculum development to teachers to enable them to incorporate local issues in teaching materials. Local languages used by relatively small groups of people, as in Nigeria, have been officially recognised in schools. Social Studies, Aesthetic Studies and Pre-vocational Studies have all been geared to local cultures and work opportunities.

In practice it is the teachers who have to reconcile policy objectives for schools which are intended to convey both national and community concerns. This is, perhaps, easiest in small countries with homogeneous populations, which have no great social inequalities and a school system providing access to all children. The task is, perhaps, most problematic in multi-ethnic, multi-lingual, multi-faith societies, with great social and economic cleavages and a school system providing restricted and discriminatory access and opportunities to children from different communities. In such situations it is likely that local community values and interests may conflict with national ones. And then teachers have to find the balance. For example, their responsibilities to inculcate modern scientific attitudes might run counter to revered local medical or agricultural practices or local deference to the wisdom of the elders. In such situations teachers have to be sensitive to community sentiments and find ways of introducing new ideas without alienating powerful local interests.

Not that local communities are always united in values and interests. Local elites may try to monopolise access to schooling or prevent teachers conveying ideas which would threaten existing power relations in the community. If, for example, the Social Studies syllabus suggested that pupils should learn techniques of social surveying by studying local patterns of land-owning, the teacher who carried out this scheme without careful preparation and explanation in the community, might well experience hostility and opposition from local elites.

Teachers have to beware of seeming to take sides with any particular community factions. They also have to cope with conflicting pressures from community and local supervisors. Local people, for instance, may be whole-heartedly in support of the school because it regularly gets a high percentage of successes in national examinations. Local inspectors, however, acting on national policy to increase enrollment and retention of all children in school, may file adverse reports on teachers in schools which appear to neglect the needs of children who repeat grades, fail tests and drop out of school prematurely.

It is interesting to hypothesise that teachers in primary and lower secondary schools probably have most pressures on them to reconcile national and community values. This is because this level of schooling is terminal for most young people and it is at this level that schools are required to convey a sense of both national citizenship and community identification. Upper secondary schools are more single-mindedly concerned with preparing pupils for higher education and the occupations which will inevitably lead them out of their own communities. It is likely also that teachers in small rural communities are less insulated from community pressures than teachers in large, often urban, schools. Rural communities often render teachers highly visible and accessible. In cities, communities lack identity in the sense of sharing a common culture and outlook; also, there, teachers often live outside the neighbourhood of the school and can remain anonymous.

It has been suggested that, in some circumstances, teachers are unable to give service to the communities to which they are posted because they are strangers in them. They may speak a different language and, by up-bringing and education, they may have little sympathy with local culture and traditions. This account of the situation in a rural Peruvian school is typical of many all over the world where teachers fail to participate in the life of the community and, as a result, provoke local criticism (Gall 1974:11).

... the best teachers come to school from Monday to Friday, whilst those called 'tourists' come only two or three days per week or only in the mornings ... The routine of the teachers is: arrival at Vicos on Mondays between 7 and 10am, some on bicycles and others on foot from the nearby town of Macara, where the bus brings them. They come with the idea of staying in Vicos until 3pm Friday, but the majority return to their homes two or three times in the week, usually after mid-day. This situation could never be controlled by the school director, because he does the same.

The problems generated for teachers in reconciling their duties as teachers with their participation in the community are probably nowhere more acute than in the poorest of rural communities. To illustrate this proposition, let us take the case of a fairly typical village primary school teacher in Bangladesh (Dove 1980b). Government policy is now to have primary teachers recruited at upazilla (sub-district) level and for them to be posted as near their homes as possible. Transfers away are sometimes used as disciplinary measures.

The typical teacher comes from a farming community. He has up to twelve years of schooling and possibly a year of teacher training. He has been teaching for a number of years and hopes to become a school principal before he retires. As a government employee his salary has improved over the years but hardly enough to cater to the needs of his family. When he first became a teacher he was posted far away but after many visits to the local education office he managed to get a transfer home. He has about four miles to walk from home to school. During the monsoons the paddy fields become waterlogged. Then he stays at home. He has crops to tend and he coaches the children of the local Union Parishad (Council) Chairman. These supplements to his income are welcome. They help to feed and clothe his eight children and other members of his household who have no paid jobs. Local officials understand only too well how hard it is to make ends meet and turn a blind eye to occasional absence from school when conditions are bad.

Of course, there are problems in working so close to home. People know him as the youngest son of a respected local smallholder. They criticise him at the slightest opportunity if he appears to fall short of the high standards of personal conduct characteristic of his father. They also tend to blame him for the poor performance of pupils in government schools and sometimes suspect him of being on the side of officialdom against community interests.

But on the whole the teacher prefers to endure the minor inconveniences of surveillance by the community than to work as a stranger elsewhere. For then he would lose his sources of additional income and be dependant on others for his accommodation, food and security. He would have to spend time and cash on visiting his family. He would have to acquaint himself with the local dialect and start all over again in getting to know local officials and community leaders, for they can be very powerful in deciding where teachers should be transferred.

STATUS IN THE COMMUNITY

This picture of the village primary schoolteacher illustrates the delicate web of community relationships which affect the lives and work of teachers. All teachers need sensitivity to the communities in which they work. In poor communities teachers cannot command a salary which enables them to maintain an adequate standard of living and accommodation and superior education for their own children. They often have to develop links with the community through establishing small businesses, coaching children for examinations or managing small-holdings. Such activities may interfere with their educational duties during school hours. In such circumstances teachers face a major challenge in reconciling the social and professional demands on them and in maintaining local good will and patronage on which they are dependent for their personal well-being.

The question is often posed as to whether the status of teachers has risen or gone down. This is a complex issue to which we shall return in Chapter Five where we examine the occupational status of teachers in terms of their educational responsibilities in society today. What the discussion emphasises so far is that status, in the restricted sense of the esteem, respect or honour in which people are held by others, depends partly on their position in society and partly on their relationships in the community in which they work. Teachers who combine teaching with their work as monks, gurus, mallams or priests, derive their status partly from the worth which society places on the religious values which they represent. In a highly religious Islamic community, for example, the religious teachers enjoy high status because of the position which Islam ascribes to them as priests, be they of very humble economic status. Teachers who entered politics in the pre-independence era were esteemed because they represented their communities at national level and brought benefits to them, not only in the form of schools, but also roads, hospitals and employment.

But the status of teachers in the local community also depends on their personal achievements. Teachers who participate in community life and make positive contributions to it are more likely to gain respect than teachers who try to separate themselves off from local people. Personal qualities are very important in terms of establishing good relationships if teachers are to gain respect. In the past, teachers were sometimes the only educated people, especially in remote rural communities. Through their voluntary efforts in contributing to the community as letter-writers, advisers to the people on dealing with officialdom and taking a lead in community affairs, they were able to achieve high status as individuals. Today, although there are very many more educated people to play such roles in the community, teachers are often still judged by their contribution to community affairs. The other way in which teachers earn respect or status is, of course, through their achievements as educators. In any community the word gets round, through pupils and parents, about the worthwhileness of individual teachers. This one may be judged good because of his kindliness and patience; that one may be respected for her great understanding of literature and her ability to communicate this to pupils; another may be admired for his ability to get pupils through public examinations.

This excerpt from the biography of Jasim Un-Din (1974) who grew up in Bengal illustrates emphatically how much the personal qualities of teachers contribute to the status which they are able to achieve in the communities which they serve.

> In the next class, Yogendra Nath Sen taught me Bengali. He had a Chittagong accent but he was able to make the more difficult points of grammar as clear as water. I became enthusiastic about Bengali literature after studying in his class ... In the school holidays, I went to his house and studied with Mr Sen. I took one of the ripe mangoes from the mango tree there and also fruit from his jamrul and he did not say anything. In my life I have never met a better teacher. He was not very learned but whatever he knew he was able to fill his pupil's mind with.

In this chapter we have examined the social and political context which affects teachers' work and status. In Chapter Three we examine in more detail

the educational roles of teachers in contemporary
society.

Chapter Three

EDUCATIONAL ROLES

In Chapter Two we argued that it is critically important for policy makers and planners, and indeed for teachers themselves, to understand the complicated relationships which teachers have in both the wider society and in the communities in which they work. This understanding is a prerequisite for establishing realistic assessments of teachers' capabilities to carry out their roles in the school and community. In this chapter we investigate contemporary policies, research and ideas about the roles of schoolteachers in their strictly educational tasks. In Chapter Four we examine their roles in community development.

CORE ROLES

The reader may feel that it is almost platitudinous to state that teachers <u>have</u> educational roles; after all, put at its simplest, teachers are surely hired to teach. But in some of the voluminous literature to which we shall allude in the following chapter the idea that <u>the teacher's core role is to educate</u> is often buried in the rhetoric, which has been flowing ever since the development of modern school systems, about the roles of teachers in community development and, latterly, social integration and nation-building.

People's occupational roles tend to emerge from society's expectations of them and their own image of themselves (Westwood 1967a; Westwood 1967b; Wilson 1962). There is plenty of evidence that both society and teachers themselves see their prime responsibility as being the education of schoolchildren and that all other responsibilities are peripheral to this core role. A plethora of official reports emphasise

44

this, sometimes deploring the multitude of additional roles and tasks which take teachers away from their central educative responsibilities. A document prepared by the Ministry of Education, Thailand (1975) illustrates such concern. It suggests that the teacher is,

> ... a substitute parent ... a registrar of students' academic records, social backgrounds and sometimes political leanings, a book-keeping officer, a canteen manager, a dormitory supervisor, a student welfare officer, or a social worker, a school building construction overseer, a community development leader, a disciplinary proctor, a fund raiser for needy students, a counsellor in academic problems as well as students' personal ones, a participant in ... in-service programmes ... or a dignitary in social functions.

Some of the tasks identified for the Thai teacher are administrative. They arise from the increased bureaucratisation of schools within national systems of education, which require files and accounts to be kept for purposes of control and accountability. We shall return later in this chapter to the question of whether or not such tasks are the proper responsibility of the teacher. Other tasks concern the roles of teachers in the community, with which we deal in Chapter Four. But tasks such as being 'a substitute parent', 'a counsellor' and 'a registrar of student's academic records' are ones which society in general, parents and the professional educational community at large nowadays perceive as an integral part of the teacher's core educational role.

Societal Expectations

The point emphasised here is that the teacher's educational role has widened in scope and increased in complexity as the school has become increasingly caught up in socio-economic change and development. As we have seen, in societies where the wisdom of one generation was sufficient for the well-being of the next, the educational role of the teacher was limited to passing on a time-honoured stock of knowledge, either, by example, orally or through texts. But in contemporary society teachers' educational roles are more diffuse (Wilson 1962). Let us note one or two examples of the effect of social change on society's conception of the proper educational tasks of teachers.

Custodial Role. It is a common phenomenon that joint and extended families tend to become dispersed as younger members move away from home for schooling and jobs in the modern sector. Parents can no longer rely on regular help from relatives in child-minding and rearing. Often both mother and father go out to work. Thus, teachers are expected to take over the custodial and socialising functions, formerly the reponsibility of the family. This is particularly the case for teachers in pre-schools, primary schools and residential schools.

Selection Role. Another example is the way in which teachers' educational tasks are often narrowly defined in terms of helping pupils pass examinations, by teaching strictly to the syllabus. The universality of this phenomenon is well-documented (Dore 1976). It occurs because parents (and pupils) perceive schools primarily as instruments of upward social and economic mobility. They judge teachers successful, and teachers tend to judge themselves successful, insofar as their pupils gain good educational qualifications which give them opportunities to compete for higher education and high status salaried occupations.

It is important to note, however, that people do not perceive the teacher's educational role in this restricted and instrumental way when they do not expect schooling to bring much in the way of socio-economic returns. Research documented by Brooke and Oxenham (1984) suggests that social demand for schooling certainly tends to be highest when parents perceive a positive link between educational qualifications and desirable employment; but that, nevertheless, the role of teachers in imparting an education good, in and of itself, irrespective of extrinsic benefits, is still seen as important. They quote studies from all over the developing world and notably from Botswana, Brazil, Ghana, Mexico and Peru, where parents have low expectations from schooling as a tool of upward mobility for their chldren, but nevertheless value education as good in itself.

Basic Skills. We may diverge briefly here from the

main theme to suggest on the basis of such evidence that pupil 'wastage', as defined by planners in terms of the inefficiencies of schools where pupils drop out after only a few years, may not accord with parents' definitions of the situation. It may be tentatively hypothesised that where parents see few economic returns from sending a child to school, they may nevertheless decide on a limited investment in schooling on the grounds that a 'good education' is worthwhile in itself. Thus, if children who attend school for two or three years reach a certain useful level of permanent literacy, numeracy and 'get-on-ability' in their own socio-economic situation, that investment is not 'wasted'. One major implication here is that qualitative improvements in education in the early grades of schooling may be the key to reducing wastage, not only in narrow costs terms, important though these are, but also in terms of human resource development.

Professional Expectations
But to return to the main theme. We have pointed to one or two examples of the effects of socio-economic changes on society's expectations of the teacher's educational role. We must also, however, remember that professionals in education, researchers in universities and institutes of education, teacher educators and practising schoolteachers interested in pedagogy, have contributed greatly to a broader conception of the educational tasks of teachers. Again, only a few, if important, examples must suffice.

Health and Welfare. There is now a great deal of indisputable evidence which indicates that pupils' abilities to concentrate and learn are affected by their general health (Balderston, Wilson, Freire and Simonen 1981:66-71; Levinger 1984). The implication of this is that part of the educational role of teachers is involvement in activities such as the diagnosis of malnutrition, mental and physical disability, participation in school feeding programmes, cooperation with parents and social welfare agencies and the development of curricula intended to enhance the health of pupils (Gurage 1984; Pollitt 1984).

New Teaching Methods. The fact that governments are

47

now committed to policies for mass schooling has
stimulated some limited research and experimentation
in teaching methods, assessment and diagnostic
techniques and educational technology. Traditional
teaching for memorisation sufficed when schooling
was highly selective; when the ablest of children
could succeed, almost in despite of rigid and
unimaginative teaching. But teachers today are
expected to stimulate learning in pupils from across
the whole range of abilities and social backgrounds.
The activity of teaching requires much more variety
of approach than formerly. As research into processes
of learning and teaching continues, teaching becomes
ever more complex.

Indeed, it is quite probable that many teachers
who used to believe that they were doing at least an
adequate job have lost confidence in the face of the
inconclusive and ambiguous messages they receive
through professional networks about the variety of
new approaches to teaching which are advocated. In
one good, down-to-earth and widely used teacher
training textbook used in Africa, for instance, the
reader is introduced to the activity method, the
discovery method, the project method, small group
learning, peer group learning, individualised
learning and programmed learning (Farrant 1980:133-
144). It is doubtful that teachers being trained with
this text are able to participate in practical
exercises on all these teaching styles. And the
majority of practising teachers rarely have the
opportunity for sustained guidance in adding to their
repertoire of teaching techniques.

Much play is made about the idea of education as
liberation. There are those who would deny that
schools can ever be liberating institutions and would
like to see an end to them (Illich 1971; Reimer
1971). But many people prefer to assume that schools
as institutions are likely to survive and that
liberation must come through improvements in
teaching and learning. One aspect of liberation has
to come through the encouragement of pupils to move
from lower level intellectual skills like
discrimination and memorisation to higher level ones
such as analysis, synthesis, evaluation and problem-
solving (Bloom 1956:17-20; Gagne and Briggs
1979:106-115). Although research into learning and
teaching is still in infancy, teachers are encouraged
to undertake discovery and enquiry methods of
teaching, to use complicated questioning techniques
and project work with the intention of stimulating
pupils to be creative in thought, to cope

constructively with a fast-changing adult world and to be active participants in national development (Goble and Porter 1977:17-72).

Role Strains

Not only does the activity of teaching appear to be ever more strenuous for teachers, but some teaching techniques advocated as appropriate for the development of intellectual skills may appear to conflict with teachers' duties towards the social development of pupils. Lee (1982:60), for example, commenting on Science education in Malaysia suggests,

... there also exist social attitudes and cultural traits in Malaysia which may be antithetical to the spirit of Western science. One cultural trait is that not only is it not right for the young to question their elders but teachers also share the same conservative attitude and are used to being directed from above. It is doubtful that this attitude of acceptance of authority can be conducive to the development of inquiry-discovery learning of science among pupils.

Lee is, of course, assuming that transfer of learning takes place from a specialist subject to civic and social education. Too little is known about the transferability of skills to judge whether her doubts will be borne out by events. Nevertheless, they are echoed in many a country. The main point is that for the teachers there appear to be internal contradictions in their educational roles which can be sources of doubt and confusion (Adams 1970; Spaulding 1975).

We have pointed to examples of ways in which the expectations of society and those of the professional educationists have changed conceptions about the core educational roles of teachers. We turn now to examine in more detail two of the most important ways in which the core educational roles of teachers have expanded.

CURRICULUM DEVELOPMENT

In the mid-twentieth century, with independence and the expansion of school enrollments, many governments began to set up institutions to plan systematic and centralised curriculum reform on a national scale. A new breed of curriculum specialists arose who usually worked from newly established Curriculum Development Centres or Units within Ministries of Education. Their first tasks were to formulate national plans for the school curriculum within the framework of national policy; to select from the prevailing culture those elements deemed most worthwhile for the younger generation to learn through the school.

The main thrusts behind increased attention to what pupils should learn were the need to bring school curricula in line with national goals for socio-economic development, to update specialist subject matter in line with the world-wide knowledge explosion, especially in science, and to replace foreign influence and bias with themes fostering national integration and cultural identity.

Approaches to curriculum reform ranged from gradual, subject by subject change, to wholesale overhaul to the whole curriculum. For many countries reform was urgent, far-ranging and on a national scale. Barbados is but one example of many countries which attempted radical changes in a very short time span. The National Curriculum Development Council was set up in 1974. By 1979 it had revised existing curricula for primary and secondary education, developed new syllabuses and guidelines, identified textbooks and teaching materials. There were ten new subjects in primary schools and nine in secondary schools at the pilot stage, one in its final form (Dove 1980c:38).

Hawes (1979:33) has identified six processes which are involved in curriculum planning and development. Briefly, these are,

1.   gathering basic information about the context in which the changes are to take place and about their feasability;
2.   deciding aims and objectives;
3.   planning a strategy for change; resources in manpower, materials and time must be correctly deployed;
4.   developing the curriculum. This involves designing syllabuses and teaching materials and trying them out;
5.   implementing the curriculum with learners; this involves selecting appropriate teaching-learning activities to translate the aims of the curriculum plans into reality;
6.   evaluating the planning and development at

every stage in terms of the appropriateness, practicality and effectiveness of the whole strategy from the adequacy of the basic information, through the formulation of aims, to implementation; evaluation provides the information on the basis of which the process of curriculum development becomes one of continuous reform.

In the early days of large scale, centralised curriculum reform, many mistakes were made for a variety of reasons. Policy targets were too ambitious, time scales were too short, resources allocated were inadequate and vital stages in the development of curricula, such as situational analysis or monitoring and evaluation were neglected. The outcome was that very many plans for new curricula remained on paper, in syllabuses and textbooks and teacher's guides. Implementation failed in the sense that teachers went on teaching and pupils went on learning much as before.

Teacher Participation

In the 1950s and 1960s, with large numbers of under-educated and untrained teachers entering classrooms as school systems expanded, it was only too easy to make the teachers the scapegoats for the non-implementation of curriculum reform. Some countries experimented with packages of materials for schools which even the poorest teachers could use. But often these 'teacher-proof' materials lay neglected while teachers continued to use familiar materials and teaching routines. Curriculum specialists designed, and still design, teachers guides intended to support teachers in understanding and utilising innovatory material and teaching methods. But many of them remain unused.

By the 1970s a great deal of research and evaluation, much of it in countries with established and resource-rich school systems, was revealing the difficulty and complexity of curriculum change (CERI 1972; CERI 1975; Harris, Lawn and Prescott 1978). Empirical research into processes of educational innovation was providing clues to the conditions under which reform was likely to be successful (Hurst 1978). Among other things, it was indicating that even in countries where teachers were not in short supply and were well educated and trained, they were unlikely to take up curriculum innovations unless they were fully involved in the whole process. At a governmental level the participation of teachers in curriculum development is nowadays fully accepted.

51

In an ILO/UNESCO survey (1983:17) 40 out of 52 countries confirmed 'some form of participation of teachers in the process of curriculum development and the selection of textbooks and teaching methods.' But Kerr (1969:4), commenting on the opposite situation in many developing countries, emphasised that, (the) 'crucial factor ... is the need for a high measure of teacher involvement and participation. Curriculum development cannot proceed unless the teachers are available and willing to participate (author's underlining).

Teacher availability appears to be an obvious sine qua non of successful reform but curriculum plans laid at the centre often neglect the fact that schools in remote and disadvantaged areas are short of teachers. Teachers with over-large classes and little administrative support are unlikely to be enthusiastic about new teaching materials and methods which will require extra work and effort. Even more so if they have not been informed or involved in planning the changes. They are unlikely to be keen to utilise new materials which arrive unexpectedly in the school if they do not understand or sympathise with the reasons for the changes. Even if they do try to use the new materials they may find that they do not match the needs, language, culture and aspirations of their pupils.

There is increasing realisation today that teachers cannot be expected by planners at the centre to be implementers of curriculum reform without being involved in the whole cycle of planning, development, implementation and evaluation. They are more likely to develop positive attitudes if they participate in formulating the aims and strategies for change. They are more likely to develop a stake in the reform if they participate in designing materials and trying them out in their own schools. They are more likely to be enthusiastic if they acquire skills in utilising new methods of teaching or new subject matter through on-the-job training and practice.

Styles of Curriculum Development

Observers of the curriculum development process have identified three dominant styles or strategies utilised for reform. Each of them makes different assumptions about the roles of teachers in curriculum development (Havelock 1971; Maclure 1972; Lewy 1977).

Research, Development and Diffusion. The Research,
Development and Diffusion (RD&D) strategy has been
widely used for large-scale reform. It is 'top-down'
and scientific-experimental in approach. Experts at
the centre explore strategies, research feasibility
and set curricula aims and ojectives. They design
materials and try them out in pilot schools. After
feedback, revision and field trials, new materials
are disseminated to all schools. At the dissemination
stage, orientation and training in the new curriculum
may be provided for teachers.

This bare outline does not do justice to the
variety of ways in which the RD&D style of curriculum
development has been utilised in practice.
Nevertheless, it does indicate that the majority of
teachers are not invited to participate in the reform
until the materials are disseminated. Teachers are
not even implementers in the full sense of the word,
meaning that they have a part in deciding what
innovations are appropriate to their own schools,
what materials are best and how they will introduce
them. In other words, the teachers are relegated to
the status of mere technicians, transmitting to
pupils the content of materials which they had no
part in developing and without regular means for
providing feedback on their experience for revision
purposes.

The RD&D strategy does typically involve a few,
selected teachers more fully. These teachers often
serve regularly on panels.

> Operating at national level, they are mainly
> concerned with specialised subjects ... Under
> the direction of the national curriculum
> centres, representatives of the education
> ministry, school inspectors, lecturers at
> teacher training centres, experienced head-
> masters and teachers, curriculum specialists
> and experts ... cooperate in the task of
> elaborating new curricula. In some countries
> e.g. Botswana, the work of such panels covers
> the entire range of curriculum development ...
> preparing teaching contents ... elaborat(ing)
> and test(ing) new instruction methods and
> directives for the teaching staff (Bude
> 1983b:26).

These teacher representatives are often unusual
in their energy and enthusiasm. They are often from
urban schools conveniently situated near the
Ministry of Education. They are sometimes out of

touch with the constraints in schools in rural areas where most teachers work. Teachers in pilot schools used for testing materials are also more involved than the ordinary teacher. They are often enthusiastic and resourceful innovators. Their cooperation is invited in providing feedback from testing. Their schools receive good publicity and extra resources. They come to have a sense of ownership with regard to the new materials and may gain in status when undertaking training and dissemination responsibilities at the later stages.

Because of resource constraints in disseminating new materials to a large number of schools, teacher orientation and training in a typical RD&D strategy may be neglected. At best, most teachers may attend a short crash course where they have lectures on the innovation and take a look at some of the new materials. They have little chance to practise new skills or to have support and advice when attempting to use them in the classroom. At the worst, the training may be not only too little but too late. The teachers are summoned to attend courses some time after new materials have been distributed and the novelty effect has disappeared.

Social Interactionist. The Social Interactionist style of curriculum development evolved partly from attempts to compensate for the weaknesses of some RD&D style reforms which had neglected the roles of teachers (Rogers and Shoemaker 1971; Harlen 1977). It lays emphasis on the notion that teachers are the best judges of what innovations are desirable and feasible in their own classrooms. They will reject or neglect interventions from outside which appear unnecessary or irrelevant but will readily adopt or adapt ideas and materials which prove useful.

The Social Interactionist perspective is compatible with centralised curriculum planning and materials development but it allows for teachers' initiatives as well. Very crucially, it assumes that there is in existence a supportive institutional network through which teachers may interact to share experiences and participate in preparation and evaluation of curriculum materials. Teacher training colleges, teachers' centres, education resource centres, subject associations, professional magazines and expert 'mobile' teams are examples of institutions which may provide decentralised support. Through 'social interaction' teachers may participate in all the processes of curriculum

planning and development. An early attempt to create
a network of support for teachers was the creation in
1967 of the Curriculum Research and Development
Division (CRDD) within the Ghana Education Service.
'Teachers were organised in subject associations
whose membership was tapped in curriculum writing
workshops' (Ntumi 1983:191). At secondary level
teachers' associations have provided the forum for
teacher involvement in curriculum development.
Science teacher associations in Nigeria and
Hongkong, for example, have made notable
contributions. At primary level teachers' centres,
groups and clubs have provided a meeting place where
teachers can discuss innovations, write materials
and evaluate their experiences (Dove 1977; Thompson
1982; Greenland 1983).

Localisation of curriculum development through
teacher interaction may not lead to uniform and tidy
innovation nation-wide but it does encourage
teachers to be more than mere passive recipients of
materials, it harnesses their initiative, resourcefulness and experience to create real changes in
teaching and learning, and provides local
institutional support where they can gain skills and
develop professionally.

Problem Solving. The Problem-Solving style of
curriculum planning and development is perhaps the
most teacher-centred of all (Havelock and Huberman
1977; Bolam 1981). Its basic assumption is that
teachers are encouraged best to innovate when they
experience a problem to be solved, a need in the
classroom to be met. It assumes, even more than the
Social Interactionist approach, that teachers have a
spirit of initiative and a confidence to seek
solutions to problems which they themselves
identify. Either individually or as a school-based
team, teachers initiate their own research into
curricular problems, utilise a wide network of
professional resources - curriculum and teachers'
centres, training institutions, advisers and
consultants - to help their search for possible
solutions. In the absence of tailor-made materials,
they design, test and develop their own.

Such an approach assumes that even the poorest
untrained teachers can benefit from involvement in
planning, designing, developing, implementing and
evaluating school-based curriculum materials.
School-level leadership for such professional
development is critical. Innovation cannot rely on

the energy of individual teachers or the charisma of a particular principal. Principals and senior teachers responsible for specialist areas of the curriculum have a responsibility for training and supporting the teachers as a team in curriculum reform. They have to create a climate in which teachers can feel free to take initiatives and experiment - a difficult task in contexts where schools operate under highly centralised and bureaucratic systems of management.

Teacher Participation in Practice

The curriculum styles outlined above are ideal types. In practice, reform strategies have contained elements of all three. Even the RD&D approach which appears to rely least on teacher participation can, in practice, and with careful planning, maximise teacher involvement. The Social Interactionist approach can most easily combine elements of centralised reform with teacher participation. The Problem-Solving approach does not, on the other hand, sit easily with centralised planning.

There is a great wealth of descriptive case-study material detailing large and small scale plans for reform in many countries. There is equally a great dearth of evaluative material on the process and outcomes of reforms. The three case-studies outlined below are selected not because they are in any sense typical or even successful but because they exemplify the diverse way in which teachers may participate in curriculum reform whatever the dominant style.

Caribbean Project. The University of the West Indies pioneered a large-scale regional project in 1980 to improve the quality of the primary curriculum in nine Caribbean countries (Shorey 1982). First, teacher trainers and selected classroom teachers participated in regional workshops to set overall guidelines for new syllabuses and to write sample materials. Then teachers in each country participated in workshops to review the syllabuses and develop materials relevant to their own islands. Later, after testing the materials, workshops were held for teachers at local level to devise teaching activities and supplementary materials appropriate to their own pupils.

The style was essentially an RD&D one but teacher involvement in the planning, design, testing

and use of materials was maximised as the new
curriculum was disseminated from regional to local
level. Shorey (1982:54) claims that the approach was
effective.

The close and intimate involvement of classroom
teachers throughout the whole series of
activities has resulted not only in better
understanding of how the materials can be
effectively used but also a willingness on the
part of teachers to be innovative, with
noticeable impact on classroom teaching. It has
also significantly improved teachers' understanding of curriculum development and has
resulted in a higher level of acceptance.

Benin. In Benin the reform of primary education since
1975 has linked the preparation, consideration and
circulation of new curricula, the preparation of
teaching materials and the selection and
introduction of innovations in teaching (Houeto
1981:195-196). The reform 'involves all teachers at
all stages. The teachers thus become active
"practising researchers" in the various fields
required by a sound application of the educational
reform'.

This strategy has elements of both 'top-down'
and 'bottom-up' approaches. For instance, the first
stage in planning new curricula is undertaken at the
school level where teachers meet together. Each
school puts together proposals which go to District,
then Provincial levels prior to incorporation in
National plans. Since 1980 new curricula for the
first four years of primary schooling have been in
the schools. They are under 'constant evaluation by
the teachers themselves and all those responsible for
supervision and guidance'. From the centre, the
National Institute for Educational Research and
Training (INFRE) organises seminars to clarify new
curricula and specialist teaching consultants design
specimen lesson notes to meet the needs of new
teachers. A mobile INFRE team also collects
innovations introduced by teachers in isolated
schools. INFRE is developing a sound library of
innovations which loans cassettes to teachers and
publishes Education Beninoise, which includes
teaching notes, stories and poems. 'This review,
which is a real help in teacher training and self-
training, consists largely of articles by teachers
... and reports on work done by specialists ...'

57

Ethiopia. The Benin reform is an ambitious national scale scheme to integrate the development of teachers' skills with their participation in curriculum development. Ethiopia is but one of many countries which like-wise plans for the in-service training of teachers to go hand in hand with curriculum development (Selassie 1985). But in this case the aim is to involve teachers at local level in materials development. Each <u>Arwaja</u> (District) has an <u>Arwaja</u> Pedagogical Centre (APC). The APC managers are normally drawn from the teaching force. Their task is to bring local teachers together to appraise syllabuses and textbooks produced by the National Curriculum Development Centre and to develop materials which will conform to national guidelines but will also be relevant to the linguistic and cultural backgrounds of their own pupils.

The scheme is founded on sound principles of teacher involvement but there are some difficulties of a practical nature. For example, the APC managers are themselves in need of support. They lack a clear understanding of their own role and career development. The APCs are often lacking in amenities and materials and teachers do not find it easy to attend frequently.

Constraints
Such practical difficulties have to be recognised and understood if we are ever going to formulate realistic strategies for full teacher participation in curriculum change (Lillis 1985; Jennings-Wray 1984; Hawes 1979:143-160; Dove 1983a). Otherwise expensive and unworkable schemes will continue to frustrate the expectations of those who rely on teachers to improve the quality of school curricula.

Political. What are the non-teacher-related constraints on full teacher participation on curriculum development? Some of them are political in origin. For example, governments and aid agencies often rush to achieve unrealistic targets for curriculum projects within, say, five or so years. Yet the evidence is that the time needed for full implementation is far longer than that. Sometimes governments adopt international fashions for new curricula without adequate consultation and research to discover if they will be acceptable to the people. Changes in political direction at national level sometimes mean that developments underway are suddenly curtailed or starved of resources.

Administrative. Other constraints are managerial or administrative. Experimental projects are often started up outside established curriculum development institutions or without regular budgets. After the experimental phase there is a danger that progress stops because of failure to institutionalise projects so that they can expand with adequate finance and personnel. Resource constraints may be most severe at local level. In centralised systems administrative arrangements for the distribution of materials, for example, may not be flexible enough to ensure that they arrive in the local area at the time they are needed. In decentralised systems an additional problem is often lack of funds out of restricted local budgets to support curriculum development activity (Griffiths 1975).

In addition local administrators and principals of schools may find themselves involved in additional work in the name of a curriculum development project of which they had little fore-knowledge and with which they lack sympathy. In situations of teacher shortage their training and experience may encourage them to insist that teachers' time should be fully utilised in direct teaching activity rather than on 'luxuries' such as research in the community or workshops on curriculum development.

Teacher Training. Teacher-related constraints on their participation in curriculum development also vary in any particular context. However, there are a number of general factors which are very important. These are all inter-linked.

Firstly, if teachers have low levels of general education and are untrained or inadequately trained, they are likely to lack confidence and ability in undertaking any activities other than those which involve familiar and 'safe' teaching routines (Ejiogu 1980; Beeby 1966). If their training has not provided them with understanding and sympathy for the crucial part they can play in translating curriculum plans into reality, then they are likely to resist attempts to impose on them additional and unconventional tasks.

By training and experience, through pressures on them from administrators, parents and examination systems, teachers may have very restricted conceptions of their responsibilities as professionals and which limit their preparedness to take part in innovatory activities. In any case, as we have suggested, curriculum roles are often expected of teachers by planners and administrators, without adequate consultation and orientation. Yet it is very clear from the experience of innovatory educational programmes that unless those involved in implementation are clear about the intended aims of the activity and have the skills to undertake the relevant work, failure is inevitable (Gross, Giacquinta and Bernstein 1971).

Leadership. In many countries teachers suffer from low morale due to a variety of factors such as dissatisfaction with pay, conditions of service, lack of status and job-satisfaction. This is discussed further in Chapter Five. Low morale inhibits resourcefulness, initiative and a team-spirit, all of which are necessary if teachers are to play a full role in curriculum development. Low morale is often, at least partly, caused by poor leadership. The willingness of teachers to involve themselves in curriculum activities is crucially affected by the encouragement they receive from principals and local administrators, inspectors and specialist advisers. It is such people who determine whether teachers see themselves as imposed upon by extra and unwanted responsibilities or as invited to participate in important educational developments.

A Realistic Role
We have discussed at some length the role of teachers in curriculum development in contexts where there are very severe constraints in terms of financial and materials resources, administrative and managerial capacity and trained personnel. We turn now to the more positive aspect to suggest briefly the conditions under which teachers can participate fully and in what ways.
i) In their initial training all teachers should have orientation to the constructive, indeed critical, role which they have in curriculum development. They should be encouraged to understand that their role is not a passive one of merely transmitting the contents of syllabuses and textbooks into the heads of their pupils, but an active one involving decision-making about the planning, implementation and evaluation of teaching activities. Their training should involve some

experience of curriculum activity.
ii) All teachers should have in-service training
opportunities to extend their skills in solving
teaching-learning problems which they themselves
experience. Most of these opportunities should be
available at local level and should be school-
focussed or school-based. Depending on their levels
of competence, some teachers will need up-grading in
subject matter, others will benefit from using and
evaluating centrally produced materials, and a very
few will be able to take personal initiatives in
developing their own materials.
iii) All teachers, whenever expected by the
authorities to take part in particular curriculum
projects, should have an initial orientation to their
aims and to the precise tasks which they are to
undertake. Just as importantly, they should have
follow-up training and regular on-the-job support in
carrying out their responsibilities.
iv) Principals or potential principals should have
training to prepare them for their leadership roles
at school level. This training should enable them to
involve all teachers in their schools in regular
school-level planning, development and evaluation of
annual programmes across the curriculum. It should
enable them to support teachers in developing their
individual schemes of work through advice to
individuals, team conferences and workshops. It
should enable them to provide national or regional
curriculum planners with information about school
facilities, equipment, materials, the home
backgrounds of pupils and socio-economic and
cultural factors affecting the practical aspects of
curriculum implementation.
v) Teachers of whatever level of seniority should
be eligible for participation in prestigious
national curriculum development projects on the
grounds of their achievements and potential at school
level. A professional climate should be encouraged in
which teachers would welcome participation for the
contribution it would make to their effectiveness as
teachers and the enhanced opportunities for their
pupils to do well in school.

An Essential Role for Teachers
These guidelines are very general and can only be the
starting point for adaptation to specific contexts.
The thesis developed here is that teachers have a
role to play in all stages of curriculum planning and
development. Without the teachers even the best of

materials will not be used fully. However, the core educational role of teachers in curriculum development is in the manipulation of curriculum materials in school-level teaching and learning activities. All teachers should receive training and support in selecting appropriate teaching strategies to achieve the goals they judge to be appropriate for their own pupils. If all teachers were able to undertake a full role in school-level curriculum development this would do far more to improve the quality of education than any number of teacher representatives on national panels and committees.

There has been a tendency to belittle the role of teachers in curriculum implementation at classroom level, as if implementation were somehow a simple, lower order activity than national level planning or evaluation. What needs to be recognised is that implementation, properly done, is a very complex and skilled activity requiring high order decision-making at every stage in the cycle of curriculum development.

Whilst some teachers should continue to be involved in aspects of curriculum development beyond the school level, it is in school where investment in curriculum development is likely to have the greatest spin-off. Many countries will continue their reform efforts within a framework of centralised planning. Curriculum specialists will continue to be needed. But the major investment of the future should be in the development of institutions which can support school-based curriculum development and, above all, in the training of teachers to undertake their core educational role.

EXAMINATIONS AND ASSESSMENT

A major influence on how teachers interpret the curriculum in practice is the examination system. In this section we discuss the influence of examinations on teachers and argue that they must play an active role in examinations and assessment if they are to help improve the quality of teaching and learning in schools.

Examinations exert pressures on teachers. One hallmark of the good teacher in the eyes of parents, pupils and, indeed, teachers themselves, is the ability to help pupils pass examinations - especially public examinations. This is because examinations are used as certificates to mark the level of schooling which pupils have attained and as selection devices whereby scarce places higher up the school system or scarce jobs are allocated. In Sri Lanka, for example, the Grade 10 General Certificate of Education Ordinary (O) Level examination leads to a school leaving certificate to mark the end of the basic cycle of schooling. In practice it serves as a selection instrument for entry into pre-university grades. Over 40 percent of pupils repeat the O Level year in the desperate hope that they can attain the top marks needed to find a place in Grade 11. They know that the chances of getting a job with mere O Level passes are very small. O Levels are worthless because employers can take people with higher qualifications when youth unemployment is very high (Lewin and Little 1984).

As more countries lengthen the basic cycle of schooling from five or six to nine, ten or eleven years the pressures of selective examinations in the early years of schooling are alleviated somewhat for teachers and pupils alike. Primary Leaving Certificates which also served as selective entrance devices for secondary schools can be abolished. Then the selective pressures of examinations tend to be felt at the lower secondary level, on those rungs of the school ladder where most pupils must leave school because there is no room for them higher up. It is sometimes suggested that examination pressures affect teachers at higher secondary grades most. Certainly this is correct where public examinations are concerned. But in certain circumstances, examination pressures exist even at the lowest grades.

Where there are wide inequalities and status distinctions between schools and competition for entry to schools with high reputation is fierce, examinations provide the means whereby these schools can select their intake. They are in a position to set their own standards for entry through their own entrance tests. They may be government schools located, perhaps, in a capital city. Or they may be prestigious private schools. In Bangladesh, for example, the competition from middle class parents in cities to get their children into private English-medium primary schools is so fierce that very small children sit examinations in English, Bengali and Mathematics, each up to three hours long. It is only in rather unusual situations when schools compete to attract enough pupils that examinations do not serve as selection devices. The Grade 8 examination in Nepal, for example, is like this because there are more school places than pupils (Somerset 1984:66).

Backwash Effects on Teachers

Because examinations serve to allocate life-chances they are very important to parents and children. How does this affect teachers, especially those teaching in examination classes or involved in periodic testing of pupils?

The reputation of schools tends to vary according to their success rates in examinations. The teachers in the top grades of primary or of lower secondary or upper secondary schools tend to be there because they have proved their ability to get a high proportion of pupils through the examinations. They themselves enjoy high status in the community and in the school and are likely to have better than average promotion prospects. In contrast, teachers who teach in lower grades where there are no public examinations, or in non-examinable areas of the curriculum, do not have such opportunities to achieve high status, even though their contribution to the educational development of children and the life of the school is just as important.

Examination pressures affect the way teachers manage the curriculum. They concentrate on examination classes and neglect other areas of the curriculum (Morris 1985). One example of this very common phenomenon came to light recently when the Malaysian authorities reviewed the reasons why teachers were neglecting Civics in secondary schools; even though it was a compulsory subject it did not figure in the public examinations (Leong 1982). Within each examinable subject teachers concentrate on the parts of the syllabus which they estimate to have the greatest weighting in the marking system. They coach their pupils on items which they believe are likely to come up on the examination paper and which appear to attract high marks and are therefore 'easy'. Several months in advance of the examinations, coaching and revision concern them more than moving forward to teach new areas.

Examinations also affect the way teachers react to their pupils. Because their own reputations are at stake they may feel obliged to give more attention to the 'brightest' pupils whom they judge to have a good chance in the selection competition. They neglect those for whom their expectations are low. Some of these pupils will be repeating a grade for the second or third time; others will have been automatically promoted even though they had failed to master the curriculum of the previous grades. In mixed-ability, all-age and multi-grade classes teachers may gear their teaching towards the high-fliers, setting, in the process, unattainable learning objectives for the majority of pupils. In streamed classes the best teachers may teach the ablest pupils and the poorer or least experienced the slower or 'difficult' ones.

Of course, in some situations, teachers may gear their teaching to the repeating group in a class. This is a rational response, for example, in school systems where the majority of pupils are <u>expected</u> to repeat several times in their school careers; simply because of shortage of places in higher classes, everyone expects to wait in the queue, even the high fliers. Somerset (1984:78-81) produces data for Nepal, for example, which show that pupils in the rural schools normally spend two or three years in Grade I.

Table 3.1: Nepal: Transition from Primary 1 to Primary 2, 1976-1977

	% promoted to Grade 2	
	Boys	Girls
1st year in Grade 1	33	26
2nd year in Grade 1	42	40
3rd year in Grade 1	44	35

In Morocco it takes approximately eight years for a pupil to complete the five-year primary cycle. About 25 per cent of pupils repeat Grades 1 to Grade 3, 30 per cent repeat Grade 4 and 50 per cent Grade 5 (Morocco, Ministry of National Education, 1981). There are end-of-year examinations in all grades. Pass rates are set by the schools to allow promotion to the next grade according to the places available. Thus pass rates, and probably repetition rates too, vary from school to school. The bottleneck at the end of primary school is severe because parents and teachers hold back pupils from the final examination, which determines who can find a place in the lower secondary school, in the hope that additional study time may increase their chances of success.

Examination pressures may affect teacher-parent relationships. Some teachers may give private tuition to children whose parents can afford the fees. Other parents who cannot, may resent this as unfair, complaining that the teachers are neglecting their responsibilities to their own children in school in favour of others out of school. Principals, in particular, may experience severe pressure from parents, especially those with influence in the community. They may want their children to somehow by-pass the examination or at least have the opportunity to repeat.

Quotas

Yet despite all these examination-related pressures on teachers, examinations are widely accepted because they are perceived as the fairest means available of rewarding merit. Other forms of selection such as quotas have the disadvantage that they appear to select candidates unfairly, even though their aim is to give greater opportunities to certain pupils in disadvantaged areas or from disadvantaged groups. For the 'disadvantaged' pupils, quotas for selection are generous. This gives them an advantage. But, by the same token, places are more restricted for 'advantaged' pupils, with the result that even very able learners may fail to be selected. This happens, for example, in upper secondary school examinations in Sri Lanka, where able pupils from 'advantaged' areas like Colombo become 'failures' because of the restricted quota there. In Papua New Guinea, after some years of experiment, discontent with the quota system has led to a reversion to an examination-oriented system of selection to high schools (Bray 1985).

But the issue is not just one of fairness. It also concerns legitimacy. The ritualism and heightened anxiety associated with examinations gives them something of the character of <u>rites de passage</u>. Those who survive are perceived to have earned their success; whereas quotas appear to deny some of those who survive their legitimate rewards.

Non-Cognitive Selection Criteria

It is, of course, arguable that pupils should be selected not only for their intellectual attainment but also for their social and physical achievements. After all, in most school systems, teachers are held responsible for the all-round development of children. In theory, there is no reason why innovative assessment procedures could not measure all-round achievements. In practice, it has so far proved very difficult to find acceptable ways of doing so. China and Tanzania, for example, are two countries where character assessment of pupils has been combined with examinations for selection purposes. This procedure, however, can expose teachers to charges of subjectivism and favouritism. In addition, teachers may use such assessments to encourage conformity and to discipline non-conforming pupils, who, though possibly very able, prove, in one way or another, to be 'nuisances' in school.

Inadequate Tests

One reason often put forward as to why examinations are necessary has little to do with their use as selection devices. The fear is that, without them, teachers will lack motivation, direction and a sense of standards to attain. However, teachers who have received adequate training so that they are competent to judge the capabilities of their pupils against the demands of the curriculum, should not lack direction and an understanding of standards possible at any level. Examinations may, indeed, give them an added motivation to apply themselves but cannot in themselves make up for poor preparation.

The greater problem is that examinations often encourage methods of teaching and learning which inhibit the full educational development of children. This is not the fault of examination systems per se but because particular examinations are poorly constructed or teachers misconstrue the type of learning required for pupils to do well. Somerset (1974; 1979; 1984) has shown in some detail how poorly constructed test items have negative effects on learning. They may be unreliable. For example, candidates may be able to do well by mere guesswork. They may be invalid. For example, an item intended to measure ability to make logical inferences may in fact allow a pupil who has merely memorised a passage on the topic to gain good marks. They may be biased in terms of subject matter. For instance, rural children may be disadvantaged in answering comprehension passages well because the topics are all about city life.

But even the best constructed tests may fail to encourage children to develop their full intellectual potential. If teachers have only a textbook on which to rely and are used to equating memorisation of factual knowledge with the requirements of examinations, they may not be able to teach their pupils in any other way. Somerset (1979:65) noted that the changeover from achievement to aptitude tests in Kenya in 1977 increased the gap between pupils in the best schools and in the less good.

A lesson in science asks what will happen if all the leopards are killed, given the following facts: leopards eat baboons, and baboons eat crops and wild fruit. The answer here can be inferred by logical reasoning but <u>poorly educated and trained teachers</u> ... tend to drill their pupils in 'facts' such as 'All leopards are carnivorous and all baboons are herbivorous'.

Such 'facts' memorised in isolation do not help the pupils to learn to think from cause to effect. The old-style CPE (Certificate of Primary Education) called for this rote learning ... and so did not penalise children who were <u>badly taught</u> whereas the aptitude test which tests abilities that they are never called upon to use penalises them heavily (author's italics).

Teachers and Assessment

It is sometimes suggested that the use of examinations as selection devices inhibits teachers from offering pupils a genuine education (Dore 1976; Oxenham 1984). Without examinations, so the argument goes, teachers would be liberated from pressures to contort the curriculum to what they see as the requirements of the examination syllabus. But the challenge to those who argue thus is to suggest a legitimate and feasible alternative mode of selection. None has yet been offered.

True, as they currently operate, school-leaving and other public examinations often merely certify the number of grades through which pupils have passed. They measure their perseverance in staying in school. They do not always record their mastery of intellectual skills and understanding of subject matter. Even internal school tests tend to measure pupils against each other, encouraging competition over efforts to master knowledge and skills. Examination pressures on teachers and pupils, which are so serious as to inhibit their respective performances, must, of course, be reduced as much as possible. But some anxiety and tension will almost inevitably remain and may even be a positive stimulus.

The proposition we put forward here is that tests and examinations are important tools in the hands of teachers. In their responsibilities for examining and assessing pupils they have potentially a most powerful means of improving <u>educational</u>

standards in schools. Far from deploring the importance which society places on examinations, educationists should turn them to educational advantage. In relation to teaching activities, examinations are the tail that wags the dog. Tests which are technically and educationally sound can do much to improve the quality of teaching and learning. But this alone is not enough. The most important ingredient is the training of teachers to understand why their work in testing and assessing pupils is an integral part of their core educational role and training them in sound assessment techniques.

Whether periodic examination or regular testing is involved, assessment by teachers, done properly, can make an invaluable contribution to qualitative improvements in education. It can help in three ways.
i) Diagnosis of pupils' strengths and weaknesses in terms of mastery of skills and content and identification of the causes of learning difficulties. This is most important if teachers are to set learning objectives and choose teaching-learning activities which are appropriate to what children can already do. It helps teachers to pay attention to individual children and not to assume that all pupils in the same grade irrespective of age, previous experience and background are at the same level.
ii) Evaluation of the curriculum and materials in terms of their appropriateness to pupils. This includes evaluating whether the objectives and content are appropriate to the levels of ability of pupils and to their experience and interests.
iii) Evaluation of teaching activities. Through tests and examinations teachers can assess whether or not their teaching is successful and identify whether alternative methods are needed to improve their pupils' learning. Testing also helps them avoid bias in their personal reactions to pupils. It helps them adjust their expectations of pupils according to how they actually perform rather than whether they are likeable or not.

In sum, the proper use of techniques of assessment can do much to improve the performance of teachers as educators and, consequently, their status as professionals. They do not need to learn highly sophisticated techniques in order to improve their professionalism. The most useful aspects of assessment are well within the scope of any teacher to acquire. This is not the place for a detailed description but we may identify a few of the more important concepts which all teachers need.

Most teachers are familiar with terminal or end-of-course or end-of-year assessment. Such evaluation is summative; it sums up how well learners have learned. Used in conjuction with a pre-test, a summative assessment, or post-test, can serve as a measure of how much pupils have achieved as a result of a particular course of study. Continuous assessment, in contrast, involves testing learners regularly during a course or period of study (Rogers 1974). One advantage is that teachers are able to assess pupils' progress as well as final achievement. They receive feedback which enables them to change their teaching as necessary.

Normative and criterion-referenced tests are another pair of useful concepts. Normative tests spread pupils across a measure of achievement (Eggleston 1974). Each person's score is related to a standard. Most teachers are familiar with such tests because they are used for selection. They compare the performance of learners against one another. They differentiate the 'distinctions' from the 'passes' and the 'failures' and the 'top' from the 'average' and the 'bottom'. Criterion-referenced tests, in contrast, do not primarily compare pupils one with another. Instead, they measure an individual's performance in terms of how well he or she can do against a standard of performance. The test may measure understanding of concepts, intellectual or motor skills. An illustration of a very simple criterion-referenced test of the motor skill of jumping would be whether pupils could jump one, two or three feet high. The purpose of such tests is to inform teachers which of their pupils have achieved the performance objective set. They are then able to judge the effectiveness of their teaching methods and take remedial action with individuals.

Another useful concept is that of profiling. Strictly speaking, profiling is not an assessment technique but a method of presenting the results of assessment (Macintosh and Hale 1976; Clift, Weiner and Wilson 1981). Profiling involves teachers in systematically compiling cumulative records of pupils' progress and achievements. The profiles are useful for teachers themselves, parents and prospective employers, in gaining an overall picture of pupils' performance and personality. They are multi-dimensional. They record a variety of aspects of pupils' progress and attainments, both cognitive and non-cognitive; they also present the information in a variety of ways. Visual presentations, such as graphs and histograms may be used to present test

scores. Written reports may be more suitable to
record information about, for instance, participation in extra-curricular activities.

A Crucial Role
In his teacher training manual, Principles and
Practice of Teaching, Robinson (1980:96-134) devotes
20 per cent of his space to a discussion of the
practical aspects of assessment, evaluation and
record-keeping. This is a measure of the great
importance he places on these aspects of teachers'
work in the Nigerian context. He emphasises that
teaching involves using regular and organised
assessment techniques based on scrutiny of
curriculum objectives and teaching materials. He
then gives practical advice to trainees on how to ask
questions, how to administer tests and how to keep
records.

> Questions promote thinking among teachers and
> pupils. Teachers have to think of the content of
> their lessons, the goals they have to achieve
> and suitable ways of presenting these
> questions. On the part of pupils, teachers'
> questions not only arouse their interest but
> also arouse their thinking to find the correct
> answers and the best solutions. Questions from
> the teacher may even encourage the pupils to ask
> questions.

He gives guidelines for setting tests and
examinations

> 1. The test or examination must focus upon the
> areas that have been covered during the month,
> term or year. It is not very good practice to
> spring surprises on pupils ...
> 2. Draw up questions that have a great
> possibility for all to be attempted
> 3. ... give sufficient notice to your pupils
> about an imminent test ...
> 4. It is good practice for some revision to be
> done before an examination.
> 5. ... avoid all ambiguities in your
> questions.
> 6. Attempt to answer all questions or work out
> all exercises beforehand to make sure that they
> are within the range of ability of your pupils
> ...
> 7. Remember that tests are not to penalise;

71

they are meant to assess, diagnose and reinforce.
8. ... go over questions, marks, grades and comments with (your) pupils after a test or examination.

He discusses the rationale for regular marking of pupils' work.

Marking is a form of record-keeping. The regular marks and grades in a pupil's books give a record of his performance ... (Marking) enables the teacher to compare a pupil's progress at different times and also to compare the performance of one pupil with that of another. Where ... promotion depends on continuous assessment ... the marks teachers award their pupils ... become a vital instrument ... Knowing their mistakes helps pupils learn by them ... Pupils stand to benefit a great deal from the marking of the teacher.

On record-keeping, he emphasises their usefulness in supplying accurate information on pupils' educational progress, their character and conduct. Apart from mark books and other records on students he urges on teachers the importance of keeping their own <u>Record of Work</u> books to help in planning future teaching, revision and setting of tests. Good records inform other teachers, principals, inspectors and parents precisely what pupils are learning.

<u>Teacher Training</u>
Both pre-service and in-service teacher training are essential for a number of reasons. These include:
i) The trend away from public examinations administered from metropolitan centres in favour of regional or national ones. In new Commonwealth countries, for example, the Cambridge Overseas Certificate is gradually being replaced at secondary level by bodies such as the West African Examinations Council and the Caribbean Examinations Council. What this means is that there is much more opportunity for teachers to teach for local relevance and more coordination between the requirements of the curriculum and examination syllabuses.
ii) The trend towards more school-based types of assessment. In Nigeria and Botswana, for instance, the practical aspects of science subjects are

assessed by the teachers. In Barbados and other parts of the Caribbean teachers assess pupils' projects for secondary level local history. This means they are able to judge the projects on fair and educationally sound criteria.
iii) The fact that many classes contain pupils of various ages, ethnic, linguistic and social backgrounds. At primary level in particular and in small one- or two-teacher schools, individualised and small-group teaching methods are necessary to accommodate the range of pupils in any one class. It is important for teachers to have good assessment techniques at their fingertips if they are to gear their teaching to what pupils can cope with. Otherwise, irregular attendance, drop out and repetition reduce the effectiveness and efficiency of the school.

Teacher Sensitisation
One innovative method of sensitising teachers to the importance of assessment and the linkages between teaching and examination performance was the CPE (Certificate of Primary Education) Newsletter, produced annually in Kenya before the abolition of the primary leaving examination. In the mid-1970s the Kenya National Examinations Council decided to do something about the poor performance of pupils in the CPE. As we have seen, because of a combination of poorly constructed multiple-choice questions and poorly trained teachers, pupils were passing the CPE by rote learning, but not developing higher intellectual skills.
The Kenyan authorities re-introduced a variety of testing methods such as comprehension and essays. The CPE Newsletter aimed to keep the teachers in primary schools informed about the philosophy, style and approaches used in the CPE examination. The examination was geared closely to the primary curriculum in order to promote good teaching. The Newsletter was very practical. It highlighted subject by subject problem areas in the previous years' examinations. It advised teachers on how to teach particular topics better. It explained test items where even teachers appeared to have missed the point and in later issues gave statistical data on national performance in the examination. In the Introduction to the 1982 edition of the CPE Newsletter, the Secretary to the Kenya National Examinations Council commented,

The main reason for sending these publications to you is to guide you into ways of making CPE a part of the learning process for your pupils ... The Newsletters have discussed the underlying principles in each of the papers. They have also discussed in quite a lot of detail, the reasons for including the various questions and made suggestions on how to tackle them. We hope this has made the teaching and revision for CPE more meaningful.

CONCLUSION

In this chapter we have surveyed the many ways in which the educational roles of teachers are expanding and becoming more complex. In particular, we have examined their core roles in curriculum development and in the assessment of pupils - two vital and interlinked roles which demand of teachers far more than merely imparting textbook information in the classroom. We have argued that, unless teachers take their full part in curriculum development and pupil assessment, there are likely to be few improvements in the quality of education in schools. All teachers should be involved in school-based curriculum development and evaluation activities and these responsibilities should count in the eyes of educational administrators as important complements to the direct teaching of pupils. In order to equip them to undertake these roles teachers need training and support.

Chapter Four

COMMUNITY ROLES

Society in general sees the classroom as the proper place for teachers to be. But the central thesis of this chapter is that the core educational roles of teachers extend out of the school into the community. If teachers confine their work solely to the classroom they cannot fulfil their full respons- ibilities. On the other hand, a clear distinction has to be drawn betwen those tasks of teachers in the community which are strictly educational and those which are not. It is argued that teachers cannot and should not have to undertake all manner of community tasks unrelated to their core educational roles. Such non-educational work takes time and effort away from their most important tasks and does little to enhance their professional status.

NON-EDUCATIONAL COMMUNITY TASKS

On an informal and voluntary basis teachers sometimes find themselves acting as advisers and counsellors to adult members of the community over a whole range of matters. This is especially so, as we have seen, in remote rural areas where there are few alternative sources of advice, few social services and where adults in general lack skills and confidence in dealing with modern society. It is also a mark of the personal esteem in which individual teachers are held because of their long-standing support of the community.

A recent survey of primary school teachers in rural areas of Cameroon revealed that they participated in a whole variety of non-educational and semi-educational support to the community (Bude 1982). They gave help in writing letters, providing

75

financial assistance and school fees, interpreting government regulations, supplying medicine, finding jobs and resolving family and agricultural problems. In urban and more developed communities people are not so dependent on teachers. They can turn to a variety of social agencies. Teachers may have no more knowledge or familiarity with the ways of the wider society than the general community. Secondary school teachers may not be local people and may be somewhat isolated from community affairs.

As discussed in Chapter Two, teachers who willingly and sensitively carry out tasks informally in the community cannot but enhance the respect in which they are held. However, as communities develop, specialist services expand and general levels of education rise, it is likely that teachers may gradually relinquish their informal roles as community counsellors, at least under normal circumstances.

On the other hand, it is likely that teachers may be called upon increasingly to carry out non-educational tasks assigned them by government. Whether administration is centralised or decentralised, lower level functionaries at the local level are often in short supply. Teachers are a very large group at grassroots level. They often find themselves called away from their schools to participate in activities of many kinds, from counting votes to collecting census data, from organising 'Clean Water' campaigns to promoting National Youth Day. Such tasks may possibly provide a little increased status and visibility in the community. There may even be a little extra income. But when teachers are caught up frequently and at short notice in such duties, classrooms may be left empty and their educational work may suffer. In the long run this may do harm to the educational hopes of school children and the professional standing of teachers.

Historical Tradition
The history of attempts to involve teachers in the community, especially primary teachers in rural areas, goes back as far as the beginnings of formal schooling and is fully documented elsewhere (Sinclair with Lillis 1980:21-77; Thompson 1981; Thompson 1983). Its expression has varied from context to context. Sometimes teachers' roles have been limited to providing educational services to adult members of the community, sometimes they have been utilised as extension agents in health,

agriculture, and integrated rural development (Loveridge 1978).

As early as the mid-nineteenth century, the British colonial authorities, for example, encouraged the missionary societies to introduce practical craft and agriculture into schools. The idea was to fit rural school children for life in their own communities; to slow down the disintegration of rural communities and the urban drift of primary school leavers in search of modern sector employment.

In the different international climate of the 1920s British, French and Belgian colonial thinking encouraged the development of adapted education (Bude 1983). This is how the Phelps-Stokes Reports on Education in Africa expressed the concept (Lewis 1962:29-31).

> The first step in the adaptation of education to the needs of rural communities is a genuine appreciation of the importance of rural life in the general development of Africans ... Next ... is the demand for a clearly defined programme of school and community activities for the improvement of African villages. In addition to the training of the individual, it is important that the school shall be organised so that its activities also extend out into the homes and institutions of the community ...
>
> Every part of the school curriculum may be made to contribute to an increased respect for and interest in the rural environment of the school ... The natural outcome of a school whose curriculum reflects genuine interest in its community is the organisation of its activities without the schoolroom that blend intimately with the life of the groups from whom the pupils come.

Schoolteachers were to teach with practical relevance to community life. They were to enhance respect for local culture using local languages and introducing traditional customs and festivals into the life of the school. They were to teach adult illiterates, demonstrate good health, nutrition and agricultural practices in the classrooms and in the school gardens. But they did not always find such roles easy or acceptable. In the first place they were often untrained and unskilled. Secondly, such work did not always accord with their own conception of their proper roles and status. Thirdly, they

sometimes met with community resistance; in the eyes
of local parents, teachers who did not give their
pupils the opportunity for upward mobility out of the
community were failing in their duties.

In the 1950s and 1960s there was still a great
deal of optimism that school teachers could somehow
lead the way in community development (Batten 1953;
Houghton and Tregear 1969). Gandhian ideals which saw
teachers as inspirational leaders in basic education
at village level spread across the world. UNESCO
programmes to eradicate illiteracy utilised teachers
in adult education. Integrated rural development
projects involved them as members of teams to
encourage development efforts across all sectors.

More recently some countries have looked for
radical alternatives to the colonial or western type
of school which tends to alienate youth from its
traditions. The Cuban Schools in the Countryside, the
Peruvian Nuclear Schools and the Cameroonian
community schools are examples (Figueroa 1974;
Leiner 1975; Bizot 1975; Lallez 1974). The Tanzanian
Community Schools Programme, inspired by the Chinese
model of the 1960s, has perhaps attracted the most
attention (Ishumi 1981). The schools were set up
within the context of a national policy of ujamaa
(self-reliance). Village committees managed them on
the basis that the boundaries between school and
community, formal and non-formal education should be
reduced. The new school curriculum linked education
to life. Teachers provided basic education for
children and adults. The school and community planned
production targets together, shared facilities such
as workshops and poultry units, and worked
cooperatively to make the village self-sufficient.
Teacher training emphasised community service and
cooperation (Mrutu 1979).

Teachers as Community Development Agents

Experience shows that such radical attempts to
involve teachers in all-round community development
challenge conventional ideas, attitudes and
practices on the part of both teachers and community.
Unless conditions are right, teachers do not easily
become community animateurs. The interested reader
may refer to various analyses and case studies which
set out the complexities of the challenges involved
(Bude 1982; Dove 1980b; Lauglo 1982; Watson 1983;
Martin 1984). Here we can only summarise some of the
main factors involved.
i)   Change agent and leadership roles have to be

undertaken by people with high status and prestige in the community. School teachers, particularly in primary and lower secondary schools where most initiatives for community development are directed, often lack the social standing.

ii) Similarly, such roles require outstanding personal qualities and skills. Teaching does not attract the highest calibre recruits and it is unusual for teacher training to provide adequate preparation for teachers to fulfil the demands of community development roles.

iii) Schools tend to reflect the socio-economic, cultural and political environment of the wider society. Nationalised school systems with central-ised administration do not accommodate very easily to local and minority needs. Schools may be responsive to wider social change but are rarely able to initiate transformations for which society is not ready or prepared.

iv) Where teachers are government servants and are subject to bureaucratic authority, symbolic, administrative and financial support from national or regional authorities is crucial to their effective involvement in community development efforts. This is especially important in inter-sectoral pro-grammes. The coordination and integration of ministries and agencies across sectors is a complex task at both national and local level. School teachers may find themselves without support from their own administration, without clearly defined responsibilities in cooperative activities and burdened simultaneously with taxing tasks in both school and community.

iv) Community support is also important. If the development programme is initiated 'from above', it may not be wholly acceptable in the community. Teachers closely associated with it may find themselves caught up in conflict, tension and rivalry. Even if the programme is initiated in the community, there may be divisions of interest and opinion. Teachers may be accused of factionalism and partiality.

vi) Role ambiguities exist for teachers who attempt to combine their work as school teachers with roles in community development. Ideally at least, teaching presupposes a measure of professionalism and autonomy in classroom practice. Top-down community development usually requires agents who are able to work within an administrative structure where tasks are carried out in accordance with fairly rigid rules and regulations. Grass-roots-initiated community development requires creative, responsive and committed participation of a type which teachers may find difficult to reconcile with their regular duties.

Except in very special conditions, teachers' participation in all-round community development is unlikely to be successful. Furthermore, as has already been emphasised, the educational tasks of teachers are extremely complex and demanding, so much so that it must require superhuman efforts for them to combine teaching with community development. The thrust of the following pages, however, is not that teachers should be excluded from any community roles at all but rather that their roles should be clearly defined and the communities which they serve should be precisely identified.

THE COMMUNITY

What is the community today? Certainly it is rarely the small, homogeneous, close-knit group of people with a common language, culture, shared values and a sense of identity and belonging, as nostalgically remembered in romantic legend. In a world where national boundaries have divided ethnic groups and economic change has led to mass mobility, many communities have in common only their place of residence. In urban centres, in particular, communities may be diverse in language, culture, social origin and occupation. Ties of family and kin give way to linkages based upon the work-place or occupation. Changes in rural areas mean that strangers, government officials, extension agents, representatives of commercial firms and voluntary bodies reside, at least temporarily, alongside local people. In communities defined in terms of locality or administrative unit there is as much likelihood that there will be conflict of interests and values as that there will be harmony. This is especially so in societies divided by race, caste or class. Nomadic people too often clash with settled communities.

The People's School
The notion of the People's School is inspired by contemporary ideas about popular participation and accountability. These have been especially prevalent, perhaps, in Latin America. In Peru, for example, the Community Education Nuclei were managed by Community Education Councils on which the

representation was 40 per cent teachers, 30 per cent parents and 30 per cent local organisations (Bizot 1975). In other parts of the world too, participation has been a key theme. In the Philippines, for example, where community participation is encouraged by the authorities, school facilities and resources in the Barrio High Schools are shared cooperatively with the community (Manuel 1968; Manalang 1977). In Bangladesh, where village communities tend to lack interest in the 'government' primary school, School Managing Committees have recently been set up to encourage popular participation and a sense of involvement (Bangladesh, Ministry of Education 1983).

It is reasonable to assume, that if communities have a say in the running of schools, management will be more equitable and more just. But the danger is that community elites may dominate management committees and claim a disproportionate amount of educational resources for themselves and exercise patronage over the teachers. The schools then become the 'property' of the community elites and others are excluded. A situation like this occurred in Rajasthan, India in the 1970s (Roy 1980; Roy 1984; Naik 1983). The conventional school had official opening times which suited wealthier families whose children's labour was not needed in the fields and home. Unconventional village schools were set up under the guidance of the National Council for Educational Research and Training (NCERT). They would cater to the needs of the very poorest village children who could not attend schools in normal hours. The teachers were selected from among the villagers and given special training. Most villagers were enthusiastic but the village elite, local politicians and the teaching profession opposed the scheme because it threatened to spread educational resources more thinly. However, in this case, the schools succeeded

> (Attendance) in the morning school doubled, and the evening school drew a number of children who came despite the fact that they sometimes fell asleep in the last half hour ... Initially the parents were surprised and irritated by the fact that the school did not teach their children from books and slates, and that there was no hum of learning by rote. Learning through games also had to be explained to parents ...

Success in breathing life into the principle of

a people's school was largely, due in this case, to the commitment of the village teachers and the support of a national agency. Putting into practice ideals of democratic participation and account- ability involve teachers, and especially the principals of schools, in new ways of working (Beynon, Branch, Page and Jack 1977). They have to be clear about precisely which groups in the community they have responsibilities towards. They have to withstand attempts by powerful pressure groups to take over the school. At the same time they must be prepared to listen to and be accountable to the community members on matters which they have hitherto regarded as their exclusive professional concern. Lastly, but by no means least, they have to reconcile community demands on the use of school resources with the administrative regulations.

TEACHERS AND COMMUNITIES

Despite all the complexities involved in attempts to link schools with communities, it is the argument here that teachers must be involved in certain, precise ways with the various communities concerned with the school. Without this involvement teachers cannot fulfil their educational responsibilities.
There are three 'communities' with which teachers have to be involved. The first is the school community itself, including pupils, other teachers, and adult assistants. Secondly, there is the community which extends from pupils to their brothers and sisters, parents and families. Thirdly, there is the larger group of people who live in the catchment area of the school. At some time or other many of them are pupils or parents of pupils. Why are these three communities important if teachers are to fulfil their educational responsibilities and what are the implications of such community relationships for the tasks of teachers?

Creating a School Community
A priority for teachers is to foster a sense of community, an esprit de corps, in the school itself. This is because education is not merely concerned with academic development but with personal, emotional and social growth. There may well be opportunities for teachers to encourage character building in the formal curriculum, through such subjects as Civics, Social Studies, and Physical

Education. But, aside from the formal curriculum, the 'hidden curriculum' of the school also has a powerful influence on social learning (Lister 1974; Burton 1981). The hidden curriculum includes the social climate of the school, the nature of relationships between teachers and pupils, how discipline is maintained, how daily life is organised, co- and extra-curricular activities and the emphasis on competition or cooperation.

The principal and teachers need to act as a team, deliberately to create the type of community life which will encouarge the social development of pupils. Of course, the issue of what constitutes desirable social attitudes and conduct differs from context to context. But there are some widely held basic values such as respect for others, honesty and truthfulness which any school community can foster. Generally, schools can most easily encourage values and conduct which are legitimated by the wider society. For example, African Socialism in Tanzania and Humanism in Zambia are official philosophies which are mirrored in the life of schools. However, under dynamic leadership, or the charismatic vision of a particular school principal, some schools have succeeded in purveying a community spirit which runs counter to prevailing social trends.

The Swaneng Hill School, set up in Botswana in 1963, nurtured for a time a counter-culture of this type. The school, which was founded with official support, owed its vitality as an educational community to the energy and enthusiasm of its founder, Patrick van Rensburg. He has stated (1983:5) that the 'perhaps naive aim' of the school was 'to counter the growth of an elite by inculcating commitment to development and by providing the analytical and practical skills to match'. He and his teachers,

> sought the means in the curriculum, activities, organisation of the school, in the relations between staff and students and in the participatory involvement of students in decision-making, to give effect to these aims. We actually succeeded in building two large secondary schools involving students in construction making equipment, producing food, cooking it and cleaning and maintaining the school, and involving them in work and development in the community.

The early success of Swaneng Hill School was

undoubtedly due to its leadership. But van Rensburg himself suggests (1983:7-8) that the later decline of the distinctive character of the school was due to a reduction in political support for its aims and adverse economic conditions. In its later days it lost its production centre and, in accordance with the wishes of the wider community, became a conventional academically-oriented school.

The argument here has been that an important core educational role for teachers is to foster a sense of community in the school itself. By deliberately creating a positive school environment teachers contribute to what, we believe, is a major responsibility to develop the social, moral and spiritual dimensions of their pupils' lives. Unusually, in the case of Swaneng Hill School, the values purveyed through the school community ran counter to the incentives of the wider society. Most schools cannot attempt to transform society but do have an influential role in encouraging those values which the wider society prizes and in discouraging conduct considered anti-social.

Community Relevance

There is an important pedagogical reason why teachers should infuse their teaching with community relevance. Even though it is extremely difficult for them to decide on what criteria they should judge relevance, they have to tackle the issue, if they are to fulfil their core educational role (Sinclair with Lillis 1980:21-22). The case here is based on the proposition that one of the central roles of teachers is to develop concept learning and intellectual skills which, to paraphrase Paulo Freire, enables learners to become critically aware of their own reality and to be able to act upon it (Freire 1974).

The challenge for teachers in the community relevance issue is how to harness community resources to encourage critical awareness and intellectual maturity in learners. They have to relate the curriculum to the experience and interests of their pupils; they have to bring the curriculum home to them. By moving from the familiar to the unfamiliar they can encourage understanding (Bruner 1972:68-97). By relating abstract concepts of community issues and problems they can encourage children to practise intellectual skills and apply knowledge to issues in the community related to their own lives (Naik 1983).

This excerpt from Teaching Primary Science

(Young 1979:23) illustrates how teachers can encourage learners to be aware of the context in which they are growing up and develop a particular intellectual skill.

With older children

Tracks are useful for teaching inference. We can learn a great deal about animals from the tracks which they leave. By 'tracks' we mean anything which an animal leaves as a result of its activity. This may include scratches, droppings, rubbings, remains, parts of homes, footprints. For example, an ant-lion pit is a good example of a track (Fig 2.29). We do not know for sure that there are ant-lions at the bottom of these pits but it would be a reasonable inference.

You could begin by making a footprint in a tray of sandy soil ... Point out that if (the children) saw such a footprint on the ground, they might infer that somebody had walked that way ... Can they find tracks round the compound? ... Can (they) find animal 'homes' e.g. nests or cocoons? What can they infer from these homes?

The second example of a community-relevant approach comes from the CHILD-to-child programme (Aarons and Hawes, 1979:29). It is an approach which aims to involve children, in school and out, in action research to improve community health and hygiene. It encourages children's investigative, analytical and problem-solving skills.

All CHILD-to-child activities need to start with a discussion by children leading to an understanding of the purpose of their activity. Before starting the activity children need to discuss: What helps our school (or our village) to be a healthier place? How can we find out about the health of our school (or our village)? What can be done to make it better?

Making a health map.
Children can map their local community. They can use copies of maps already prepared to make their own maps. First the children should discuss what they will show on the map. This will help them to decide what is to be done to make their community a better place in which to grow up. Children can find out and mark on their maps: areas where animals and insects live that

spread diseases; areas where accidents can
easily happen to young children; areas where
people spread diseases ...

Jamaican primary schools recently participated
in a project to integrate the curriculum around
topics and themes with community relevance
(Jennings-Wray 1984). Pupils' comments showed how
learning had come alive for them. They learned from
experience. 'The lessons are more about things we
know and so are easier ...' 'I get to interview
people in my area and learn more about them'. 'Its
fun. I learn lots of things from it.'
The argument that the curriculum should relate
to community concerns should not be interpreted to
mean that learning should be restricted to parochial
horizons. Teachers have a responsibility to
encourage critical awareness of wider national and
international communities too. As pupils grow older
and their horizons widen, they should be able to
transfer and apply to the broader scene the
intellectual skills acquired in learning about the
immediate community. For the majority of children who
leave school after a few short years, the development
of transferable intellectual skills at an early stage
is crucial to their future capacity to develop as
effective members of both the local and wider
community.

Preparation for Life
The argument so far is that teachers must infuse the
curriculum with community relevance because this
enhances the process of learning and lays the
foundations for children to become well-educated
adults. As pupils get nearer to leaving school, their
focus of interest becomes what the school can do to
prepare them for adult life and, in particular,
earning a living. The fact that this becomes a need
and interest to young people is justification enough
why teachers should include 'the world of work' in
their teaching (Gardner 1981). But this is not to
suggest that school leavers should be subjected to
neo-colonial versions of adapted education,
preparing them for a life hewing wood and drawing
water in the immediate community. Nor is it to
suggest that general education should restrict
pupils to skills of narrow vocational relevance. In
any case, this is not really feasible. Employers
often prefer to recruit young people with good
general education and to train them on the job in

specific skills. School teachers do not normally have aptitude in teaching vocational skills. Good quality vocational training is very costly. And, moreover, narrowly vocational curricula have rarely proved popular in societies where general educational qualifications are more likely to lead to desirable jobs (Lauglo 1985).

A curriculum which ignored pupils' aspirations, anticipations, hopes and fears about their future lives, would be without interest and relevance to them. The role of teachers here is to help school leavers gain information and awareness of alternative occupations and associated life-styles, to introduce them to various occupational possibilities in the local and wider community and to help them to understand what sorts of skills are needed in different fields. Pupils may then make decisions about their lives on a realistic basis and choose elective subjects which may be of vocational relevance to them.

Evidence is accumulating that a curriculum which has such practical relevance may be popular if it reinforces, rather than distracts from, the process of gaining a good general education. For example, a small pilot project in Papua New Guinea, the Secondary Schools Community Extension Project, aimed to create positive attitudes and generate skills useful to school leavers in their own communities, as well as tackling the problem of an irrelevant academic high school curriculum (Vulliamy 1981). Teachers had designed the practical subjects in such a way that they reinforced the core knowledge and skills required of pupils in the conventional subjects, thus enhancing their chances of doing well in examinations. Another example, a recent evaluation of Industrial Education in Kenya's academic secondary schools, indicates that it is a popular subject (Lauglo 1985). It attracts some of the most academically able pupils in a country where interest in 'technical' jobs amongst school leavers in general is increasing. The issue which requires further examination, however, is why successful graduates of Industrial Education fare relatively badly in the job market.

Involving the Community in the Education of its Children

Teaching for community relevance and preparation for life may well involve members of the community in the education of school children. In areas such as

History, Geography, Social Studies, History and
Religious Education teachers may arrange for pupils
to learn from community members. School visits and
field trips enable pupils to learn from them in their
own institutional settings. Alternatively, community
members may visit the school.

There is another compelling educational
justification for involving the community in the
education of their own children. Research quite
clearly shows that well-directed parental interest
in children's schooling has a positive effect on
their motivation and achievement levels (for
example, Seng 1985). It follows that teachers have a
direct responsibility to collaborate with parents to
extract the maximum educational benefit for pupils.

The effort has to go much further than the
conventional Parent-Teacher Association, which
involves only a few, ambitious parents and serves
primarily as a fund-raising mechanism. Teachers must
organise regular contact with all parents. In Zambia,
for example, this is a duty of school principals. It
does not mean merely sending out information about
the school or having annual meetings where parents
can discuss their children's progress with teachers.
It also means encouraging parents to understand,
sympathise with and, where necessary, clarify the
aims of the school. It means inviting parents to
identify ways in which they can help and may
unwittingly hinder their children's learning. It
means encouraging them to take initiatives in drawing
the attention of teachers to learning difficulties
which their children may experience.

Parental collaboration with teachers in the
educational support of their children appears to be
most widespread in pre-primary and the early stages
of primary schooling. One fairly typical example was
part of the Compensatory Education Project in
Malaysia (Dove 1982a:24). The project aimed at
improving educational opportunities for the children
on rubber estates and paddy farms in rural
communities. Pre-school centres were set up and
parents' participation was encouraged. The project
capitalised on the high level of interest which
parents had in their children's education and
attempted to increase their knowledge and confidence
so that they could make a real contribution. Primary
schoolteachers helped to run workshops for parents.
Mothers learned to make simple learning materials and
took them home. The materials formed the link around
which teachers and parents were able to collaborate
in creating a positive home and school environment

for learning.

In this case the goal was to involve parents directly in the teaching-learning process. More often, perhaps, parents can be invited to play a supportive role in less direct ways. For very young children who need to be encouraged to form habits of school attendance, parents may organise a rota to accompany groups of children to school. This may be especially valuable in countries where, for cultural reasons, girls hesitate to make the journey to school alone or where the journey is long and hazardous. Teachers may involve the health care services in encouraging parents to detect physical and mental handicaps or other difficulties which, if undiagnosed, may lead to permanent learning disabilities. For older children who have homework and revision for public examinations, teachers can collaborate with parents in arranging for the best possible learning environment at home.

Close collaboration between teachers and members of the community of the type advocated here is relatively unusual. It occurs most frequently if there exists political and administrative support or if an individual principal succeeds in inspiring both teachers and parents with enthusiasm. There are a number of reasons why it is an unusual phenomenon. Parents often feel, especially at higher levels of schooling, that they have little contribution to make. Some feel that it is best to leave to teachers what they are paid to do. Schools do not always welcome parental involvement. Sometimes this may be because it takes managerial skills or administrative capacity which they do not have. Sometimes teachers develop a siege mentality, born of insecurity, about their proper educational role and status. Sometimes they want to keep parents away from the school because of misguided fears about dilution of their professional status.

The central thesis of this chapter so far is that teachers have core community-related educational responsibilities. They should foster the development of the community comprised of the school itself. They should ensure curriculum relevance to the community for pedagogical and social reasons. They should encourage parents to collaborate in supporting the educational aims of the school.

Involving Teachers in Community Education

Finally, we argue that, in certain circumstances, it may be appropriate for teachers to be involved in the education of the community. This argument is put forward cautiously for two main reasons. One is that teachers' core roles are already demanding. Their main concern should be the education of their pupils. The other is that it is only in special cases that school knowledge is directly of interest and welcome to adult members of the community.

The most obvious example of a possible contribution which teachers can make to community education is to open up school resources for general use. Apart from the cost-reducing arguments for community sharing of facilities and equipment, there are valid educational reasons why the school sports centre, its musical instruments or its technical workshops should be available to members of the community who wish to improve themselves. What must be recognised is that such sharing has to be underpinned by an efficient system of management of time and space if the needs of both adults and children are to be coordinated.

In many countries teachers have participated in efforts to eradicate adult illiteracy. With adequate training, time and material reward, there is evidence that teachers can make a real contribution. To give just one piece of evidence for this, an evaluation (Sjostrom 1983) of a non-government literacy drive in Ethiopia between 1962 and 1975 found that the most progress was made in improving adult literacy in areas where the schoolteachers were skilled and committed to the programme. Only too frequently, however, teachers are obliged to participate without adequate training, preparation or support. They teach reluctantly because the work is additional to their normal school teaching and they depress the motivation of adult learners because they use teaching methods and materials unsuited to their needs and status.

Factors like these tend to reinforce arguments against wholesale conversion of conventional schools to, and utilisation of teachers in, Community Education Centres except in very favourable circumstances. For them to be successful there must be, as a minimum, a radical change of attitude by teachers and community about the basic functions of the school. There has to be a strong management and coordinating framework. And, finally, school teachers have to be supported by others with skills in adult education if the range of community learning needs are to be met.

Notwithstanding all the constraints, however, the magic mix of circumstances do sometimes combine to achieve a close integration of school and community learning. We complete this discussion on the role of teachers in community education with a description by the Director of the Health Education Department (Darras 1985), New Caledonia, of a remarkable nutrition education programme. With careful preparation for teachers and the support of other extension agents, school children achieved a change in the dietary habits of the whole community through what they themselves learned in school.

The South Pacific region is becoming quite rapidly urbanised, and this is causing a decline in the general nutritional status. For this reason, a comprehensive nutrition programme has been set up, which is aimed at local agricultural and health personnel, and at school teachers. It should be said that the rural health educators and the 'Vigiles de Sante' volunteers work quite effectively at the community level. Nutrition education is a very recent activity in schools.

My objective, as the person responsible for health education , was to promote nutrition through the schools, thus involving the community in promoting health. This would be very difficult if we worked only with the health educators at the community level. We thought that by using the schools we would be able to make the link between the schools and the community.

We have been trying to make the teachers realise that it is necessary to teach nutrition in the schools, and to have within the education programme at primary level a part especially reserved for nutrition and health education. At the same time, we are working on the production of a health education curriculum. We are very fortunate in that the medical and educational sections are working so closely together.

Of course, there was a problem initially because the teachers had not been trained to teach nutrition, and because they lacked the resources. We therefore started to produce resource materials in my Department, and to make it easier for the teachers we opened it up so that they could come and see everything we have ...

The teachers are asked to volunteer. This is because real motivation is needed to teach health education. It is not yet compulsory to teach health education in schools if teachers do not want to do it; it is useless to force them to do so. I feel that in a situation in which we can easily control what is happening, it is better to wait until there is the motivation. I must say that such motivation is coming faster than had been expected at the beginning. Volunteer teachers can attend training sessions organised by the Health Education Department.

My Department has been crowded with teachers every Wednesday (their free day). They come to my office for slides, documents and so on, and we have had to set up a special service within the Department for health education in the schools. A section attached to the Teachers' Training College was created to collect all the educational materials that could be used by teachers, and to prepare new materials, such as slides and pamphlets in collaboration with the Health Education Department.

As far as the method of teaching is concerned, I trust the teachers to use an appropriate method, based on the pedagogic methods used in primary schools, which start from "what do we know? what do we see? what has to be done?", and ensure that pupils learn by doing. As long as they are given the necessary theoretical knowledge of nutrition, they will be able to use it effectively with the children – indeed more so than either the doctor or myself. I would like to give an example. Recently I visited a school in which there are twenty two children. This school is very close to the local community, which has a population of 126. The school lunch was found not to be balanced, so together with the teachers we decided to see that the children had a balanced diet, at least for their lunch, by the children themselves making discoveries. As soon as they understood the idea of a balanced diet, they realised that their lunch was not balanced. They also saw that what was missing was available in the community, and that the parents were not preparing those foods and putting them into the children's lunch baskets.

The children first said that their parents should be told what to eat. And indeed, the health educators have already explained it to the parents, but people's food habits are very difficult to change. When they have some money they buy tinned food and similar things. If they have four or five children at school, they cannot afford to give all of them a good lunch - because they do not use locally produced food.

During a month of observation, we left the parents alone. The children realised that their lunch had not changed. The children then said that as they had no green leaves or raw vegetables in their lunch, why could they not grow them at school? They decided to grow their own vegetables (such as carrots and lettuces) at school. They then realised that if they grew vegetables at school, they would also have to prepare them there. The teachers were willing to help them (with me behind, pushing them a little). We had hoped that would happen, so had already prepared a small store, but we waited until the children asked to grow the vegetables.

On another occasion, a child said to me that a lot would have to be planted to feed his family of ten. That led us to the importance of family planning: the children could see that family planning and nutrition are very closely related.

The children also learnt (and we have put a lot of emphasis on this) about the frequent problems of anaemia and so on. We asked them what was still missing in their diet. They said that eggs were needed, so they decided to keep a little poultry. The parents gave some money, a small enclosure was built, some chickens were brought from their homes, and the children then had eggs in the school. The teachers were very surprised at all that was happening.

Parents became curious and came to the school at lunch time to observe what was happening. We thought that they would say now the school was doing so much they could forget about the children's lunch. That did not happen, however, and the community has become involved in that way. It seemed that the mothers did not want to have to say that the school was providing the lunch for their children. We noticed that the lunches were changing; the mothers were putting in green leaves, eggs and so on. The result was that the school production of these things was too great, so the children started to sell their produce. This gave some of the mothers the idea of raising chickens and of selling eggs and also of growing and selling lettuces. A whole development process has begun within the community from what was started in the school. I think it is very important to make a close link between the community and the schools.

CONCLUSION

Such success stories in integrated school and community education are comparatively rare. Nevertheless, even more modest attempts by teachers to link the school with the community in educational endeavours require a certain measure of decentralisation of control over the curriculum. Over the last thirty years many countries have overhauled their curricula to replace foreign material with that more relevant to national development. More recently, there has been a great deal of experimentation in devolving responsibilty for localising the curriculum to teachers colleges and education resource centres, especially at primary and lower secondary levels which are not so constrained by the influence of universities and examinations as are higher secondary schools. But if curricula are to be responsive to community needs in the various ways identified here, the process has to go much further. The teachers in a school or a group of local schools have to be able to examine and adjust the official curriculum, within national guidelines, on a regular basis. This presupposes a measure of professional autonomy which few teachers enjoy. Some of the reasons why they do not do so are examined in the following pages.

Part Two

PLANNING AND MANAGEMENT

Chapter Five

STATUS AND THE TEACHING PROFESSION

It is often asserted that the status of schoolteachers is very low. But is it? And why should status be so important an issue? It is also a subject of much debate as to whether teaching is or is not a profession and whether it should be more professionalised, or even de-professionalised. These questions are often addressed amongst conceptual ambiguity and confusion. It is important to clarify the issues, however, because, as we shall argue below, improvement in status and increased professionalisation are essential to improvement in the quality of teachers.

STATUS

The UNESCO Recommendation concerning the Status of Teachers (1966:3) defined 'status' as used in relation to teachers as

> both the standing or regard accorded them, as evidenced by the level of appreciation of the importance of their function and of their competence in performing it, and the working conditions, remuneration and other material benefits accorded them relative to other professional groups.

This definition encapsulates most of the different but inter-related dimensions of teachers' status which are discussed here, for purposes of analysis, under three headings, personal, occupational and professional.

Personal Status

Personal status is the regard, appreciation or esteem which teachers as individuals earn from those who know them - pupils, parents and community. The level of public esteem which an individual attracts inevitably affects self-esteem and morale. Attempts to answer the question whether teachers as persons are less well-regarded today than in the past must be tentative. Personal status depends on the unique relationship which a teacher, as a personality and character, establishes with others. Personal status is earned according to who one is and how one conducts oneself across the whole range of human relationships, including work relationships.

Commonsense, however, suggests that it is, perhaps, more difficult today for teachers to earn high personal reputations. With the rapid expansion of educational services over the last forty years, teacher shortages have led to the recruitment of many people who, in the past, could not have aspired to a 'white collar' job. Many teachers are from lowly social backgrounds. In highly stratified and ascriptive societies this is a handicap to them. In more egalitarian and achievement-oriented societies, people who 'make good' as teachers operate in competitive, status-seeking environments and many fail to earn the personal status they seek. In addition, teachers can no longer rely, as we have seen, on achieving personal status because of superior education and the consequent power to act as cultural brokers. Finally, in systems where teachers are recruited, posted and deployed according to national needs, the possibility of their establishing long-standing personal relationships with local communities are more difficult.

Occupational Status

Personal and occupational status are, of course, inter-linked. It is difficult to judge a person purely as a person, distinct from what he or she does for a living. It is often claimed, moreover, that expansionary pressures on teacher recruitment have led to the selection and self-selection of people with inferior personal characteristics, lacking in motivation, drive and ability to enter more prestigious occupations.

However we judge the validity of these claims, it is true that schoolteachers tend to suffer from low morale as an occupational group - or, rather, groups in the plural, since governments, teachers associations and teachers themselves tend to differentiate primary from secondary, graduate from non-graduate, general from technical teachers. The reasons why they suffer from low morale also partly explain why teaching ranks low in prestige relative to other occupations. There are four main factors involved, salary and conditions of service, working conditions and career opportunities.

As long ago as 1967 an eminent Nigerian commentator, Babs Fafunwa (1967:84) made an observation which teachers would still perceive as correct today.

> The African teacher, like his counterpart in most parts of the world, is one of the most poorly paid of all professional workers ... Yet the services of the teachers are indispensable to a nation, for they ... influence in no small measure the lives of the nations' youth and the nation's future.

Occupational status today depends largely on what rewards those engaged in the occupation can command. Analysis of comparative rewards - pay and other benefits - is a complicated process. Few generalisations can be made from one country or region to another because the level of rewards has to be judged not only against international yardsticks but also against the unique historical and socio-economic context of each country. However, we do need to extend our research into salary structures in the teaching profession, if only because this would provide a sounder basis for policy and planning in regulating teacher demand and supply (Chapter Six).

Salaries and Benefits. The information used here comes mainly from studies by ILO and UNESCO (ILO 1978; ILO 1979; ILO/UNESCO 1983). The data relate to public school teachers. But it should be noted that this does not cover a sizeable proportion of the total number of teachers, those in private schools whose salaries may be much higher or lower and foreign teachers who usually enjoy higher remuneration.

The ILO/UNESCO (1983:25-32) survey revealed that governments tend to set teachers' salaries in line with those for other public servants. Twenty-three governments across the industrialised and developing world gave information on teachers' salaries relative to those of public servants with comparable qualifications (see Bame 1979). Amongst developing countries, in Bangladesh, Chile, Egypt, Jamaica, the Philippines and Venezuela, the two groups have comparable salaries. In Cameroon, Kenya, Mexico and Papua New Guinea, teachers are relatively better paid. In Colombia, Guyana, Nicaragua, Peru and Sri Lanka they are, relatively poorly paid. Nineteen countries compared their teachers' salaries with those in the private sector. In Cameroon, Colombia, India, Jamaica, Kenya, Nicaragua, Sri Lanka and Thailand, teachers' salaries are lower than those paid to similarly qualified persons in the private sector. In none of the developing countries surveyed are they higher. However, in some recently developed oil-rich economies in the Middle East, public sector salaries, including teachers', are higher than in the private sector.

Table 5:1 is adapted from an ILO analysis of teachers' salaries against average earnings in manufacturing industry. In Bangladesh, Kenya, Nicaragua and Pakistan, primary schoolteachers at the start of their careers in 1980 earned salaries ten per cent or less than the average level of earnings in local manufacturing industry. In Bangladesh and Pakistan the situation was the same for secondary school teachers. However, scale increments may eventually work in teachers' favour in some situations. In the case of Argentina, salaries are fixed according to the number of hours worked.

The most frequently used criterion for fixing teachers' salaries is the level of academic attainment, education or training (ILO/UNESCO 1983:25). Length of service is also important. Other criteria are levels of responsibility, (Cuba, Guyana), the level of the school (the Philippines), personal conduct, political and social activity and the nature of the post occupied (for example, special schools). Chile and Kenya mention merit rating.

Most of the countries replying to the survey questionnaire stated that there are formal arrangements to adjust teachers' salaries to the cost of living. In most cases, salaries or cost of living allowances are reviewed regularly. In Chile they are adjusted whenever prices rise by a given percentage. In Cameroon, Pakistan, the Philippines and Thailand adjustments are made on an ad hoc basis. In Venezuela they are negotiated with the unions. But the main finding of the survey is that in general, the cost of living has risen faster than teachers' salaries.

Where other benefits are concerned, sickness and retirement are the contingencies most generally

Table 5.1: Gross Monthly Salaries of Schoolteachers compared with Average Monthly Earnings in Manufacturing Industry, 1980.

Country & Currency	Primary School teacher		Upper Secondary School teacher		Average Earnings in manufacturing industry	Remarks
	Initial Salary	Final Salary	Initial Salary	Final Salary		
Argentina (pesos)	593,130		666,252		353,000	Sec. teacher for 18 hr. week
Bangladesh (takas)	300	540	625	1,315	700 (est)	Secondary: highest level
Cuba (pesos)	148	171	211	250	150	Pry. Grad 3; Sec. Grad. 7
Ecuador (sucres)	6,060	10,585	8,855	15,495	6,620 (Jan 81)	Pry: P3; Sec.: graduate/approved, Scale II
Kenya (shillings)	885	1,560	2,990	4,040	1,252	
Mexico (pesos)	15,000	18,000	21,000	24,000	11,965 (June 81)	Final salaries after 30 years service. Secondary: 30 hour week
Nicaragua (cordobas)	1,650	2,310	2,760	4,000	2,125	Final salary after 30 years service. Secondary: 30 hour week; manufacturing 45 hour week
Pakistan (rupees)	370	640	520	1,010	640 (est)	Primary: level 8 (certified teacher). Secondary: level 14 (Bachelor of Education)

Source: ILO/UNESCO (1983) Report of Joint ILO/UNESCO Committee of Experts on the Application of the Recommendation concerning the Status of Teachers (ILO, Geneva) pp.27-31.

provided for. Paid holidays and maternity leave are
also common. For teachers in remote or rural areas,
additional facilities and incentives are financial
allowances, accelerated increments, free home
travel, subsidised housing and regular study leave
etc. (ILO/UNESCO 1983:111).

The ILO/UNESCO (1983) survey covers information
only from the few countries which supplied
sufficiently precise data for any conclusions to be
drawn. We must remember also that such data are
quickly out-dated. Salary issues have quality and
cost implications. A global analysis is therefore
needed to document the data, including policies on
starting salaries, how and when increments are
awarded (annually, automatically or by merit) and on
compatability.

In the 1970s salaries in Nigeria were improved
considerably and had a positive impact on the
recruitment of secondary school graduates into
teaching. In a survey at the end of the decade Nwagwu
(1981) found that the position of teachers was again
deteriorating against other comparable occupations.
We complete this discussion with an excerpt from his
conclusions which emphasise a general problem in many
countries where problems of implementation,
efficiency and equity exacerbate the salary problem.

> The Federal Ministries of Education and
> Establishments have ... advised the State
> Ministries of education to implement decisions
> and policies meant either to improve service
> conditions of teachers or to bring the
> conditions in line with those enjoyed by civil
> servants. Such directives are occasionally
> ignored or the implementation is delayed by
> State Governments for one reason or another. For
> example, some State governments have not
> implemented the Federal Ministry of Establish-
> ment's Circular No. 15 of 1977 which provided a
> new structure for Nigeria Certificate of
> Education (N.C.E.) teachers up to Grade 11 ...
> Shortage of funds has often been given by
> state governments for non-payment of teachers'
> entitlements such as annual leave allowance ...
> This is of course unacceptable to both the
> serving teachers and the secondary school
> students we expect to recruit for training as
> teachers. For example, it is plain
> discrimination if a newly promoted executive
> officer in the civil service on Grade Level 07
> is able to receive a car loan a few weeks after

his promotion yet a graduate teacher or a
headmaster on Grade Level 08 has to wait for
years to receive his own car loan from the same
government (Nwagwu 1981:85-86).

WORKING CONDITIONS

In the past, to be a graduate secondary schoolteacher
was considered a respectable aspiration. Teaching at
this level compared well in prestige with other
professions. Today, with the expansion and
democratisation of schooling to even the remotest
rural areas, schoolteaching at any level cannot
compare in working conditions with these
occupations.

Part of the problem is the inadequate physical
environment of many schools which lack amenities,
equipment and materials (see Chapter Nine). Another
aspect is crowded classrooms. Sometimes this is
because of lack of physical space, at others lack of
teachers. The permitted maximum sizes of classes are
high in most of the countries represented in the
survey by ILO/UNESCO (1983:154 and 68-79). In the
majority of the developing countries the actual
average class size is also extremely high (Table
5.2). In most countries average class sizes and
pupil-teacher ratios are close to the permitted
maxima. The ILO/UNESCO (1983:125-135) survey
reported that a number of the developing countries
studied, including Bangladesh, Barbados, Cameroon,
Chile, Cuba, Egypt, Guyana, Indonesia, Jordan,
Nicaragua, Pakistan, Peru, Philippines, Sri Lanka,
Thailand and Tunisia, experience teacher shortages.
(This is a theme we take up again in Chapter Six).
Table 5.2 indicates, however, that, except in
Bangladesh, Cameroon, Indonesia, Kenya, Nicaragua
and Pakistan, these shortages are not general.
Rather, they relate to specific levels or subjects or
to particular geographical areas or isolated
locations.

Career Opportunities

Schoolteaching tends to have low occupational status
because it does not offer good career opportunities
whereby a majority of able and ambitious people can
expect to attain posts of responsibility and
commensurate remuneration. In most countries, the
only formal limitation on promotion is the possession
of the requisite qualifications for transfer to

Table 5.2: Permitted and Average Class Sizes (and/or Pupil-Teacher Ratios in Replying Countries, 1980).

| (1) | Maximum Permitted Class Size | | Actual Class Size | | Remarks |
	Primary (2)	Secondary (3)	Average (4)	Public schools (5)	(6)
Argentina	40	40	19	31	Col. 4: urban 26, rural 8
Bangladesh	40	40,50	52 urban / 36 rural	42 urban / 32 rural	
Barbados	30:1	25:1	25:1	19:1	Pupil-teacher ratios
Cameroon	50	40	51	40	Includes state-supported private schools
Chile	45	45	-	-	Pupil teacher ratio
Cuba	varies with classroom size		18:1	13:1	Col. 4 & 5: pupil teacher ratios for public and private schools
Ecuador	40	40	33:1	15:1	
Egypt	50	40,36	-	-	Col 4: classes in urban areas up to 130 pupils, Col. in principal towns, 40
Gabon			45	30	
Guyana	40	35	30.8	29.7, 40.9	
India	50	50	30-40	30-40	Pupil-teacher ratios Cols 2 & 3: the higher the level of class the higher the permitted maximum
Indonesia	not fixed	not fixed	33	41,38	
Jamaica	-	-	45-55:1	30:1	
Jordan	variable	variable	34.1	31.3, 35.3	
Kenya	50	40,35	-	-	
Madagascar	70	70	45	45	
Mauritius	-	-	40-45	40-45	

| (1) | Maximum Permitted Class Size | | Actual Class Size | | Remarks |
	Primary (2)	Secondary (3)	Average (4)	Public schools (5)	(6)
Nicaragua	35-45	35-45	41:1 urban	41:1	Cols 2 & 3: minimum and maximum Cols 4 & 5: rural is 48:1, pupil -teacher ratios
Pakistan	not fixed	not fixed	40-50 31.2:1	40-50 25.8:1 16.2:1	
Papua New Guinea					
Peru	30-45	30-45	23	39	Cols. 4 & 5: includes public and private, private range 25-70
Philippines	40	40	–	–	In emergencies, classes of 50 permitted. In 2 shift schools, some teachers have 2 shifts of up to 30 pupils
Sri Lanka	55	45	25.3-30.5	19.2-28.5	
Tanzania	–	–	45	35-40,22-25	Since 1977 average class sizes in primary have risen sharply due to introduction of UPE
Thailand	–	–	45	40	Cols 4 & 5: actual range 20-50
Tunisia	30-38	40,36	33.8	34.2	
Venezuela	30	30	–	–	Col. 2: Grades 1-8, Col 3, grades 9-10

Source: ILO/UNESCO (1983) Report of Joint ILO/UNESCO Committee of Experts on the Application of the Recommendation concerning the Status of Teachers (ILO, Geneva), pp. 69-77

another level of schooling or specialism (ILO/UNESCO 1983:14-15). This means that secondary teachers tend to have better prospects than primary because they are in general better qualified. This creates problems when senior posts in primary education are monopolised by highly qualified people who lack primary experience. But at every level the overall number of senior posts, whether in teaching, administration, supervision or related fields, tends to be small. Thus, promotion opportunities, in practice, are restricted to only a very few.

The ILO/UNESCO (1983) data indicate that academic qualifications, length of service and performance are the main promotion criteria. In Thailand, seniority is the only fact taken into account. The authors of the survey suggest that seniority or length of experience is, in fact, a principal criterion in many countries. This has adverse implications for the career prospects of female teachers who often have to interrupt their work to assume family responsibilities. In Guyana, for instance, the frequent absences and lower performance standards 'to which women teachers with family responsibilities are prone' adversely affect their chances of securing promotion (ILO/UNESCO 1983:113). We return to this theme in Chapter Seven.

In most countries which responded to the survey, promotional posts are filled from within the teaching profession. In Columbia, however, a number are reserved for governmental recommendation. Promotion procedures vary. The judgement of inspectors, school managers and principals frequently play a part. Ecuador and Venezuela use competitive examinations. Jamaica relies on Ministry decisions on the advice of the National Teaching Council on which the teachers' organisations are represented. Teachers' organisations have a role to play, also, in Guyana, Mexico, Nicaragua but not in Tanzania.

The claim is frequently heard that teaching offers poor career opportunities relative to other occupations. We have little comparative data to go on. But, in any case, it all depends on which other occupations are taken as the yardstick. The civil service is probably the one most commonly used by teachers' associations. But, arguably, for pre-primary and primary teachers, qualified field posts in agriculture and health might be appropriate.

The need to provide better career opportunities in teaching are well recognised. They would attract better qualified recruits and reduce wastage of people of calibre. In a number of countries the situation is being tackled. In Kenya, for example, innovations included new M.Ed. and B.Ed. degrees for able and experienced primary teachers who were previously unable to gain access to leadership positions in primary schooling and teacher training because they lacked the necessary formal qualifications. Other countries in Africa are also developing in-service programmes for the profess- ional development of primary education personnel, including supervisors and inspectors (Chapter Ten).

Bangladesh provides another example of a country where the authorities have recognised the need for primary education leadership to come from primary specialists. In 1978 the Academy for Fundamental Education, later re-designated the National Academy for Primary Education (NAPE), was set up under the Ministry of Education (Dove 1983b). Its main functions are to train primary teacher trainers, develop and test materials and conduct evaluation and research in primary education. NAPE is now the apex institution for primary education; but the problem still remains that it cannot draw upon primary teachers for its staffing because they do not normally have the Batchelors and Masters degrees necessary to be upgraded for service in a high status institution like NAPE. Currently, degrees in education in Bangladesh concentrate on secondary teaching, except, that is, for an option within the Diploma and Masters degree programmes of the Institute of Education and Research, University of Dhaka. Bangladesh urgently needs to establish opportunities whereby limited numbers of primary school teachers selected for leadership positions can be encouraged to specialise in primary education at graduate level.

Such re-structuring and institutional develop- ment is a long term endeavour. Meanwhile, however, Bangladesh has taken steps to create some limited promotion opportunities for primary school teachers. In 1981, new Assistant Upazilla Education Officers were appointed for the first time and school principals were made eligible for promotion into the ranks of primary school administration. In 1984, plans were afoot to provide new job descriptions and responsibility allowances for principals, who, till then, had reached their position by virtue of seniority alone. Thus, measures are being taken which will for the first time enable classroom teachers to rise up the career ladder of primary education.

PROFESSIONAL STATUS

We began this chapter by asking whether the status of teachers is poor. We have seen that, in general, this is the case and we have examined some of the factors which create status anxieties for the teaching profession. Low professional status has partly to do with low salaries, poor working conditions and poor career prospects. It has also to do with the low levels of qualifications and lack of professional training of many teachers. Because of recent expansionary pressures and teacher shortages, many teachers, as we have seen, are teaching age groups, levels and specialisms for which they are not trained. In some situations, heavy reliance on better qualified foreigners detracts from the image of the local teaching profession. In others, feminisation of teaching, especially at primary level, contributes, as we shall see in Chapter Seven, to a public image of teaching as an occupation for people with low commitment and willing to accept low salaries (Birdsall and Fox 1985; Smock 1981: 209-245). Furthermore, the teaching profession itself has not as yet generated a sound body of theoretical knowledge and a set of technical concepts which would help to legitimate its claims to professional status.

In the following pages, the argument is that full professionalisation is a goal which governments and teachers themselves should jointly pursue, as fast and far as is possible within the cost constraints. It is an important goal. Failure to move forward is to prejudice the quality of teaching and learning in modern education systems.

PROFESSIONALISATION

The term 'professionalisation' refers to two related but distinct phenomena. One is the pressure by teachers and their unions and associations for better pay, conditions of service, working environments and promotion prospects. The other is the process of professional development whereby teachers as individuals improve their teaching competence and the teaching 'profession' as a whole improves in quality (Hoyle 1980). By 'quality' here we mean improvements in the way teachers teach. The desired outcome is better educated pupils. We are concerned here with the second meaning of the term 'professionalisation' and the relationship of professional development with improved professional status. Of course, in practice, the two senses of the term 'professionalisation' often merge, especially in the long-standing debate about whether or not teachers are 'true professionals'.

This debate has its roots in North American and European sociological analyses of a whole range of professions and semi-professions (for example, Etzioni 1969; Jackson 1970). Western analyses were imported to clarify the status of teachers in developing countries (for example, Peil 1977:205-6); Blakemore and Cooksey 1980:135-6). Not all of these analyses were uncritical of the difficulties of applying theses developed about professional groups in western industrial societies to the very different contexts of, say, post-independence West Africa (for example, Johnson 1973; Shils 1963). Nevertheless, in the author's opinion, the debate about whether teachers are true professionals has been largely arid and misguided, based on false premises. But because so many words have been spent on it, it cannot be ignored.

The Older Professions
Much of the debate has been superficial, answering real questions with definitions. Schoolteachers are compared with independently practising lawyers and doctors as the 'ideal types' of true professionals. Not surprisingly teachers fall short of the measure applied and are labelled semi-professionals. The criteria by which they are judged are the supposed characteristics of the older 'learned' professions. These are, first and foremost, specialist knowledge and skills based on theory and research and a long period of training; professional autonomy in the sense that members of the profession control entry standards, selection and administer their own rules of conduct; and a 'service' ethos which means that the interests of the client come first; professional fees are commensurate with services rendered.

Prior to discussion of the issue in these terms, it should be noted that the characterisation of lawyers and doctors is inaccurate. Whilst they are certainly specialists, it is not the case that their working practice is based solely, or even securely, on guidelines derived from research and theory. Doctors have to judge between competing theories and ever-changing research findings when deciding how to utilise their expertise. Their training reflects this state of affairs for it comprises 'disciplines' as far apart as chemistry and sociology, as well as much rote memorisation and practical, hands-on, skills training. Certainly good doctors utilise their theoretical knowledge and the findings of research but they also rely on working experience, knowledge of the patient and intelligent guesswork.

Nor are many doctors and laywers the autonomous professionals idealised in the literature. Often they are employees working in government or commercial concerns, with no direct responsibility to clients nor control over their profession. Even independent doctors and lawyers do not conform to the ideal type. Johnson (1972) sees them as part of a fast-disappearing laissez-faire capitalism, rarely found today anywhere in the world and particularly not in state-dominated developing societies. According to Johnson, independent professional groups are essentially monopolistic forms of organisations, selling services to clients who can afford their fees. Illich (1977:12) goes further. He suggests that professional groups are 'disabling'; not only do they monopolise knowledge and skills which ought to be freely available in a just and caring society, but they create artificial 'needs' in clients who then have to pay the 'specialists' to have them met.

But to return to the main issue. It is quite clear, whether one takes a benign or hostile view of the motivation for professionalisation, that school teachers do not measure up (or down) to the criteria set out above. At present, the practice of teaching is based as much on rule of thumb, working experience, common sense and guesswork as on research-based theoretical knowledge. Many teachers have no training at all, let alone long periods of high level training. In almost no country do teachers control their own profession but serve under university, private agency or government bureau-cracies. Although teachers provide a service, 'education', they may also be perceived as providing a product, 'educational manpower', nor is it clear which of their many clients - those who pay their salaries, parents, community or pupils - come first.

Teaching a Profession?
Should teachers, then, seek a model for professionalisation in the older professions? In a practical sense this would be unrealistic. Under contemporary socio-economic conditions they cannot hope to attain autonomy and the high social status and incomes of doctors and lawyers. In a more

fundamental sense, it has to be recognised that teaching is unlike the service rendered when a doctor treats a wound or a lawyer solves a case. These professionals provide a service but do not share their specialist knowledge. They do not have to engage in any direct relationship with the client as a person. Even a psychiatrist is only concerned with treating specific conditions. Teachers, in contrast, have to be concerned with enabling learners to develop to their full potential as human beings. They have to engage with their clients as persons. Their ultimate aim is to pass on their specialist understanding and skills and to teach people how to learn.

Does it follow from this line of argument, then, that teachers do not need training and, in particular, a theoretically-based training? Are personal charisma and intuition more important? Are teachers born, not made? It is the opinion of the author that none of these assumptions are correct. Even if the very best of teachers do have a natural gift, it does not follow that their skills cannot be encouraged by training, just as gifted musicians benefit from theoretical understanding and practice of their skills. They need a deep understanding of the structure of the subject matter in which they specialise and of the implications for practical teaching of research into learning and human development. They need to acquire insights into the various roles of teachers in society and, of course, they need training in pedagogy.

In summary, then, we have separated out some of the issues involved in the complex question as to whether the status of teachers has declined. We have distinguished personal from occupational and professional status, though, of course, they are closely inter-related in reality. The fact that these issues have a high priority for teachers themselves reflects their anxieties about their status (Spaulding 1975). As we have seen, teachers suffer from a lack of public sympathy about their roles in school and in the community, they often fail to meet the high aspirations which people have of them in terms of examination results, and, in addition, though many of them are ill-equipped by education and training to fulfil the challenges society sets them, they feel dissatisfied with the rewards they get for their services.

111

DE-PROFESSIONALISATION?

It is sometimes suggested that professionalisation is not an appropriate goal for teachers and that teaching should be de-professionalised. But what does this really mean? There are at least three dimensions to the issue.

The first usually springs from concern by the authorities about the potential political power of teachers as an occupational group. In some Latin American and Asian countries, for instance, labour unions have strong traditions. Teachers organise for both occupational and broader political goals. But, in general, it is more common for teachers to have difficulties in organising themselves because of their lack of cohesion, their fragmentation by qualification, level and specialism. In particular, secondary teachers tend to keep a status distinction between themselves and more poorly qualified and more poorly paid primary teachers.

Many governments do, in fact, allow teachers to be members of professional organisations (ILO 1977:ILO/UNESCO 1983:21). Some countries limit the power of organisations to act independently of state machinery. Some allow freedom of association but not the right to strike. Some allow only one organisation to exist. In general, however, few governments breach international conventions, except in emergency situations, or seek to 'de-professionalise' teachers by denying them the right to their own professional association at all.

A second strand in the argument put forward for de-professionalisation emphasises the costs of increased professionalisation. Lower occupational status and, presumably, less organisational strength, means lower salaries, fewer fringe benefits and less costly training. Although few governments would seriously contemplate this as a deliberate policy, nevertheless, chronic neglect or starvation of resources to the education system can result in demoralisation and creeping de-professionalisation.

The argument for de-professionalisation on the grounds of cost is sometimes supported by the claim that the 'barefoot doctor' model is, in any case more appropriate to the role of teachers in countries attempting to provide a basic education to all. Teachers of basic literacy and numeracy, working with illiterate adults as well as in school, teacher 'animateurs' involved in community development and mobilisation, should not, it is claimed, distance themselves from the community by emphasising occupational and professional status distinctions. They should live like the people. They require only modest training for the modest expertise required and, commensurately, modest salaries. Whilst one can agree that teachers should not live in style too dissimilar from local people, the claim that only modest expertise is needed to teach basic skills to adults and children is quite false. In addition, they perform a valuable service which deserves adequate reward. And, in any case, such a model is hardly appropriate, if at all, to teachers of <u>different</u> specialisms at <u>any</u> level of the school system.

In Chapter Four reference was made to the ways in which lay community members can contribute to the life of the school. Unfortunately, the argument for the greater utilisation of teachers' aides or paraprofessionals is often regarded by teachers as a threat of dilution or de-professionalisation. Such fears have prevented the full use of non-professional aides to teachers in a number of countries (ILO/UNESCO 1983:63-67). This has been a problem in countries, for example, where the innovative Project IMPACT has been tried out (Cummings 1984). This project is a carefully-conceived alternative strategy to provide low cost basic education utilising teachers' aides from amongst the local community, peer learning and self-instructional modular materials. In the Philippines it has flourished in a form fairly close to the original conception but, notably, in Indonesia, Liberia, Indonesia and Jamaica, there is little use of teachers' aides. In Project IMPACT in Bangladesh, where the potential cost-saving on teachers has to be an attractive feature to government, primary school teachers have so far resisted attempts to introduce 'teacher substitutes' into their schools.

In Project IMPACT teachers' aides were intended to carry out quasi-teaching tasks such as keeping pupil records, hearing pupils' read and managing the use of learning modules. It is, therefore, understandable that teachers should feel the threat to their professional and occupational status. But there is also a whole range of less threatening, non-educational tasks which paraprofessionals may usefully undertake and which would release teachers' time and energy for more centrally educative tasks. These include the physical care and welfare of learners, the care of equipment and materials and community liaison and mobilisation. Some tasks would demand a measure of skill such as the maintenance of laboratory equipment; others would require little skill, such as accompanying very small children to and from school.

The suggestion put forward here is that teachers associations have an important and constructive role to play in investigating the potential of a wider use of paraprofessionals to support (not substitute for) teachers. By accepting the hard but inevitable economic fact that countries are going to have to limit the expansion of their teaching forces, by concentrating on pressing for the very best training, conditions of service and working environments for a high quality teaching profession, and by taking the initiative to set out the conditions under which paraprofessionals may be effectively utilised, teachers' associations could lead the way in ensuring that the quality of educational services is maintained and, hopefully, improved, possibly at lower unit cost per pupil.

Unfortunately, there has been little systematic research in developing countries into the conditions under which paraprofessionals are acceptable and useful (but see, Lauglo and Gartner for OECD, 1977). A variety of case studies in a variety of settings, indicate their usefulness in pre-school education (Zambia, Ministry of Education, 1975; Sestini 1985; Sattar 1982) though even here there are dangers of creeping professionalisation.

It would also be helpful to examine the lessons of experience in other sectors where paraprofessionals are established, such as medical and health care, ante- and post-natal mother and child care, agriculture and community development (Brekelbaum 1984; Dillon 1984; Aarons 1983). Indications are that the following factors are important:

i)   precise descriptions of tasks and competencies are needed to avoid tension and ambiguities;

ii) the local community should have a say in the selection of paraprofessionals and if possible they should be recruited locally;

iii) teachers should be involved in initial orientation and in supervision; they should liaise with the community.

iv) teachers should be trained to manage paraprofessional personnel. In particular they should understand the limits to their responsibilities and be sensitive to the distinctions between volunteer helpers, paid auxiliaries and unqualified teachers.

CONCLUSION

This chapter has explored approaches to some of the complex questions about the status and professionalisation of teachers. These issues are by no means relevant only in developing countries. But in such contexts, severe resource constraints, particularly in terms of the resources available for training and remunerating teachers, combined with the unstable and insecure nature of the teaching force in a changing educational environment, accentuate the status ambiguities and anxieties of teachers. Such problems must be faced, for poor status affects morale, recruitment and teacher quality.

We have suggested above that de-professionalisation, however this concept is interpreted, is not the answer. Rather, governments, the public and the teachers themselves should pursue full professionalisation. The crux of the issue is that teachers should be able to do a good job and win public recognition for this. They should not be required to be 'jacks of all trades and masters of none'. Top priority should go to better training and professional development - a theme explored further in subsequent chapters.

But it is not just training institutions which have a role to play in pursuing greater teacher professionalisation. The authorities responsible for managing recruitment and deployment must also play a part in ensuring teachers work in conducive environments (Chapter Seven). Universities can do much to legitimise Education as a worthwhile and serious field of study and publicly endorse the importance of training for teachers. They can lend their authority to the teaching profession by participating in policy-formulation and research. This would be especially valuable for primary education which, as a largely non-graduate occupational field, has suffered chronically from a poor public image.

Finally, but by no means least importantly, teachers' unions and associations have a crucial role to play. It is sometimes suggested that unions alienate public sympathy by selfishly campaigning for improvements in members' salaries and conditions of service. The view taken here is that they should continue to press for improvements in the occupational status of teachers and resist attempts by the authorities to take advantage of teachers' goodwill by paying them less than they are worth. But alongside these traditional activities unions should also take the lead in pressing for greater professional autonomy. They should propose ways in which the teaching profession could set its own standards of competence and conduct and enter into partnership with the authorities in supervision, monitoring and evaluation. Alongside this strategy they should consider pressing for salary and promotion reforms which would discriminate between the most competent and the average and below average teachers. They should welcome, and if possible, promote and sponsor research into teaching and learning, based on teacher participation relevant to national and cultural considerations. These are all activities requiring a great deal of skill, sensitivity, public relations and negotiation. But by pursuing greater teacher professionalisation on all fronts in a whole-hearted way, teachers' organisations can fulfil their potential for leadership of a self-improving, self-regulating and self-confident teaching profession.

Chapter Six

PLANNING TEACHER SUPPLY AND DEMAND

The argument in Chapter Five was that greater professionalisation of teachers could do much to improve overall quality. But this also depends on effective planning and management of the teaching force in terms of recruitment, deployment and the provision of a positive working environment. In this chapter and in Chapter Seven we examine some of the main implications of this proposition for those who plan and manage teacher training and the supply of teachers.

In this chapter, the discussion focusses mainly on issues in the national or regional planning of teacher training, supply and demand, whilst issues of more concern to those responsible for the day to day management are dealt with in Chapter Seven. In practice, of course, planning and management issues are integrally linked. Nor can national level planning be isolated from local level considerations. Furthermore, the reader should remember that the issues discussed below have to be interpreted within the general framework for planning and management in any particular country. Naturally, there are many different ways in which countries establish machinery for planning, management and coordination and in degrees of centralisation or decentralisation of authority. Finally, it should be noted that the main focus here is on school systems financed largely from the public purse. This is not applicable to all situations. We have to remind ourselves yet again that in some countries, for example in Latin America, planners have to take into account long-established private provision of teacher training and schools (Gimeno 1983); and in other countries, the private sector is still growing, as, for example, in Kenya (Wellings 1983). But a focus on planning for the public sector is, nevertheless, still appropriate for the majority of countries and, therefore, occupies our attention here.

WHY PLANNING?

Put at its simplest, planning is the process of regulating the future supply of teachers to meet demand, regulating requirements, identifying train-ing needs and resources. In an age when governments are committed to the provision of schooling to all as a basic human right, the free play of market forces is allowed to determine the number of teachers available in only one or two countries. In a number of others, including Cameroon, Cuba, Tanzania and Thailand, educational planning forms an integral part of national economic and social planning (ILO/UNESCO 1983:47). Without regulation, unaccept-able inequalities and imbalances in the availability and distribution of teachers would occur, with discrimination against those least able to pay for them. Planning is also a way in which teacher training can be developed to meet the needs of the schools in accordance with national policy.

This is not to suggest that planners are able totally to control events. Indeed, we show below that this is far from the case. Nor is it to suggest that planning is merely a technical matter. Although planning techniques continue to become ever more sophisticated, as the literature on technical aspects shows (UNESCO 1974; UNESCO 1978; Williams 1979), it also involves political acumen and sensitivity. To illustrate these points we turn briefly to examine two case studies in the history of educational planning in West Africa.

Ghana
Ghana, the then Gold Coast, was a pioneer amongst English-speaking sub-Saharan African countries to launch universal primary education (UPE). In 1950 primary school fees were abolished. Up till 1955 enrollments expanded rapidly, outpacing the increase in certificated teachers. Uncertificated teachers were recruited and the proportion of certificated teachers in the total teaching force fell to 40 per cent (Williams 1977). Subsequently, however, from 1955 to 1960, the growth in enrollments slowed down, allowing the proportion of trained teachers to improve by ten percentage points.

118

At this point, Williams suggests, two uncoordinated policy decisions were made which led to unplanned shortages of trained teachers. First, in an effort to improve teacher quality, the authorities introduced a compulsory four-year pre-service teacher training course to replace the former two-year course. Second, the government announced compulsory primary schooling. Although compulsion was not, in fact, enforced, in 1961 enrollments suddenly doubled, just as the training colleges were phasing down their output of two-year trained teachers and when the four-year course was not yet producing graduates. In fact, the output of new teachers from the teacher training system did not reach the 1960 level again until 1968.

The effect of this lack of coordination between policy decisions and planning decisions resulted in yet another deterioration in the proportion of trained teachers from 50 to 37 per cent.

Nigeria

In the 1960s Nigeria had serious problems because of the poor levels of education of primary teachers (Fafunwa 1974). After many years of debate and vacillation the Government announced in 1974 that UPE was to come into effect in 1975. After protests from the planners that the timescale was too short, the deadline was set for September 1976. In 1974 there were five million pupils in school and 150,000 teachers of whom 80,000 were qualified. Hawes and Williams (1974) estimated that an additional 70,000 to 80,000 teachers per year for six years would be needed, in order to enroll all six-year-olds in school. With only 12,000 new teachers per year graduating from training colleges, they predicted that many unqualified and under-qualified teachers would have to be recruited.

This turned out to be correct. In 1976 the expansion of primary education was so rapid that even primary school leavers were being recruited as primary teachers. By 1980 there were an estimated 11.5 million children in school but the chronic problems of poor teacher quality had greatly increased.

The experience of Kano State in the north of the country illustrates both the achievements and the problems involved for planning teacher training and supply (Bray 1981). In Kano State there was only a shallow pool of educated people available to become teachers. In 1974 a crash programme to increase the supply of teachers was implemented. Between 1974 and 1979 the number of colleges rose from 15 to 25 and enrollments of teacher trainees increased three times to over 15,000. These were massive achievements in view of the fact that new facilities had to be built, trainers identified and training programmes developed.

Nevertheless, the situation in terms of trained teacher shortages turned out to be chronic. The colleges had to take recruits who had failed their West African School Certificate. To speed up output, the training course was shortened to one year. A two-year course was designed to attract primary school leavers. In 1976 the proportion of trained teachers including Arabist (Islamic) teachers was only 13 per cent. In 1977 it deteriorated to 9 per cent. In 1978 the situation improved slightly with one third of the teachers trained.

The Nigerian case demonstrates how planners may manipulate the length and level of teacher training courses to influence the speed at which new teachers may become available. It also reminds us that there are a number of different potential sources of supply which may be tapped to meet crisis situations. These include recruitment through the normal teacher training, 'crash' courses in teacher training colleges, the recruitment of 'failed' as well as successful teacher training examination candidates, untrained West African School Certificate and Standard VII school leavers and Arabist teachers. In the Nigerian case, as in the case of Ghana, the cost of the strategy lay in the poor quality of teachers taken into the system in the short term, who would need further upgrading in the long term. Finally, the Nigerian case illustrates clearly how planners are affected by political decisions in what they are able to achieve. What they are able to achieve today influences what will become the policy issues and problems for tomorrow (Akangbou 1983).

EXPANSIONARY PRESSURES

In 1980 the World Bank estimated that, between 1960 and 1975, average annual increases in pupil enrollments were nearly five per cent at primary level and nearly seven per cent at secondary; aggregate increases were over 100 per cent at primary and over 200 per cent at secondary (Table 6.1).

Table 6.2 gives an indication of how much developing countries achieved in the drive towards

Table 6.1: Size of Enrollments and % Annual Increases in Developing Countries, by Income Level, 1960-75

Level of education and group of countries by income level	Number of students 1960 (millions)	Annual increase 1960-65 (percent)	Number of students 1965 (millions)	Annual increase 1965-70 (percent)	Number of students 1970 (millions)	Annual increase 1970-75 (percent)	Number of students 1975 (millions)	Annual increase 1960-75 (percent)	Aggregate increase 1960-75 (percent)
First level	117.0	6.5	160.0	4.3	197.9	3.6	236.4	4.8	102
Low income	58.5	7.1	82.4	4.0	101.0	3.6	120.7	4.9	106
Lower middle income	17.4	4.9	22.1	4.1	27.0	4.0	32.8	4.3	88
Intermediate middle income	30.3	6.8	42.2	5.4	54.9	3.7	65.7	5.3	115
Upper middle income	10.8	4.3	13.3	2.6	15.0	2.6	17.2	3.1	59
Second level	22.6	10.0	36.5	6.7	50.7	6.4	69.0	7.7	205
Low income	15.0	9.5	23.7	5.4	30.9	4.6	38.6	6.4	157
Lower middle income	2.1	11.6	3.6	8.5	5.4	8.3	8.0	9.5	281
Intermediate middle income	3.5	11.4	6.0	10.6	9.9	9.5	15.6	10.5	346
Upper middle income	2.0	10.3	3.2	7.1	4.5	8.4	6.8	8.5	240

Source: World Bank, <u>Education Sector Policy Paper</u> (Washington, 1980) pp 102-103

Table 6.2: Primary and Secondary School Enrollments, 1965-1982

	Number enrolled in primary school as percentage of age group						Number enrolled in secondary school as percentage of age group	
	Total		Male		Female			
	1965	1982	1965	1982	1965	1982	1965	1982
Low income economies	62	85	77	103	47	77	20	30
China and India		98		111		83		33
Other low-income	45	70	59	80	31	58	9	19
Sub-Saharan Africa	40	69	52	79	28	56	4	14
Middle-income economies	84	102	90	109	77	99	20	42
Oil exporters	70	102	79	111	60	103	15	36
Oil importers	95	103	99	107	91	96	24	48
Sub-Saharan Africa	44	96	54	99	34	81	5	17
Lower middle income	74	103	82	109	65	98	16	35
Upper middle-income	96	102	100	108	92	100	26	51
High-income oil exporters	43	76	60	86	25	65	10	44

Source: World Bank, World Development Report 1985 (Oxford University Press, New York)

Table 6.3: Annual % Increases in Pupil Enrollments and Teacher Stocks, 1970-82

	Developing Countries		Africa		Asia		Arab States		Latin America		Oceania including Australia & New Zealand	
	1st level	2nd level	1st level	2nd level	1st level	2nd level	1st level	2nd level	1st level	2nd level	1st level	2nd level
Annual % 1970-75												
Pupils	5.3	7.8	6.5	14.3	5.0	7.3	5.8	10.0	5.1	3.3	-0.1	3.4
Teachers	7.2	7.5	7.6	11.6	6.8	7.8	7.2	9.8	8.2	0.9	3.1	6.4
Annual % 1975-82												
Pupils	2.2	3.9	7.6	12.2	1.2	2.7	4.2	8.3	2.5	6.4	0.6	0.8
Teachers	2.9	5.5	8.2	12.2	2.3	4.5	5.9	10.0	2.1	5.9	1.6	2.6

Source: <u>UNESCO Statistical Yearbook</u> (1984), Paris

universal schooling between 1965 and 1982. Over these decades, countries at all income levels made progress at primary level, though the very poorest countries still had one third of the age group outside school. Female enrollments lagged behind male. Progress at secondary level was great in terms of absolute increases but only the richer developing countries had achieved near 50 per cent enrollment whilst around 70 per cent of children in the poorer countries did not participate in secondary schooling.

TEACHER CONSTRAINTS

To what extent have teacher supply constraints affected the expansion of enrollments and to what extent is it likely that they will do so during the future? These are not easy questions to answer. However, Table 6.3 provides some insights on a regional basis for developing countries.

At lower levels of school systems teacher supply does not appear to have been a limiting factor on enrollment in the sense that, throughout the entire twelve years, teacher stocks have grown annually faster than pupil enrollments. Only in Latin America was there a marginally slower rate of growth of teachers from 1975. Fredriksen (1981:13) gives some support to this suggestion for primary education for the period 1965 to 1977. He points out that pupil-

Table 6.4: Pupil-Teacher Ratios in Primary Education (a)

Region	1965	1970	1975	1977
Asia	40	37	37	37
Africa	39	40	39	39
Latin America	32	32	28	28
Arab States	36	34	32	31
(Industrialised countries)	(25)	(23)	(21)	(21)

Note: These ratios are weighted averages for each region.

Source: Fredriksen B., 'Progress towards Regional Targets for Universal Primary Education: a statistical review' International Journal of Educational Development, 1:1, 1981, p.12.

teacher ratios actually declined somewhat, probably because pupil enrollments did not expand as rapidly as planned, whilst targets for teacher recruitment were probably exceeded (Table 6.4).
Table 6.5 suggests that this situation may continue in the 1980s, with pupil-teacher ratios around 20:1 in a majority of developing countries, unless, of course, teacher stocks are not in future allowed to grow. We explore this possibility below.

Table 6.5: Frequency Distribution of Pupil-Teacher Ratios in Developing Countries

PTRs	-11	11-20	21-30	31-40	41-50
First Level					
1970	-	12	24	3	1
1980	-	23	16	1	-
1982	-	24	15	1	-
Second Level					
1970	4	81	61	7	1
1980	9	77	53	14	2
1982	8	80	55	82	2

Source: UNESCO Statistical Yearbook (1984), Paris

At higher levels of school systems the rate of growth of teacher stocks from 1970 to 1975 lagged slightly behind pupil enrollment (Table 6.3). But in the later period, teacher stocks expanded faster than enrollments. It appears that teacher constraints may be operative here with a high proportion of countries experiencing pupil-teacher ratios of over 30:1, and even up to 50:1 (Table 6.5). The observation, moreover, is supported by the data presented in Table 5.2 where, it can be seen, average class sizes often approximate to the permitted maxima.
These statistics are useful indicators. But they cannot confirm conclusively whether teacher supply has been the only critical supply side constraint on enrollments. There may also be demand side factors which affect enrollments. Finally, global statistics do not show bottlenecks in enrollments due to imbalances in the deployment of teachers within a country.
And the future? Between 1985 and 2000 in

developing countries, there will be an additional 87 million 6-11 year olds and 56 million 12-17 year olds, 16 and 11 per cent increases respectively. Thus, to maintain 1985 enrollment and pupil-teacher ratios, teacher supply must increase by the same percentages. Given the severe financial climate, this is unlikely. It is more likely that enrollments will continue to increase but teacher supply will not. If so, the quality of schooling will decline unless existing teachers become more effective.

Trained Teachers
Global statistics showing trends in the recruitment of trained and untrained teachers are not readily available, partly because of problems of comparability in what counts for training from one country to another. However, it is clear from Table 6.6 that the proportion of teacher training enrollments at secondary level has not kept pace with overall secondary enrollments.

Table 6.6: Teacher Training Enrollment as % Secondary Level (Normal) Education

	Developing Countries	Africa excluding Arab States	Latin America	Arab States	Asia excluding Arab States
1970	1.9	6.2	5.6	2.1	0.6
1980	1.9	6.2	4.2	1.8	0.6
1982	1.8	6.4	4.0	1.8	0.4

Source: UNESCO Statistical Yearbook (1984), Paris

A number of factors may lie behind this. In Latin America, for instance, the decline in teacher training enrollments between 1970 and 1982 was at least partly due to the increased recruitment of graduate teachers in preference to trained non-graduates. In all regions, too, the decline may also be due to increased attractiveness of general secondary education, as it expands. Wider opportunities in non-teaching employment fields may also be important factors. However, for those countries where non-graduate teachers predominate at the primary and lower secondary levels, it does appear that teacher training enrollments have not kept pace with secondary level expansion in general. What are now needed are comparative country surveys to indicate whether or not teacher training, both non-graduate and graduate, is keeping pace with the growth of pupil enrollments and whether or not teachers are teaching in subjects and levels for which they are trained. There is a certain amount of limited evidence for sub-Saharan Africa, at least, which we review in Chapter Ten, to indicate that a great deal of in-service training is going on to upgrade the many untrained primary teachers in the schools.

COSTS

Even if the numbers of qualified people available to be recruited as schoolteachers are adequate, cost constraints are likely to be the major limiting factors on expansion in the coming decades. In the 1960s and 1970s public recurrent expenditure on education relative to total public expenditure rose to 20 per cent, even 30 per cent in some countries. And up to the mid-1970s the annual growth in educational expenditure far outstripped growth in gross national products (World Bank 1974:18-19; Simmons 1980:27-80; World Bank 1984:268-269). Tables 6.7 and 6.8 show the global growth rates in public educational expenditure as a proportion of gross national product and per inhabitant.

Table 6.7: Estimated Public Expenditure on Education as % GNP

	1970	1975	1980	1982
World Total	5.4	5.7	5.7	5.8
Developed Countries	5.7	6.0	6.1	6.2
Developing Countries	3.3	3.9	4.0	4.3
Oceania including Australia & New Zealand	4.3	6.2	5.9	5.8
Arab States	3.5	4.7	5.1	5.1
Asia excluding Arab States	3.5	4.7	5.1	5.1
Africa excluding Arab States	3.5	4.0	4.1	4.4
Latin America	3.3	3.5	4.0	4.2

Source: UNESCO Statistical Yearbook (1984), Paris.

Table 6.8 Estimated Public Expenditure on Education per Inhabitant (US$)

	1970	1975	1980	1982
World Total	57	109	183	181
Developed Countries	137	264	456	455
Developing Countries	7	19	38	40
Oceania including				
Australia & New Zealand	103	331	460	490
Latin America	20	44	90	96
Asia excluding Arab States	10	29	59	59
Africa excluding Arab				
States	7	16	34	31

Source: UNESCO Statistical Yearbook (1984), Paris.

It is likely that countries which are still attempting to improve participation ratios at all levels of the education system will continue to make some increases in educational expenditure from the public purse. But there are reasons to believe that the last two decades of the twentieth century will see an overall levelling off (Lewin, Little and Colclough 1982). The global economic recession, monetary inflation and high levels of international indebtedness inhibit the growth of spending in all sectors, especially in real terms. Also, governments today are less optimistic than formerly about the returns to be anticipated from educational investment. This reduces the chances that education will maintain its current share of scarce resources in competition with other sectors.

Efficiency
In this sober economic climate, all governments, in rich and poor countries alike, are looking for ways and means of reducing educational costs (Stromquist 1982; Tang 1985). Efficient use of available resources is the target: the maximum output from current levels of resources and the minimal necessary input of additional resources to attain target outputs.

Primary and secondary schooling together absorb some 80 per cent of total education budgets (Simmons 1980:30). Teacher salaries comprise between 70 and 90 per cent of recurrent educational expenditures. Secondary teachers on average cost more than primary, largely because of higher qualification levels. As

the teaching force ages, the costs of benefits,
including retirement, rise. In addition, as more
teachers are trained, costs of training generally
rise. Given these facts, it can easily be understood
why governments monitor teacher costs closely.
Teacher-related factors form a large part of
anxieties about the recurrent cost implications of
increased educational development (Jennings 1982;
Adiseshiah 1974). Future school expansion,
therefore, could well be limited by contraints on
governments to pay for more teachers. There are
already plenty of signs that policies are being
directed less towards the overall expansion of
teacher numbers and more toward more intensive
utilisation of existing teachers.

A dramatic example of the problems involved is
provided in a 1982 UNESCO study, Costs and Financing
Obstacles to Universal Primary Education in Africa.
The analysis shows that for many countries with low
gross enrollment ratios but targets to provide access
to school for all children, cost reductions per pupil
have to be made, given limits on the overall
expansion of educational expenditure. The study
takes the case of Berkina Faso, then Upper Volta, as
an example. In 1977, there was a gross enrollment
ratio of 16 per cent for primary education. It was
estimated that an 84 per cent reduction in costs per
pupil would be needed to provide for an enrollment
ratio of 100 per cent, given a constant level of
expenditure on primary education.

> What would a reduction of 84 per cent in costs
> per pupil imply? The pupil-teacher ratio ... in
> 1977 ... was 51, and the proportion of
> expenditure on primary education accounted for
> by teachers' salaries was around 90 per cent.
> Thus, if the 84 per cent reduction in costs per
> pupil were to be carried entirely by the pupil-
> teacher ratio - while holding salaries constant
> - then the pupil-teacher ratio would have to
> increase from 51 to 319 (UNESCO 1982:7).

Clearly this is an extreme case where there is
no possibility in the immediate future of teacher
supply being able to meet educational needs. Nor is
an increase in the pupil-teacher ratio to over 300:1
possible given current educational technologies.
But in other contexts there are signs that policies
are being directed less towards the overall expansion
of teacher numbers - and hence salary costs - and
more towards teacher upgrading (Chapter Ten) and more

Table 6.9: Maximum Teacher-Class Contact Hours in Public Schools,
1980-1981

	Daily hours or periods	Weekly hours or periods	Remarks
Argentina			
primary	4x60 min	20x60 min	
secondary	6x60 min	30x60 min	
Bangladesh	5x40 min		Attendance requirement 37 hours per day 6-day week
Barbados			
primary	7x40 min	35x40 min	
secondary	6x40 min	30x40 min	
Chile (grades 1-8)		30-35 hours	Classwork requirement varies by grades. Grade I, 30; grade 8, 35. Total working week 30 hours min; 40 hours max.
Colombia			
primary		30 hours	
secondary		20-24 hours	
Ecuador		35 periods	Spread over 5 or 6 days per week
Guyana		25 hours	Somewhat less for secondary
Indonesia			
primary		min 25 x30 or max 40 x40 min	
secondary		min 18 x45 min max 40	
Jamaica	5 hours		Min 5-day week
Jordan			
primary		26 periods	36-hour working week
secondary		24 periods	

	Daily hours or periods	Weekly hours or periods	Remarks
Kuwait			
primary		30 periods	actual teaching hours
secondary		37 periods	pry 16-22, lower sec. 10-18; upper sec, 10-21
Mauritius	6x50 min		
Nicaragua			
primary	5 hours	25 hours	
secondary	8x45 min	40x45 min	
Philippines	6 hours	30 hours	In emergencies, teachers may be required to teach 2 hours per day, above the maximum (overtime pay)
Sri Lanka			
primary		22 hours	Working hours 6 per
secondary		25 hours	day and 30 per week, including preparation time
Thailand		35 hours	35 hours per working week
Tunisia			
primary		30 hours	
secondary		18 hours	
Venezuela			
primary	6 hours	30 hours	within 36 hour week
secondary		16 hours	

Source: ILO/UNESCO (1983) <u>Report of Joint ILO/UNESCO Committee of Experts on the Application of the Recommendation concerning the Status of Teachers</u> (ILO, Geneva), pp. 79-84

131

intensive teacher utilisation. Teacher upgrading may or may not be associated with some increase in salary costs, depending on policy. Some information about the extent of teacher upgrading through further education and training was provided in the survey by ILO/UNESCO (1983:54-65). Provision is mainly free. Much is in the form of evening course, day release, short courses and correspondence or radio and television courses. The survey also provides some information on how intensively teachers are used through data on the maximum permitted teacher-class-contact hours (ILO/UNESCO 1983:78-86). In many countries class-contact time is much less than total working hours normally available for preparation, extra-curricular activities and related professional tasks. Longer class-contact time, ceteris paribus, would reduce teacher costs.

Whilst these data are not sufficiently comprehensive for conclusions to be drawn about the actual degree of teacher utilisation in developing countries in general, they do indicate that there may be scope for planners and teacher organisations to work together to create greater efficiency in the teaching force. However, there are dangers in such a strategy. Some of these are the erosion of non-teaching time available for other complementary professional activities, including study leave, preparation time, curriculum development and community liaison.

Bangladesh. The primary teacher situation in Bangladesh illustrates the efficiency issue, in terms of the need for greater utilisation of existing teachers. Bangladesh launched the first phase of its UPE programme in 1981 and the second phase in 1986. One major lesson of the first phase is that the presence of teachers in school and the quality of their teaching are important factors in improving enrollment, particulary in a country where effective social demand for schooling is weak (Dove 1981).

In 1986 there are approximately 9 million out of 16 million children enrolled in primary school (author's estimates). The teaching stock is approximately 156,000. On low population growth projections, the primary school age group will increase to 17 million by 1991. Another 4 million children must enroll in school if an enrollment ratio of 75 per cent is to be achieved.

What does this mean for teacher requirements? To maintain a pupil-teacher ratio of 50:1, the stock of teachers must rise to 260,000, an additional 104,000 or 21,000 annually over five years. The Primary Training Institutes (PTIs) have the capacity to produce 9,000 one-year-trained teachers annually. Thus, the shortfall per year is 12,000.

These statistics give some picture of the magnitude of the problem for the government in achieving UPE. Moreover, the situation has been simplified because no allowance has been made for the fact that there may be up to ten per cent of under- and over-age children in school, nor for increases in attendance rates as well as enrollments. If we were also to include wastage rates for teachers and teacher trainees and acknowledge that the PTIs are not always filled to capacity, the situation would appear even more serious.

What if teachers were utilised more intensively by an increase from 1986 of the pupil-teacher ratio to 60:1? The teaching stock would have to rise to 217,000, an additional 61,000 or 12,000 a year over five years. After the PTI output is accounted for, this leaves a shortfall of 3,000 teachers per year.

A rise in the pupil-teacher ratio thus appears to reduce the problem of teacher supply to more manageable proportions. But, it may well be argued, this would be unwise in that it would seriously impede the quality of learning. But would it? Let us examine very carefully the actual situation in schools. First of all, it is quite common for classes in Grades 1 and 2 to have 50 to 100 pupils. And there are no guidelines from research to suggest that teachers' capacities to handle 50 or 60 pupils are greatly different, given, at least, the current teacher-centred, didactic techniques (Haddad 1978). Above Grade 2, due to drop-out, class sizes are much smaller, with sometimes no more than a handful of children in Grade 5. Teachers are trained to teach all subjects and all levels but in practice they tend to teach a particular subject specialism or level. Sometimes a double shift operates with the first two grades in the earlier hours of the morning and the higher grades in the late morning and early afternoon. But teachers rarely teach both shifts. In addition, time-keeping is irregular and some schools operate for no more than four or five hours a day due to lack of supervision.

A pragmatic approach to meet the immediate problem of teacher shortage would be to acknowledge that <u>in fact</u> pupil attendance, and hence class size, is likely to remain much lower over the next years than enrollment statistics suggest. A rise in the pupil-teacher enrollment ratio to 60:1 would not therefore appear unreasonable, at least as a temporary expedient. But there are a number of other options available to policy makers and planners which would help to alleviate the problems of teacher supply at the same time as maintaining quality.

Intensive Teacher Utilisation

i)   The Ministry of Education may fill all vacancies for school supervisors and principals and ensure that the maximum number of schools per supervisor is 15 to 20, depending on the locality. This would improve teacher attendance and timekeeping.

ii) Supervisors and principals should be made responsible for ensuring that teachers teach more than one subject and level. The experience of Project IMPACT in Bangladesh suggests that teachers can teach multi-grade groups successfully (Cummings 1984).

iii) The double shift system should be enforced for teachers so that the actual teaching load is increased to official limits.

iv) The official time-allocations for core subjects, Bengali and Mathematics in particular, may be increased for the early grades (even at the expense of other subjects which teachers often neglect anyway). Thus teaching-learning time in basic skills may pay off in higher achievement and lower repetition and drop out.

Alternatives to Regular Trained Teachers

i)   Given the increased teaching-learning time implied by the above measures, the primary cycle may be reduced to four years. Alongside this measure, the authorities could give positive encouragement to the use of paraprofessionals for the kindergartens. Bangladesh has had good experience on a small scale of the use of educated village women as feeder school paraprofessionals, chosen and paid for with community support (Sattar 1985).

ii) Secondary school leavers may be recruited as volunteer teachers on a temporary basis, receiving a small honorarium or payment in kind for community service. There are a number of examples of countries which have used this expedient successfully. For example, Botswana compensates for shortfalls in trained primary teachers by utilising Form 5 school leavers during their compulsory community service.

iii) The government has already authorised the recruitment of untrained Higher School Certificate holders and graduates to serve alongside regular, trained teachers.

Increasing the Output of the Training System

i)   Several new PTIs are being developed as a long term strategy.
ii) The current one-year training could be reduced to six months, thus enlarging training capacity by 100 per cent to 18,000. If the curriculum of the primary schools were tailored to the basic core subjects and in-service, recurrent training were developed to reach all teachers, as currently planned by the Ministry of Education, the quality of new teachers would not be seriously impaired. (In addition, it should be noted that the minimum educational qualification for entry to teacher training has already been raised from Secondary School Certificate to Higher Secondary Certificate level).
   Some of these options challenge conventional ideas about the organisation of primary schooling and teacher training. Effective supervision is important to enforce regulations already in place. The most difficult challenge for the government is negotiation and agreement with the teachers themselves. However, without bold and unorthodox policies, Bangladesh is unlikely to achieve UPE in this century, if only because of teacher constraints.

TEACHER REQUIREMENTS

The term 'teacher shortages' may be utilised by planners to mean a variety of different types of constraint in the teacher supply situation. In addition to overall shortages of teachers to fill classroom vacancies, there may be, for instance, shortages of trained teachers, teachers of particular specialisms such as Music, pre-school teachers, or teachers of the handicapped. Shortages, in other words, are definable relative to policy concerns and educational needs.
   The 'needs' for teachers also vary in the same way. The overall educational need for teachers is usually much greater than the number of teachers society can pay for. The demand, or requirement, for teachers are the terms used to specify the numbers and types of teachers necessary to achieve specific educational results.
   Table 6.10 reproduced Sri Lankan data

Table 6.10: Teachers Available and Required for Sri Lanka According to Qualification Category and Medium, 1984

Total for Sri Lanka	Graduates				Non-Graduates English			
	Science	Arts	Commerce	Sc/Maths	Grades 3-5	Grades 6-10	Primary	Art
Sinhala								
Available	2,086	18,139	1,330	12,828	10387	6,440	38,912	896
Required	2,032	4,691	989	12,813	7,394		49,509	681
Def./Ex.	+54	+13,448	+341	+15	-3,363	-84	-10,597	+215
Tamil								
Available	668	1,807	205	2,351	2123	1,501	8,337	136
Required	558	864	176	2,745	2,678		15,131	99
Def./Ex.	+110	+943	+29	-394	-1,934	-122	-6,794	+37
Sinhala and Tamil								
Available	2,754	19,946	1,535	15,179	125	10	47,249	1,032
Required	2,590	5,555	1,165	15,558	10,072	7,941	64,640	780
Def./Ex.	+164	+14,391	+370	-379	-5,297	-206	-17,391	+252

	Non-Graduates							Supervisory Staff		Total
	Music	Dancing	Agri-culture	Home Science	Commerce	Handi-crafts	Others	Sectional Heads	Principals	
	1,322	1,198	2,067	2,117	1,549	1,389	10,376	2,160	6,989	113,745
	1,164	1,001	1,530	1,419	858	955	12,708	7,489	6,989	118,662
	+158	+197	+537	+698	+691	+434	-2,332	-5,329	-	-4,917
	363	76	539	638	275	226	1,963	262	2,566	22,535
	293	83	336	408	215	119	2,728	1,710	2,566	32,210
	+70	-07	+203	+230	+60	+107	-765	-1,448	-	-9,675
	1,685	1,274	2,606	2,755	1,824	1,615	12,339	2,422	9,555	136,280
	1,457	1,084	1,866	1,827	1,073	1,074	15,436	9,199	9,555	150,872
	+228	+190	+740	+928	+751	+541	-3,097	-6,777	-	-14,592

Source: Sri Lanka, Ministry of Education, An Analysis of the Teaching Staff Requirements of the School System, (1984), Colombo

summarising teacher requirements by subject and medium of instruction and according to the qualification status of teachers. By measuring requirements against the available teaching stock, the excess or shortage of teachers in each category is arrived at. Unfortunately, the Ministry of Education document from which these data are derived does not set out the assumptions on which the calculations are made. In particular, we do not know what pupil-teacher ratios are used.

Pupil-Teacher Ratios

Planners estimate teacher requirements in a number of simpler and more complicated ways. The simplest ratio, and the one we have utilised in this Chapter hitherto, is the average pupil-teacher ratio (number of pupils divided by the number of teachers). Similarly, the class-teacher ratio is the number of classes divided by the number of teachers. Common planning norms are 30:1 for primary pupil-teacher ratios and 25:1 for secondary schools. Where primary teachers teach all subjects, the class-teacher ratio is 1:1, but if specialists teach, for example Music or Physical Education, the ratio may be 1:1.3. At secondary level a common standard is 1:1.5.

Pupil-teacher and class-teacher ratios may serve as norms (setting standards or targets) or as measures of the actual situation at national, regional, local or school level. The goal for planners is to bring actual ratios into line with standard or target ratios. They use the gap between targets and actual ratios as a proxy measure of the quality of educational provision.

But these simpler ratios only reflect average situations which may be misleading, as we saw in the case of Bangladesh. Another common case is where the pupil-teacher ratios in urban schools are much more favourable than the average because teachers cannot be easily recruited in remote rural schools, as, for instance, · in the Zimbabwean case discussed below. Similarly with class-teacher ratios. A common example at secondary level is where the teachers of compulsory core subjects have many classes with many pupils, whilst teachers of optional or elective specialisms have far fewer.

More complex methods of estimating teacher requirements allow planners to examine pedagogical and organisational factors in more detail. For subject teachers, requirements may be calculated by the number of periods a subject is taught per week,

Table 6.11: Malawi Government and Aided Secondary Schools: Available Teacher Stock by Main Teaching Subject, and Estimated Teacher Requirements by Subject, 1981-1982

	JCE	MCE	Total	Available Teacher Stock	High (25p/wk)	Medium (28p/wk)	Low (30p/wk)
	Estimated Class Periods/Week				Estimated Teacher Requirements		
English	2008	1512	3520	140	141	126	117
Maths	1506	1182	2688	86	108	96	90
Phys Sci	1004	900	1904	88	76	68	63
Biology	753	900	1653	59	66	59	55
Geog	753	696	1449	58	58	52	48
History	681	608	1289	47	52	46	43
Chichewa	753	756	1509	21	60	54	50
Agric	753	945	1698	54	68	61	57
Home Ec	894	456	1350	45	54	48	45
Tech	558	392	950	33	38	34	32
(MYP)	502	378	880	(50)	(35)	(31)	(29)
Other				51			
Bible K	513	532	1045		42	37	35
French	318	392	710		28	25	24
Comm	87	108	195		8	7	7
Total	11083	9757	20840	682	799	713	666

Notes: (1) All figures exclude heads. Malawian Young Pioneers (MYP) teachers are excluded from Available Teacher Stock and Estimated Teacher Requirements totals. MYPs are normally one per school.
(2) All figures represent 'full-time equivalent teachers' not actual persons. Most teachers teach more than one subject.
(3) Estimates are based on subject/period allocation by the Ministry of Education and Culture 1982. High, medium and low estimates assume alternative average teaching loads of 25, 28 and 30 periods per week respectively.
(4) Available Teacher Stock column reflects full-time equivalent teachers by main subject of qualification, derived from school statistisal returns. All optional subjects except Home Economics and Technical Subjects are included under 'other'. However, optional subject teacher requirements have been calculated separately in the last three columns, but the very small numbers of Latin and Art teachers are not shown.
(5) General Science teachers are subsumed under Physical Science and Biology.
(6) No. of schools = 54; No of classes = JCE 251, MCE 189, Total 440; No. pupils = 16338
(7) JCE = Junior Certificate in Education. MCE = Malawi Certificate in Education.
Source: Coombe, T. (1985) 'Secondary Schoolteachers: Stock, Requirements, Allocation and Flows', Planning Unit, Ministry of Education and Culture, Malawi

the number of classes taking each subject and the teaching load (number of teacher-pupil contact periods) per week. This notion of a teaching load is useful for setting standards for the optimal or minimum-maximum number of periods a teacher should teach per week. Actual teaching time may be measured against these standards and requirements calculated. Loads may be varied to take into account not only direct pupil-teacher contact time, but also, for instance, the adminstrative responsibilities of principals and other senior personnel, teachers who have to prepare laboratory experiments or workshop activities and teachers involved in community outreach or in-service training.

Table 6.11 illustrates the utility of methods of estimating teacher requirements using a ratio of teachers against the number of class periods per week for each subject on the timetable. The Notes have been reproduced from the original document in full because they set out fully all the background information and assumptions made by the planners in arriving at their estimates, thus enabling others to understand the full implications of the calculations.

The most important point for our purposes to note from the Malawian data is that different assumptions about the number of teacher class periods of contact time per week lead to different outcomes in terms of teacher requirements. For instance, less intensive teacher-class contact time for Mathematics teachers at 25 periods per week means that there is an 'excess' of teachers against current stock (108-86=22). In contrast, if teachers teach 30 periods per week the excess is very much reduced (90-86=4).

A further refinement in estimating teacher requirements would be to calculate how far the qualifications and training of teachers match the subjects and levels at which they are actually teaching. Elsewhere in the Malawian report these statistics are analysed for teachers in Government and Aided schools. Provisional estimates are that out of 929 teachers, 112 were teaching partly in a subject for which they were qualified and partly in a subject for which they were not qualified. A further 42 were not qualified in their teaching subjects. This amounted to a mismatch of about ten per cent of the teaching force.

The pupil-teacher ratio is a powerful tool in educational planning. It may guide consideration not only of the overall numbers of teachers required but also subject specialists, optimal class sizes and teaching arrangements. It is thus a tool with implications for both quantitative and qualitative aspects of education. But it cannot be used on its own in isolation from other considerations. For instance, there has to be coordination of the Science teacher requirements, not only with the number of pupils studying Science, but also with the amount of laboratory space available or planned. Similarly, changes in time-allocations in the curriculum have to be coordinated with changes in teaching load norms.

The following case studies illustrate some more of the planning considerations outlined above.

Papua New Guinea
In Papua New Guinea, the Provincial High Schools, with Grades 7 to 10, accept graduates and non-graduates with secondary teaching diplomas (Guthrie 1983). (National High Schools have grades 11 to 12 and recruit graduate teachers with some years' teaching experience). In 1980 the superintending inspector of the Provincial High Schools stated, 'the most important single factor affecting the performance of these schools is the continued shortage of teachers ... a situation which is getting worse and worse' (Bacchus 1984:129).

Bacchus (1984:199) estimates the annual teacher requirements from 1980 to 1990 for Grades 7 to 10 in all types of schools. He bases the estimates on actual pupil enrollments for 1980 to 1982 at a pupil-teacher ratio of 30:1. He comments (132)

> The PNG Government had hoped to achieve 100% localization of the provincial high schools' teaching force by the early 1980s but did not succeed in doing so. For these schools to localise their staff completely by 1990 it is now estimated that an output of about 225 teachers per year will be required.

He estimates that teacher requirements would rise from 1,400 in 1980 to 1,750 in 1990. He notes, however, that Goroka Teacher College, from which most of the Provincial High School teachers come, had recruited declining numbers of trainee teachers over recent years. By 1980 it had an output of only 150. He comments (132-133) 'If the secondary schools teaching is to be localised, then a major effort has to be made to ensure that the output ... is substantially increased and for the time being should

141

Table 6.12 Enrollments of PNG Students in all Provincial, National and International Schools for Grades 7 to 10 Between 1980-81 with Projections up to 1990 and with Estimates of Number of Teachers Needed

Grades	1980+	1981+	1982	1983	1984	YEAR 1985	1986	1987	1988	1989	1990
Grade 7	12,125	12,623	13,051	13,291	13,531	13,771	14,011	14,251	14,491	14,731	14,971
Grade 8	10,926	11,299	11,738	11,958	12,178	12,398	12,618	12,838	13,058	13,278	13,498
Grade 9	7,092	7,365	8,064	8,217	8,968	9,742	10,538	11,356	12,196	12,405	12,614
Grade 10	6,140	6,772	6,909	7,459	7,600	8,288	9,011	9,748	10,504	11,281	11,474
Total Enrollment Grades 7-10	36,283	38,059	39,762	40,925	42,277	44,199	46,178	48,193	50,249	51,695	52,559
No. of teachers employed or needed with Teacher Pupil Ratio at 1:30	1,401	1,485	1,556	1,364	1,409	1,473	1,539	1,606	1,675	1,723	1,752

Note: The same assumptions are made as in the National Manpower Assessment study at the rate of progression and three new schools with an increase of 240 additional pupils enrolled in Grade 7 each year. The only difference is that it is assumed that Grade 8 students will, after 1983 be automatically allowed to proceed to Grade 9 – but staggered over the period at the following rate: 1984: 0.75; 1985: 0.8; 1986: 0.85; 1987: 0.9, and from 1988 on at the rate of 0.95. However, the figure for the base years of 1980 to 1982 are changed to reflect the actual enrolment in these years as indicated in the Dept. of Education's Planning Services Statistics.
+ actual figures

Source: Bacchus, M.K. A Review and Analysis of Educational 'Needs' at the Secondary Level in Papua New Guinea (E.R.U. Report 48 (University of Papua New Guinea, Port Moresby), June 1984, p. 142

not fall below the 200-225 mark'.

Bacchus points out that the major cause of low recruitment to Goroka was the lack of high school graduates with suitable qualifications. Therefore, he builds into his planning model a proposal for automatic promotion of all Grade 8 pupils into Grade 10 but keeeping current pupil-teacher ratios stable at 30:1. This may appear to be a paradoxical recommendation in that it actually increases the number of teachers required to 250 per year. The rationale is that this will eventually increase the number of pupils eligible to proceed to Grade 12, who would then provide a pool of suitably qualified high school graduates to enter teacher training.

This case study illustrates how the planner has to think through the possible implications of actions taken in the present on the medium to long term supply of teachers. It also illustrates how the number of pupils graduating from secondary schools, especially in countries with small populations and general scarcities of educated manpower, can dramatically affect the supply of future teachers.

Zimbabwe

In Zimbabwe, as in Papua New Guinea, there is high attrition from secondary teaching because of attractive, alternative job opportunities for qualified people. Since independence in 1980, the attractiveness of teaching for high school graduates has markedly declined. Pupils with good 'O' level qualifications no longer choose to go to teacher training college as a first choice (Chivore 1985). This is mainly because racial discrimination has been abolished and a whole range of other career opportunities has opened up for educated Africans. Many of them no longer look to teaching and nursing as the only viable avenues of employment but to other public and private sector jobs, including apprenticeships which pay better than teaching.

Table 6.13 indicates the extent of the teacher problem in Zimbabwe. National statistics do not as yet allow precise estimates of teacher shortages by subject but they do give a broad picture of the serious imbalances in the qualification levels of teachers in different categories of secondary school. The overall proportions of graduate or trained non-graduate secondary teachers is very low in the Rural Day Secondary Schools in contrast with the Mission Boarding and Urban Secondary Schools. In addition, the trained teacher numbers include many

Table 6.13: Zimbabwe: Teachers in Lower Secondary Schools by Qualification, 1982-1984

		Graduates		Non-Graduate Secondary Trained		Primary Trained		Student Teachers		Untrained Teachers		Total	
		N	%	N	%	N	%	N	%	N	%	N	%
Government Aided (Private) Rural Day Secondary Schools	1982	79	2.9	123	4.7	1,030	38.4	28	1.0	1,417	52.8	2,682	100
	1983	102	2.4	304	7.2	1,091	26.1	338	8.0	2,341	56.0	4,176	100
	1984	185	3.0	281	4.6	1,484	24.4	839	13.8	3,278	54.0	6,067	100
Government Rural Day Secondary Schools	1982	22	6.0	64	17.5	149	40.8	7	1.9	123	33.7	365	100
	1983	74	11.0	154	22.9	201	29.9	103	15.3	139	20.7	671	100
	1984	137	13.6	266	26.4	211	20.9	180	17.8	213	21.1	1,007	100
Mission Boarding Secondary Schools	1982	708	29.3	937	38.9	186	7.7	108	4.4	470	19.5	2,409	100
	1983	804	31.8	878	34.8	332	13.7	110	4.3	397	15.7	2,521	100
	1984	893	32.7	620	22.7	605	22.1	326	11.9	285	10.4	2,729	100
Urban Secondary Schools - mainly Government	1982	1,341	44.9	1,025	34.3	364	12.2	119	3.9	133	4.4	2,982	100
	1983	1,439	42.8	1,153	33.3	475	13.6	189	5.4	163	4.6	3,474	100
	1984	1,495	37.3	1,171	29.2	457	11.4	407	10.1	478	11.9	4,008	100

Note: Percentages are rounded.

Source: Zimbabwe: Minstry of Education, Planning Division 1984

foreigners who are not categorised separately. The vast majority of teachers in all schools are either primary teacher trainees on extended teaching practice or completely untrained teachers. Again the Rural Day Secondary Schools are most disadvantaged in terms of the proportion of untrained teachers who comprised over half the total number of teachers over the period 1982 to 1984.

This case underlines a lesson for all planners when projecting teacher requirements from past trends. Before independence no one could have foreseen the scale and impact of all the changes which subsequently took place in the socio-economic and employment fields. Plans made for teacher training and recruitment before 1980 were completely overtaken by events outside the control of educational planners.

Zimbabwe is taking steps to improve its planning capacity. More detailed information, particularly on shortages of secondary teachers by subject is an urgent need. Another need is for an accurate assessment of actual teacher-pupil ratios in schools to measure against norms of 28:1 and 30:1. The planning system is being computerised to make systematic collection of information easier and to provide projections of future teacher requirements. Computers do indeed make it possible to project far into the future. Yet, as we have seen, a host of unforeseen variables can make nonsense of even the most sophisticated planning models. It is therefore imperative that planners offer policy makers a number of alternative models based on different sets of assumptions and quickly adjust their strategies to take into account new situations which arise and which should affect rational decision-making.

PLANNING AND MANAGEMENT INFORMATION SYSTEMS

Planning teacher supply is part of a larger enterprise of managing education systems to meet current and future needs. Yet sometimes planners do their work in isolation from the actual situation in the schools. They sometimes rely on out-dated conventions when estimating teacher requirements. For instance, a class-teacher ratio of 30:1 may be used long after schools which were built with classrooms to take 30 children have been replaced by open-plan arrangements where larger groups of children can be satisfactorily handled by one teacher.

145

Frequently, planners have to rely on inadequate data bases to estimate teacher requirements. Information may be available from salary records, personnel files, and the school reports filed by supervisors and inspectors. But planners must also have regular personal contact with the schools so that they can assess the validity and reliability of information collected from a variety of different sources. They need also an awareness of the limitations for their own use of data collected for different purposes and must be ready to cross-check and up-date information regularly.

Planners and managers at all levels of the school system, from Ministry Planning Units to local administrators and principals, need training in the collection, utilisation and analysis of data and statistics. Computerisation does not reduce the need for this since such systems are only as good as the information which goes into them. Planners using computer-based information need to collaborate with computer specialists to ensure that information fed into computers is organised in such a way as to be of maximum utility to the planning process. One important aspect of this is where data are disaggregated or aggregated by computer to show the variations in the teacher supply situation by district or region or by school type or teacher characteristics.

A comprehensive data base would include information about individual teachers, absences and retirements, teacher trainees, current and projected pupil enrollments and school characteristics.

i) **Teachers** - sex, age, nationality, marital status, permanent residence, language group, religion, educational qualifications, professional qualifications, in-service up-grading, terms of service (permanent, contract, part-time, volunteer), grade of appointment, salary, benefits (accommodation, travel allowance etc.), responsibility allowance, length of service, previous posts, current posting and teaching subjects.

ii) **Absences and Retirements** - study leave, maternity leave, paternity leave, in-service training, secondment; deaths, retirements, resignations, dismissals, promotion (out of service) transfers (out of education).

iii) **Teacher Trainees** - sex, age, nationality, marital status, permanent residence, language group, religion, educational qualifications, other qualifications, previous work or work-study experience, type of course, level of specialisation (pre-school, secondary etc), subject specialisation, other specialisation (handicapped etc.), preferred district of posting.

iv) **Current and projected pupil enrollments** - sex, age, nationality, language group, religion, special needs (deaf etc.), part or full-time, grade, subject specialisation (where relevant), examination grades, previous schools, work experience or paid employment.

v) - **Schools** - Structure of school system (6+3+3, 7+3+2 etc.), class pattern of schools (mixed ability; streamed etc.), class structure of school (number per grade, per subject), type of school (boarding, day, etc.) number of shifts, optimum/maximum class size per subject, optimum/maximum teaching load, optimum/maximum pupil-teacher ratios, duration of periods, number of periods per week, duration of school year, curriculum by subject, subject options by school or category of school, time or period allocation per subject per week.

In practice it is rarely possible for planners to have access to all this information. Therefore, when setting up an information system, it is important to decide on priorities in relation to information most essential for current purposes. The reliability of the information is also a consideration. Future, as well as current needs, have to be foreseen so that the system is set up to be capable of expansion. Finally, certain items of information on individual teachers and pupils should be kept confidential and safeguards should be built in to restrict access to confidential information.

CONCLUSION

In this chapter we have outlined some of the issues which arise with regard to planning teacher supply and demand to meet the needs of the school system. In general we have concentrated on identifying issues which have relevance to the efficiency and educational effectiveness of schools, alluding to the importance in planning of selecting the appropriate technical tools, such as pupil-teacher ratios and comprehensive information systems. We have also indicated that it is important for planners to balance immediate needs against long term goals. In the short term, planners have to adjust the flow of teachers into the schools to match outflows caused through resignation, retirement or death and to fulfill current teacher requirements. But longer term goals involve shaping the size and composition of the teaching force to meet anticipated and planned future educational needs.

This means that decisions taken today must always take account of the implications they may have for the future. For instance, in cost-saving exercises it is simple to reduce the salary burden by not replacing teachers who resign or retire. But this has long term implications for the age structure of the teaching force. It also "wastes" newly trained teachers who are not able to find jobs.

Thus, planners welcome strategies which do not introduce rigidities into the teacher supply and allow some short term flexibility. To give just one example, there are a variety of sources of supply of temporary teachers who can be recruited and retired as the situation demands, or are appointed for a definite, limited period only. Various schemes utilising volunteer teachers fall into this category. Malawi has its Young Pioneers. Botswana utilises Form 5 leavers during their community service. Mexico has its <u>instructores</u> <u>communitarios</u>, who serve in rural schools in return for free higher education (Chapter Seven).

Finally, we should remind ourselves that planners should always balance the decisions they make on grounds of efficiency, effectiveness and equity against what is practicable. As discussed in Chapter Five, teacher unions have entrenched interests and in many countries teachers are government servants with closely guarded rights to security of tenure. Planners have to have a political sensitivity and willingness to work actively with teachers' representatives in pursuit of goals which involve innovation and change. Otherwise, with teacher opposition, plans may come to nothing. Examples of failures to introduce greater efficiency have been numerous. One is the use of educational media. The well known programme to use television in primary schools in the Ivory Coast, begun in 1969, eventually failed. Cost and technical difficulties were partly responsible but opposition from teachers was also strong (Coombs 1985; Grett 1981). Similar opposition is occurring in some countries where Project IMPACT, pioneered in the Philippines, is being introduced as a means of enabling teachers to cope with primary class sizes of up to 100 pupils with the use of self-instructional materials, paraprofessionals and community support (Sanger 1977; Flores 1981; Cummings 1984). Teachers often see such innovations as a threat to their working

conditions and to the future of the teaching
profession.
A final but important example is the shift
system. This works well in some countries. Ethiopia,
for instance, utilised teachers over two and three
shifts per day during a period of crisis teacher
shortage. Malaysia successfully uses a two-shift
system in urban primary schools. But, for such an
innovation to be acceptable, planners must take time
to negotiate with the teachers who have to work the
system. In a number of countries double or even
treble shifts of pupils utilise scarce classrooms
intensively. But this does not necessarily mean that
the same teachers teach across two or three shifts.
Indeed, normally, different teachers teach different
shifts. Since class-teacher contact time is
generally somewhat reduced with shift systems,
teachers may work for no more than three or four
hours a day. This is clearly not intensive
utilisation. On the other hand, to require teachers
to work long double shifts could well have a negative
impact on the quality of instruction and on teacher
morale.
In Chapter Seven we examine further some of the
issues which are involved in management of the
teaching force and which often depend for their
resolution on close cooperative communication
between planners, educational managers and the
teachers themselves.

Chapter Seven

ISSUES IN TEACHER DEPLOYMENT

Teacher deployment is frequently perceived as merely an administrative routine, necessary to distribute available teachers amongst the vacant teaching posts which arise from year to year. However, in this chapter we show that teacher deployment policies and strategies have important effects on the teaching force and should be seen as an integral component of overall planning and management of teacher supply.

In the first part, we discuss selected issues which have implications for deployment policies. These are teacher wastage or attrition, the feminisation of the teaching force and teacher mobility and transfer. In the second part we identify a number of possible policy options available to planners and managers attempting to alleviate problems caused by teacher wastage and mobility. Various posting and transfer procedures are examined. But these have to be regarded as supportive of a wider package of measures relating to the recruitment, preparation and support of teachers in the field.

WASTAGE

One of the most chronic problems for planners is teacher attrition. This may be due to natural causes such as retirement and death. Planners normally allow for about five to eight per cent wastage of this sort each year when calculating requirements for new teachers. But the rate rises, of course, proportionately to the seniority loading of the teaching force. Wastage due to resignations is less easy to predict and may be very high if teachers are dissatisfied and other employment opportunities are available. Planners need to have an idea of wastage trends in order to plan how many teachers, in what specialisms and in what schools, will need to be recruited.

But wastage is not merely a problem for planning. It is very costly educationally and administratively. It often tends to occur among the younger and more recently trained and recruited teachers. Their energy, enthusiasm and abilities are lost to the schools. While it would be a mistake to suggest that older teachers who have stayed in teaching are more conservative or less able, there is no doubt that the injection of new blood is important. Individual schools need a team of teachers at various levels of age and experience. If teachers come and go frequently, morale, professional cooperation and continuity are difficult to maintain. Cooperation with parents and the community suffers. In addition, the costs of teacher training are high in relation to the short time during which teachers stay in the profession.

The problem of teacher wastage is a general one throughout the developing world. We do however need to know much more about particular causes and its precise pattern and make-up in different environments. In many countries teaching, particularly at primary level, as we have seen, is a bridging occupation - a place of short stay while the teacher looks for opportunities for further study or better jobs. Part of the reason for this is that many teacher trainees enter training only because it is a means of continuing their formal education subsidised by the state. They gain a teaching qualification but have no real intention of taking up teaching as a career.

Indonesia has a tremendous problem of teacher shortage at primary level (RIHED 1983:22). The authorities have to use volunteer teachers to meet part of the shortfall. A national teacher survey (Tjiposasmito and Cummings 1981) concerned with recruitment and deployment issues is worth describing in some depth because it illustrates some of the issues involved in teacher wastage throughout the developing world.

The majority of Indonesian teachers today are the academically able people from rural and modest-income urban homes. Those from more affluent homes (especially males) reject teaching because the pay and promotion opportunities are low. They go into more highly paid jobs. Those from poorer homes become teachers because they cannot afford the education which would enable them to compete for more lucrative jobs.

The survey showed that people were attracted to teaching for altruistic reasons, because they perceived it as a form of social service. However, they also thought that teachers suffer more material hardship than other occupational groups. Interestingly, the study found that most Indonesians who finally settle on teaching do so with the idea that it is for the long term. Only about ten per cent of teachers seriously consider resigning. Their major concerns, however, are for further training and greater promotion opportunities. Teachers do not want merely greater administrative responsibility but recognition for the quality of their teaching. Many teachers are blocked from promotion at a higher level or to principalships because they have only high school education. For promotion posts they need a university degree. Other causes of teachers' dissatisfaction are the lack of a teachers' room in school and teaching facilities and aids such as teachers' texts, teaching materials, school libraries and sports fields. Many do not teach the subjects for which they are trained.

The Indonesian study highlights poor pay, poor prospects and a poor professional environment as major causes of teacher dissatisfaction. These are issues reminiscent of those discussed in Chapter Five in the context of professionalisation. Society often sees teaching as a profession for second-raters. They are the people who cannot compete for better jobs. First-raters do not stay in teaching. Wastage tends to be high also among the least qualified and least experienced teachers with few financial commitments. For those who are inadequate to the challenges, life in the classroom becomes a daily nightmare. In desperation they drop out, reasoning that even unemployment is preferable to teaching.

This is a worldwide problem not confined to Indonesia as the following observations on the Sudan illustrate (Lyons 1981:269).

> Hitherto, teaching has been a lifetime career in the Sudan with promotion into the higher ranks of educational administration as a prospect. But a number of factors have somewhat altered this picture. The Sudan is now a source of technical assistance to some oil-producing countries as a provider of teachers. More seriously significant numbers of recent secondary leavers who have been recruited to teaching leave the profession, either to enter

higher education or to take more lucrative employment in the Sudan or the Middle East. Thus there is a tendency towards a shortage of teachers but conversely there is each year a large crop of graduates and school-leavers competing for available jobs, so that there is always a fresh supply of recruits to teaching. The problem ... is one of increased turnover amongst the less experienced and frequently unqualified teachers, so that the proportion of less effective teachers tends to be higher than it would otherwise have been.

FEMINISATION

In order to improve the enrollment and retention of girls in school, a number of countries, Sudan among them, have positively encouraged the recruitment of female teachers (UNESCO 1984:21-23; Comparative Education Review 1980; Acker 1984). In addition, teaching tends to be one of the first occupations, along with nursing, into which women move when they enter salaried employment (Kelly and Elliott 1982; Guruge and Ryan 1984). The term 'feminisation' is often used to mean that teaching is becoming increasingly a female preserve. Indeed, increased 'feminisation' of teaching is often linked directly with problems of wastage from teaching. Whether or not there is a casual link is not yet clear. This is an area where research is needed. But the idea that women are taking over the teaching profession is definitely not supported by the statistics.

Table 7.1 shows the proportion of female teachers by region from 1970 to 1982 at first and second levels of the school system. Over the twelve years, there has been only a three percentage points rise in the proportion of female teachers at first level in all developing countries. From a very low base of 28 per cent in 1970, Africa had the highest increase of 17 percentage points. The Arab States came next. Asia, from a fairly low base of 36 per cent, had only a two percentage point increase. Latin America had a four percentage point decline.

At second level the general profile for all developing countries was similar, with little change over the period. The Arab States had a five per cent increase and Asia a three per cent increase. But all other regions showed a decline.

These statistics alone are sufficient to dispel the myth that teaching is fast becoming feminised, at

Table 7.1: Female Teachers by Region, 1970-1982: % 1st and 2nd Levels

	Developing Countries		Africa excluding Arab States		Asia excluding Arab States		Arab States		Latin America		Oceania including Australia & New Zealand	
	1st level	2nd level	1st level	2nd level	1st level	2nd level	1st level	2nd level	1st level	2nd level	1st level	2nd level
1970	45	33	28	36	36	27	37	27	81	49	63	46
1980	47	34	31	33	39	30	42	32	77	47	64	46
1982	48	34	45	32	38	30	45	33	77	47	63	45

Source: UNESCO Statistical Yearbook (1984), Paris

Table 7.2: Pre-School Teachers by Region: % Female, 1970-1982

	Developing Countries	Africa excluding Arab States	Asia excluding Arab States	Arab States	Latin America	Oceania including Australia & New Zealand
1970	97	75	90	100	98	86
1980	90	95	93	44	98	100
1982	91	97	93	47	98	100

Source: UNESCO Statistical Yearbook (1984), Paris

least on a regional basis, (though, of course, the situation may be different for particular countries). However, it is important also to examine the proportion of female staff at pre-school level because many people enter this field of employment anticipating that they will move on into teaching at primary level once they have gained appropriate qualifications and experience. Table 7.2 shows us that pre-school education is dominated by female employment. In most regions it is virtually a female preserve. If, therefore, many pre-school staff do eventually move over into primary teaching, this will increase the proportion of women teachers at first level.

Davies (1985) has analysed the distribution of female teachers on a country by country basis. Table 7.3 shows clearly that in the majority of countries women form only between 20 and 40 per cent of the teaching force. Only in eleven countries do they form 50 per cent more at first and second level.

Davies also brings together convincing evidence from developing country surveys to show that women are much under-represented in senior and administrative positions. The ILO/UNESCO survey remarked on the same phenomenon (1983:1.2). Greenland (1983:56) also noted that, in English-speaking sub-Saharan Africa, women do not achieve promotion nor participate in leadership training in proportion to their numbers in the primary teaching force. In this context, many of the in-service training courses provided in Africa are referred to as headmaster training.

What are the factors holding back female participation and achievement? Socio-psychological ones are those most commonly quoted; women tend to have lower educational qualifications than men; women are not accustomed to having high career expectations and aspirations; women place their main priority on their domestic responsibilities. But Davies also argues that organisational and structural factors are important. The sexual division of labour between home and workplace traditionally militates against full female participation in a career. Time out for child-bearing hinders promotion potential and may even carry financial penalties. Women are less unionised than men. In school, women teachers tend to gravitate towards, or be encouraged towards, pastoral responsibilities, whilst men undertake more prestigious duties in curriculum and administration. Davies also discusses evidence which points to

Table 7.3: Distribution of Developing Countries by Ratio of Female
Teaching Staff

	First level	Second level	Third level
Under 10%	Mauritania Nepal	Mauritania Nepal	Malawi Mauritius Sudan
11%-20%	Afghanistan Congo	Congo Korea Sudan	Cameroon Congo India Iran Korea Sierra Leone
21%-30%	Cameroon Congo Gabon India Mozambique Papua New Guinea Sierra Leone Uganda Korea	Afghanistan Cameroon China Gabon Gambia Ghana India Mozambique Rwanda Tanzania Tunisia Uganda	Iraq
31%-40%	China Gambia Ghana Malawi Rwanda Sudan Tanzania Tunisia	Botswana Iran Mauritius Papua New Guinea Seychelles Sierra Leone	
41%-50%	Burundi Iraq Mauritius	Fiji Honduras Iraq Lesotho Swaziland Tonga	
51%-60%	Fiji Iran Tonga	Costa Rica Panama	

	First level	Second level	Third level
61%–70%	Botswana		
71%–80%	Costa Rica Honduras Lesotho Swaziland		
Over 80%	Seychelles		

Source: Davies, L. 'Women, Educational Management and the Third World: A Comparative Framework for Analysis (Unpublished ms).

institutional prejudice and discrimination against women eligible for leadership positions.

But how is all this related to the problem of teacher wastage? As we suggested above, it is often said that women teachers are more likely than men to drop out of teaching and that, therefore, a high proportion of females in the teaching force means a higher level of wastage than there would otherwise have been.

But on the basis of the facts assembled above, this proposition needs to be scrutinised with care. In the first place, women do not have disproportionately high representation; in fact, the reverse is the case in most developing countries. In the second place, systematic research to investigate the link between wastage and female teachers has yet to be done. Thirdly, even if there is such a link, it may well be explained in terms of discriminatory social, economic and organisational factors pertaining to female employment. For instance, it is often suggested that women do not take a career in teaching seriously because they get married, bear children and regard their income as merely a minor contribution to household earnings. Because of this, it is alleged, they tend to drop out of teaching after a short time, or regard it as a part-time job which they can take up or drop with little commitment.

But another way of perceiving the situation would be to regard such behaviour as a function of the way society traditionally enforces a sexual division of labour. Women are induced to feel a role-conflict between home and work. Sometimes, they are not allowed paid maternity leave. Sometimes, benefits such as accommodation are available only to male teachers. Davies provides an extreme example of the subordinate role which society accords to female careers in the case of Zaire where it is a legal provision that a woman must have the permission of her husband before she can agree to take a job.

The situation in Nepal provides some interesting clues which appear to contradict notions about the lack of ambition and 'staying-with-it-ness' of female teachers (Nepal, Ministry of Education and Culture 1983). In the early 1970s only 16 per cent of girls went to school and very few women became teachers. With a positive government policy, the situation had improved somewhat by 1976 with girls' enrollment up to 20 per cent and female teachers not only coming forward in larger numbers but also moving up from primary to secondary teaching. The main point here is that female teachers were keen to improve their qualifications, undergo further training and aspired to levels of teaching which gave higher pay. Data from a study of women trained between 1971 and 1982 under the Equal Access for Women Education Programme show that 76 per cent remained in school and only 24 per cent dropped out. Therefore, at least, in the short to medium term, female teachers showed themselves fairly committed to their careers.

MOBILITY

High rates of wastage from teaching are a drain on the school system. But high rates of teacher mobility between schools are also wasteful in both educational and administrative terms. A few years ago the author realised that some of the most frequent complaints she heard from administrators at central and local level in many different countries had to do with the amount of time they spent on teacher recruitment, posting and transfer. Education officers complained in particular about the tedious pressures under which they worked when trying to match teachers' own preferences for posting with vacancies to be filled.

To illustrate the size of the problem, again from Nepal. In 1977 in the Sankhuwa Sabha district, 40 teachers were appointed, 14 (mostly untrained) teachers resigned and 34 were transferred from one school to another (Lyons 1981:124). At the time, there were only 442 teachers in the schools, so teacher turnover was a significant problem. Classrooms were left teacher-less until replacements were found. And this itself was not an easy task, especially in the remoter schools. Most teachers resisted transfer unless they could be near their own homes, the main reason being lack of accommodation.

It hardly needs stating that rapid teacher turnover has detrimental effects on schools. Teamwork amongst teachers becomes difficult and coordination and curriculum planning are weakened. For instance, in Papua New Guinea secondary schools often experience high turnover. Academic standards suffer. One headmaster reported that five out of nine of his staff were transferred over a period of one year three months with the result that some of his pupils had three teachers during one year (Bacchus 1984:143).

Factors Underlying Teacher Mobility

There are a number of factors which contribute to high rates of teacher mobility (Dove 1982a). Here we examine them under four headings, including teachers' personal, economic and professional concerns and administrative procedures.

Personal. Accommodation was mentioned above as one of the most intractable problems. It causes teachers to persist most vigorously in requests for transfer or in resistance to transfer when the authorities need to deploy them to other schools. Transfer causes problems for married teachers who face possible separation from spouses and family. When female teachers are married to men in salaried jobs, the husbands' jobs are usually regarded as more important. The likelihood is that these families gravitate to urban areas. Hence, urban schools often have a disproportionate number of female teachers.

Other personal factors include schooling, culture and the cost of living. Teachers with children would be understandably unwilling to move to areas where schools are inferior. Teachers brought up and trained in urban environments find the living conditions in rural areas uncongenial. Teachers from different cultural groups or speaking different languages find it hard to settle down among alien communities.

To illustrate this let us dwell briefly on the problem of schooling for nomads. The authorities responsible for the education of the nomadic, cattle-herding Fulanis of northern Nigeria have great difficulty in finding teachers for their schools. Fulani teachers are very few and outsiders find it difficult to adjust to the nomadic way of life, even where 'stationary' rather than 'mobile' schools have been established.

> The reason for most teachers' unwillingness to work in rural areas is not far to seek. Rural communities lack basic amenities and the nomadic camps are even worse so. Many rural footpaths are virtually impassable both to motorists and pedestrians. During the rainy season people trudge through large pools of muddy water; in the dry season the roads are horribly dusty. In some cases access from one nomadic settlement to another may involve crossing flooded streams or deep dry valleys (Ezeomah 1983:131).

161

Nomadic communities undoubtedly provide special problems for outsider teachers but the conditions described above are only a degree worse than those in the remoter rural areas of many countries.

Economic. Economic factors are also tied in with personal reasons for requesting transfer. Young teachers often get posted to remote rural schools at a time when their salaries are relatively low. They may find the cost of living much higher in rural areas. The cost of consumer goods and accommodation may be higher in the countryside. They may spend more on travelling or sending their children away to residential secondary schools if they are not available locally. Salaries may not be paid promptly. Even if they enjoy some special allowances, they may find it difficult to make ends meet if they try to maintain a standard of living to which they have been accustomed in urban areas.

Professional. Factors to do with job satisfaction and professional advancement are also important. We have already seen how teachers in Indonesia complained of the lack of teaching materials. In remote rural areas facilities and supplies may be lacking. Teachers may feel isolated from support and have few opportunities for contact with teachers from other areas. Teachers with ambitions for promotion may feel that they would have greater chances of recognition if they were in central schools. Others may want jobs in urban areas where they can enrol in training institutions on a part-time basis more easily than in isolated rural areas.

In a Mexican study concerned to discover why rates of mobility for teachers from rural schools is so high, 15 different factors came to light (Mexico, Secretaria de la Educacion Publica 1981). Of these, at least three were broadly associated with the poor physical and social environment, such as climate and social isolation. Four factors were professional or administrative, such as the unsuitability of teachers' professional preparation and their previous service in rural schools. But the main factors were personal to do with teachers' lack of adjustment to the rural location and way of life. Interestingly, the study distinguished between all the reasons teachers proffer when asked why they would like a change and the few considerations which lead them actually to make an official request for

one. There were only a few of these: age, previous
home location, type of training and years of service
in rural areas. This discrepancy suggests that
Mexican rural teachers ask for transfer only when
they judge that they have a fair case according to
administrative rules and practices.

Administrative Procedures

Administrators, of course, are aware of the
destabilising effect on schools of high rates of
teacher transfer. They have to resist pressures from
individual teachers in the interests of schools and
sometimes also in the interests of equalising
educational provision between urban and rural areas.

But administrative procedures themselves can
and do, unfortunately, contribute to high mobility of
teachers between schools. It is, for instance, often
the practice to post new recruits to outlying schools
for a period of time, maybe one or two years. This is
sometimes a condition of service for teachers who
have been trained at public expense. In countries
which are expanding their teaching force year by
year, this practice can result in a constant redeployment of teachers who, having served their term
in more difficult areas, expect to move on to more
favoured schools.

Such a policy can lead to high wastage rates for
new teachers. Lacking support and guidance in their
first teaching posts and meeting tremendous
challenges in adjustment to strange surroundings,
new teachers cannot endure the isolation and drop out
of the profession. Therefore, today, some countries
are taking care to post new recruits to schools where
they can receive regular support and supervision. In
Sudan, for example, new teachers are posted near
towns for this reason. But, admirable though the
intentions behind this practice are, the consequence
is that many new teachers have to be re-deployed,
after an initial settling-in period, to schools which
have vacancies; and, often, these are the rural
schools, where support and supervision is lacking
(Lyons 1981:270).

Sudan also provides us with other examples of
the way in which policy and practice with regard to
teacher deployment may lead to high rates of teacher
mobility. As a condition of service in the Sudan,
teachers have to expect to be transferred after a few
years in one school. Because some districts produce
more teachers than others, this policy means that
some teachers in areas where there are few recruits

to teaching are outsiders. They naturally seek to get back to their home areas as soon as possible. The Sudanese authorities try to achieve a balance between experienced and inexperienced teachers in each school. Because of high wastage rates, particularly among new teachers, this policy implies a frequent need to re-deploy teachers. When teachers are promoted, this again destroys the balance and a new round of transfers takes place.

Other practices to do with the development of the teaching force and the management of schools almost inevitably increase mobility. In countries where a great deal of in-service training is going on, for example, teachers have to be transferred on a temporary basis to fill gaps left by those away on training. In situations of teacher shortage this means either that schools have vacant posts for long periods or that teachers are moved around from school to school. The latter procedure may be counter-productive if teachers are unable to provide continuity of teaching in particular schools if they themselves become frustrated because of frequent upheavals. Secondary schools, where teachers are deployed according to subject expertise, experience these difficulties most frequently. But the problems also increasingly affect primary schools where new types of specialisms are required. Language policies, for instance, may require the presence of local language experts in the schools or teachers able to teach an international language. In Morocco, for example, where the government intends to improve the flow of pupils up through the basic cycle of schooling, specialists in remedial instruction are to be identified and trained. Whether or not they can be deployed to the remotest rural schools which have most need of them remains to be seen.

POLICY OPTIONS

Those concerned with planning and managing the teaching force have a number of inter-related goals. First and foremost, they want to bring teacher supply into line with requirements over the short to long term. Secondly, they want some short term flexibility to meet acute shortages or excesses of teachers. A pool of 'reserve' teachers is useful for this purpose, as we saw in Chapter Six. The long term goal is the development of a stable teaching profession, of high morale, well educated, well trained and capable of further professional development. High rates of wastage and teacher mobility are signs of a malaise among teachers. They are costly in educational and administrative terms. What policy options, therefore, exist for reducing wastage and mobility in the long term?

The strategies suggested below should be seen as complementary rather than as alternatives. They divide into three groups. One is to do with the selection, preparation and recruitment of teachers. A second is concerned with better provisions and incentives for serving teachers. The third focusses on improvements in procedures for posting and transfer of teachers.

Selection, Recruitment and Teacher Preparation

Wastage from teaching, as discussed, is often attributable to lack of commitment by recruits or their inability to cope with the challenges of the work. High rates of teacher mobility are caused by a variety of factors, but, as we have seen, many of them are to do with teachers' personal circumstances and potential for adaptiveness to unfamiliar environments. It follows, therefore, that there is a strong case for educational planners and managers to scrutinise their policies and routine procedures for the selection, recruitment and preparation of teachers.

Countries with teacher shortages are, of course, not in a position to be rigorously selective about the people they recruit for the classrooms (Klitgaard, Siddiqui, Arshad, Niaz and Khan 1985). But in countries where overall expansion of the teaching force is slowing down there is an opportunity to overhaul strategies. We can find little guidance from research on the best selection criteria to use for teacher training and teacher recruitment (Landsheere 1980). But commonsense suggests that it is not sensible if we intend to reduce wastage and mobility to a minimum, to give uniform treatment to all applicants for teacher training or for teaching posts. Differential treatment is necessary according to the type of applicant and according to the type of contracts to be offered. Below are some illustrations of how this might be put into practice.

In a context where alternative employment opportunities are available and an applicant for teaching is already well qualified, it is likely that he or she views teaching as a temporary job. An appropriate response to this situation for the employing authority, therefore, would be to offer a precise, short term teaching contract. This would be renewable subject to the agreement of both parties. Professional training would be offered only after the first contract had been satisfactorily completed and would be conditional on the teacher's prior acceptance of a specific posting, possibly in a disadvantaged area where teachers are needed. Under this scheme, the authorities are able to utilise the well-qualified individual for a specific period but no expensive training nor tenure is given until he or she decides positively to undertake a longer term commitment to teaching.

In contexts where alternative job opportunities are not available, a possible way forward would be for the authorities to offer short term contracts to all recruits in their first years of teaching. Tenured positions could be earned after the qualifying period had been satisfactorily completed. This might include a commitment to work in disadvantaged schools for a minimum period. Tenure could be accelerated for those teachers willing to guarantee that they would serve in disadvantaged areas for a longer period. This scheme gives the employing authorities more scope for deploying teachers to disadvantaged schools and for reducing rapid turnover.

A third approach is for the offer of a place in professional training to be tied to a commitment by the would-be teacher to work in a particular area or school on successful completion of training. This is done in Morocco where primary teachers are needed in isolated areas. Trainees may choose three districts in order of preference. Their eventual destination depends on their final examination results, those with top marks going to their posting of first choice. Teachers may apply for transfer only after three years and, once trained, they are bonded to public service for eight years. This policy is possible in Morocco because there is no overall teacher shortage and, due to scarcities for other salaried jobs, teaching is an attractive profession.

If postings are decided prior to training or recruitment, the possibility opens up for the training to be specifically geared to preparing teachers for the precise posts and areas for which they are destined. This measure in itself is likely to cut down wastage due to lack of adjustment. It would be particularly supportive of less qualified recruits for whom pre-service training is essential and who are at high risk of drop out in the early years of teaching. It would, of course, involve some localisation of training, more school-based training and coordination between the employing authorities and training institutions.

Finally, a consideration of the possibilities of cost-sharing. As we have seen, many people apply for teacher training because it is often a state-subsidised route to further qualifications. But their commitment to teaching is not serious. If teacher training involved some contribution towards cost from individuals, those who had no intention of entering the profession would be somewhat discouraged. Of course, safeguards would have to be built in to prevent inequity towards those who genuinely wanted to enter teaching but who could not afford pay. In addition, trainees' costs could be reimbursable after completion of a specified period of teaching or if the trainee were willing to work in disadvantaged areas.

On the same theme of cost-sharing, but in this case with the community. Commensurate with their capacity to pay, communities could be encouraged to contribute towards the local costs of school-based preparation of teachers destined for the communities' schools. Accommodation and subsistence are patently the most important contributions. A travel allowance to enable trainees to get to know the local area is another possibility. Similarly, communities could be encouraged to support teachers who give guarantees that they would serve in the locality for a specified period of time.

Provision and Incentives

The Indonesian study described above recommended better pay for teachers but acknowledged that substantial increases were beyond the capacity of the education budget. Therefore, it recommended selective salary increments and allowances for teachers working in particularly difficult conditions, mostly in the outer islands.

Such incentive payments can take a variety of forms. Cash allowances may be available for teachers with special responsibilities such as management of a library or community liaison. Hardship allowances may be available for those opting to work in disadvantaged schools. These could be of various types such as accommodation grants, education grants for teachers' children, paid study leave or accelerated promotion.

It was noted in Chapter Six that teacher

requirements filter through from primary to secondary levels. Countries which have moved from differential pay scales for primary and secondary teachers to unified ones based on teachers' qualifications have enhanced the capacity to deploy teachers more flexibly between different levels of the school system. In particular, equalisation of pay encourages well-qualified teachers who have experience at primary level not to transfer to secondary teaching for financial reasons alone.

In Chapter Five we explored the problems created for teacher professionalisation by career structures which allow few the opportunity for promotion, in particular at primary level. The Indonesian survey recognised this problem and recommended the introduction of the post of 'master teacher' for teachers who excelled in the classroom.

In Chapter Ten we discuss some contemporary strategies for in-service training and professional development. In-service training specifically geared towards the preparation of selected teachers for new responsibilities in promotion posts is an important means of providing incentives. Training for principalship, for instance, is a vital provision because principals can give the vital leadership and support to teachers, which may reduce drop out and mobility.

Finally, as discussed in Chapter Five, a comfortable and efficient working environment in schools is an important provision likely to encourage teacher retention. Much can be done by principals at school level. But field administrators must carry the main responsibility to ensure that buildings are maintained, equipment is available and consumable supplies are regularly distributed. Outlying schools are often neglected in this respect and this, of course, affects teachers' morale. Field level administrators and inspectors are often overburdened and cannot visit schools frequently. Yet the costs of such undermanning in terms of poor professional morale may be very high.

The argument here has been that teacher wastage and mobility are influenced by pay, career opportunities and the working environment. Educational managers need to scrutinise incentives, the career structure and the arrangements they make to provide material support for classrooms. Selective improvements, particularly in disadvantaged schools, can encourage well qualified applicants into teaching and reduce wastage.

Posting and Transfer Administration

Administrative procedures for posting and transfer can affect teacher wastage and mobility. They can be very cumbersome and inefficient. Sometimes, they appear to be administered unfairly to the advantage of those who have strings to pull. It is not unusual for newly qualified teachers to wait for many months before being assigned a post. This lowers morale and may well encourage some to look for employment elsewhere. If applications for transfer take a long time to be processed, teachers in uncongenial posts may apply sooner than they might otherwise have done. Eventually, if their patience is exhausted, they may leave the profession altogether.

The administrative context in which teachers work is an important factor in determining morale and cannot be neglected. In particular, the efficiency of administration in outlying areas must be maintained if teachers are not to feel isolated and neglected. For this reason, some measure of decentralised administration is often preferable to centralised procedures. It should allow a better matching of teachers to schools; local level administrators should be able to check more closely on teachers' training, previous experience and references from supervisors. Also, coordination should be easier between training institutions, administrative authorities and schools.

Posting of teachers locally eases accommodation problems and adjustment to the locality. Teachers avoid the social isolation induced when there are differences in language, culture and life-style. As we saw in Chapter Two, the social pressures on teachers born and bred in a locality probably encourage them to carry out their duties responsibly. Local posting also cuts down on the need for travel allowances and leave requests. Of course, this approach is easier to implement at primary level than at secondary where specialist teachers have to be found from a national pool. In addition, the advantages of localised recruitment and deployment have to be balanced against the disadvantage of creating a fragmented and parochial, as distinct from a national teaching profession.

Volunteer Recruitment

Finally, in this section, a comment on the need for the authorities to be sensitive to the special situation of temporary, volunteer teachers. In Chapter Six we pointed out that a number of countries

utilise Young Pioneers or educated youth on Community
Service schemes. The presence of untrained and
temporary teachers in schools sometimes creates
disturbance and resentment amongst regular ones.
·They are inexperienced. They may not adjust well to
local culture and conditions. They may misuse scarce
supplies of materials. On the other hand, they may
show a spirit of enthusiasm and commitment which
poses a threat to regular teachers. Educational
planners and managers need to be aware of these
potential problems and ensure that such temporary
teachers are posted to schools where they have an
opportunity to be effective.

The authorities in Mexico were alive to the
potential problems involved when they set up the
Instructores Communitarios scheme in 1973 in the
state of Guerrero (personal communication to the
author by Juan Prawda and Prawda 1984). At the time,
the national government had 20,000 new primary
teacher posts to fill but had applicants for only
7,000. Even though there was a general shortage of
jobs, teaching in remote rural areas held no
attractions. Apart from the main urban centre,
Guerrero state has more than its fair share of remote
schools.

The authorities did not see a solution to the
teacher shortage problem in terms of improving
incentives for regular teachers to serve in rural
schools. From experience, they knew that urban-
educated teachers would not develop a commitment to
rural schools and requests for transfer back to urban
areas would increase. The result would be, either a
large number of dissatisfied and disgruntled
teachers in rural schools or a gradual migration of
teachers from rural schools back to towns. (In Mexico
regular teachers are government servants and have
security of tenure however poor their commitment to
teaching).

The Instructores Communitarios scheme was
planned to avoid some of these potential problems.
High school graduates are selected for the scheme.
Their aspirations are for higher education in fields
other than teacher training. They study over a four-
year period in return for primary school teaching in
rural areas for just two years. In the first year
they begin their degree studies and receive an
orientation to teaching including an introduction to
the teaching materials they are to use. In the middle
two years they teach for half of each day and study
for the remainder. During this time the local
community provides subsistence and accommodation. In

170

the fourth year they return to their full-time degree studies. They receive a small stipend but the government does not enter into any contractual arrangements with them.

In 1974 the scheme involved 300 <u>instructores</u>. In 1975 there were 700. By 1981 there were 17,000. But at this stage the authorities cut back to 12,000 because administrative and recruitment problems arose due to over-rapid expansion. However, the scheme has been sufficiently successful for it to be expanded to pre-school education where, in 1985, <u>instructores</u>, mainly female, were working in 5,000 communities.

The Mexican scheme has the advantage that it provides teachers to fill vacancies in schools where regular teachers are unwilling to serve. (An evaluation study showed that the <u>Instructores</u> performed no better and no worse than regular teachers). Accepting that they would not develop a long term commitment to rural primary teaching, the authorities were content to utilise their services for a two-year period only whilst making it possible for them to pursue their personal aspirations for higher education. By undertaking to share the costs, rural communities also committed themselves to taking an interest in their primary schools.

CONCLUSION

By way of a conclusion to these chapters on the issues and problems involved in planning and management of teaching forces, we review in some detail the various approaches which the Malaysian authorities have used over the early 1980s to expand and develop the teaching force. The reader should note in particular how management strategies have been utilised alongside complementary strategies for teaching training – the theme to which we turn in the following chapters.

Peninsular Malaysia is fortunate in having had adequate resources to finance its educational expansion. It has practically universal schooling up to ninth grade and is now endeavouring to raise this to the eleventh grade. But educational provision and take-up has been highest along the urbanised west coast. The east coast and rural hinterland where most of the farming Malays and plantation Tamils live are still relatively disadvantaged. Recent Five Year Plans and the New Economic Policy aim to foster national unity amongst Malaysians, traditionally

171

divided by race, religion and socio-economic status (Wang 1982). In line with this the government has been expanding educational provision in the rural areas. Bahasa Malaysia, the national language, is the medium of instruction at all levels. Non-Malay teachers who do not speak Bahasa Malaysia must take a qualifying examination in the national language and be prepared to serve in any part of the country, urban or rural.

Since the mid-1960s the government had made great efforts to increase teacher supply to meet expanding needs. Emergency training courses were held. By 1980 there was a slight surplus of trained teachers except in Science, Bahasa Malaysia and English as a second language. The Malaysian government, therefore, can now afford to concentrate efforts on improving the quality of the teaching force. Primary and lower secondary level training have been integrated and the two-year pre-service training has been extended to three years. There is at least one training college in every stage and four new ones in east coast states are being set up. A new teacher training curriculum in line with the new school curriculum has been devised. In-service training in the new curriculum is provided. A new institution, the Ministry of Education Staff Training Institute (MESTI) was set up in 1980 to provide training for principals and educational managers. The off-campus programme of the Universiti Sains Malaysia uses distance learning techniques to enable teachers who wish to gain a degree to study part-time over five years.

Teachers at primary and lower secondary levels are relatively well paid, given their level of qualifications. They enjoy good pensions and other benefits and many new rural schools are built with teachers' housing also. Fair conditions of service and pay encourage stability in the teaching force, though there is a problem of mobility among women teachers who tend to follow their husbands wherever they work. Increasingly Malay women are entering the modern sector through teaching which is regarded as a convenient and appropriate profession for women. For those from farming families, their salary is an important element in family income. For those from middle class families, it is increasingly difficult to combine family and teaching responsibilities as household servants become scarce and the support of the extended family system declines. Nevertheless, few resign, because teaching remains attractive and it is difficult to join the service again after once separated.

Newly qualified teachers for the primary and lower secondary schools are deployed by the Schools Division of the Ministry of Education according to the requests received by State Departments of Education for the filling of vacancies. Postings take place annually in April at the end of the training course year. Student teachers' final teaching practice takes place, whenever possible, in the school to which they are to be posted.

State level education officers are responsible for the orientation of new teachers but initial posting is arranged centrally according to the requirements of each state. In general, teachers are posted to their home state or neighbouring ones. This arrangement is adhered to strictly where women teachers are concerned. It enables Muslim girls from rural areas to conform to traditional customs and cope with traditional obligations in the family much more easily. Married women are also given priority and are posted near their homes. Next in order of priority for posting are certificated male teachers pursuing up-grading in universities. Last in priority are single people, men and women.

Teachers trained in government colleges are not guaranteed a job on qualification, though in practice, during the period of teacher shortage they were virtually sure of being offered one somewhere. If they are without a job after one year then they are free to move out of government service. Teachers are otherwise bonded for five years. If they refuse their posting, they have to pay a penalty to gain release from service.

Within each state the transfer of teachers is the responsibility of the State Department of Education. For inter-state transfers the Schools Division of the Ministry of Education takes responsibility. Transfer of principals (head-teachers) (though rarely requested by themselves) is done by the Education Service Commission. A high proportion of principals serve in their home states.

The Ministry of Education has to take the needs of the schools as the first priority in transferring teachers. But teachers can also request transfer. For inter-state transfers they are allowed a request only once in five years. There is a high demand from female teachers for transfer to Kuala Lumpur because their husbands get transferred there. But the demand for transfers to the cities of Penang and Malacca also is so high that to qualify teachers must serve elsewhere for fifteen or seven years respectively.

For intra-state transfers teachers can apply after three years in one school. Usually teachers ask for transfer to the urban areas in their own states. In remote rural areas the requirement is reduced to two years. Certain exceptions may be considered on compassionate grounds such as sickness, and for people nearing retirement.

The ministry and state level authorities have to interpret the rules on posting and transfer so as to strike a balance between the personal needs of teachers and the needs of schools. One aspect is the need to ensure that disadvantaged schools in east coast areas get their fair share of older, more experienced and better qualified teachers. Teacher turnover in urban schools is lower than in rural schools because most teachers want to be in the towns. Another issue is the gradual improvement in the representation of Malay teachers in the more prestigious schools from which they were previously excluded by virtue of relatively low levels of qualification compared with non-Malay teachers. However, the quality of Malay recruits to teaching should improve as more enter the three year training courses. And a positive posting and transfer policy should gradually correct imbalances.

Part Three

TEACHER EDUCATION AND TRAINING

Chapter Eight

TEACHER TRAINING: ORIGINS AND EVOLUTION

Modern school systems have had to make do for over a century with high proportions of untrained and unqualified teachers. The planning and development of teacher education and training has nearly always lagged behind the development of schools. Popular pressures have often filled the classrooms with pupils faster than teachers could be found. The first imperative of school authorities in the nineteenth century was to find sufficient literate individuals of suitable moral character willing to teach the basic skills which they themselves had learned at school. The issue of teacher training has usually come to the fore when popular complaints about poor standards have forced the authorities into action or when they themselves have become concerned to get better value from the teachers whom they employ.

It is an interesting question why, historically, teacher training has tended to have low priority. Much of the answer lies in the fact it is only part of a larger school system, responsive and reactive to developments in the schools. Another reason is that the need for training was not, until recently, convincingly put forward. Particularly at elementary level, where the earliest expansion of school systems began, the notion that any literate person could teach was, and is, widespread. A third reason has to do with political visibility. Building schools is often a highly popular measure. There is usually a blaze of publicity when a new school is built. In contrast, the training of teachers is a behind-the-scenes process, without much scope for dramatic, popular gestures.

In Chapter Nine we shall examine contemporary debates about the importance of teacher education and training. Here, we place those debates in context by outlining the origins and evolution of teacher training systems. We take as a unifying focus countries which experienced British colonial rule and inherited British-oriented systems at independence.

TEACHER TRAINING IN ENGLAND AND WALES

The term 'system' is hardly appropriate to describe the structure and provision of teacher education and training in England and Wales in its early years. (Scotland and Northern Ireland are somewhat different from England and Wales). State support for teacher training was small and ad hoc until the 1890s (Lynch 1979:6-23; Taylor 1969; Dent 1977). The first teacher training college was established in 1798. By 1888 there were 43, all of them supported by voluntary organisations and most under the Church of England. Other missionaries active in education were the British and Foreign School Society, the Wesleyans, the Baptist, the Congregationalists and the Roman Catholics. Colleges were residential, most imposed a religious test for entry, they were single sex and their staff came from the same establishments.

State support began only in 1846 (Morrish 1970). Until the 1890s, governments placed little priority on teacher training and preferred to subsidise voluntary effort rather than become directly involved. State support encouraged the development of the apprenticeship model of teacher training for elementary schools. Under this pupil-teacher scheme, able elementary pupils, who normally came of lowly social origins, were apprenticed for five years from the age of thirteen to the principal of a school. They taught part time and received a small period of daily instruction in return. At 18 years old, the best pupil-teachers took the Queen's scholarship examination for a place in a two-year course in a training college.

In 1889, four years after elementary education was made available for all, the Cross Commission Report encouraged the government to give more support to elementary school teacher training and to associate teacher training with higher education. Six day-training colleges were set up under the universities, thus uplifting the academic and professional status of teacher training. Under the 1902 Education Act, Local Education Authorities were for the first time able to provide not only elementary but also secondary education and teacher training. Many established their own training colleges. The secondary schools provided the general academic preparation of intended teachers and the training colleges provided their professional preparation. By 1923, there were 22 training colleges in 16 local authorities. Some teachers were by this time continuing into upper secondary schooling, taking university degrees and a one-year course of professional teacher training at a postgraduate level leading to qualified teacher status.

The trend towards decentralisation of teacher training and the linkages with higher education continued through the inter-war years. After the second world war university institutes began to accept responsibility for the validation and examination of college courses and the recommendation of trainees for qualified teacher status. Colleges were grouped under these area training organisations until the early 1970s. But severe postwar shortages of teachers delayed until 1960 the lengthening of teacher training courses to three years.

In 1966, teacher education and training was considered alongside overall higher education provision in the Robbins Report on higher education. The report recommended that the status of teacher education and training should be raised in order to sustain a high quality of recruits into the teaching profession. It directly encouraged the introduction of a four-year B.Ed. degree, fully equivalent to a B.A., and leading to a professional qualification. Ten years later, 23 universities had established B.Ed. degrees and many associated colleges were teaching at degree level, gaining in status and experience as a result.

The 1960s was an expansionary period but teacher training was beset with problems. There was lack of comparability in training under different universities. The teaching profession was still divided between non-graduate and graduate teachers. The B.Ed. was not yet fully accepted as academically equivalent to a B.A.-plus-postgraduate-qualification, (though it was increasingly accepted as a sound professional preparation). Graduate teachers for secondary schools were still not required to have teaching qualifications.

In response to these and other problems the James Committee of Inquiry into Teacher Education and Training produced a report in 1972 which was very influential in the re-orientation of thinking about teacher education and training. It conceptualised teacher education and training in three cycles; the first, personal education; the second, pre-service training and induction; the third, in-service education and training. It also insisted on the need for an all-graduate profession. However, the 1970s was an era of severe financial constraint. There was contraction in teacher training, partly brought about by declining birth rates and pupil enrollments. Thus, there was only modest progress in implementing proposals for systematic induction and in-service training.

The. significant feature of the 1970s was the diversification of teacher training institutions and validating bodies. By the late 1970s intending teachers could be trained through a variety of routes. There was the traditional 'consecutive' training, that is, a first degree, taking three or four years after twelve or thirteen years of schooling, followed by a one-year professional course for the award of a postgraduate certificate or diploma of education. This route was now available through universities, polytechnics, college of education and colleges of higher education. As an alternative, training could be over three or four years for a 'concurrent' B.Ed. degree at ordinary or honours level through polytechnics or colleges. A few universities offered joint degrees in Mathematics or Science for a B.Sc. with Education, leading to the award of qualified teacher status. By this time, for colleges which came under the local authorities and voluntary bodies, rather than the universities, many degrees were validated by the Council for National Academic Awards (CNAA). The CNAA allows training institutions considerable academic autonomy whilst offering degrees equivalent in status to the universities.

In the 1980s the evolution of teacher training has continued with increasing resource constraint and organisational diversity. At the time of writing, major reforms are being implemented which appear likely to strengthen central government control over teacher supply and demand and to reduce the autonomy of the universities and the validating powers of the CNAA over teacher training curricula and teacher certification.

The history of teacher education and training in England and Wales is intricately tied into the evolution of the school and higher education system. Noteworthy for our purposes are the following points. There has been a gradual rise in the status of teacher training both academically and professionally. This was initially stimulated by its association with the universities and later by the efforts of teacher training institutions themselves to raise their standards, through the university institutes and the CNAA. Teaching is now virtually an all-graduate profession and since the late 1970s graduate teachers are required to have professional qualifications as well.

Over the last nearly 200 years, reforms of teacher training have been undertaken in a piece-meal fashion. Organisational changes have frequently been disruptive of the professional work of teacher training institutions. Successive governments have neglected teacher training despite the potential multiplier effects of better trained teachers on the whole of the education system. Today, more than ever before, there are efforts to regulate national teacher supply and demand and to ensure that training institutions, including universities, are account-able for producing teachers according to publicly acceptable standards. It is unlikely, however, and perhaps undesirable, that a system of teacher training characterised by institutional diversity and a variety of paths towards qualified teacher status, will evolve towards an integrated and uniform national pattern.

COLONIAL SYSTEMS

The origins of teacher training in the colonies were similar to those in Britain. In the early days, voluntary organisations undertook teacher training for their own schools in Britain and the colonies. In Jamaica, for example, in the 65 years from 1832, nine different missionary societies set up a total of 22 different teacher training institutions (D'Oyley and Murray 1979:5-31). Many of them foundered within a few years and only four survive today. In Jamaica, the missionaries most active in teacher training were the Church Missionary Society, other Anglicans, Moravians, Baptists, Wesleyans and Presbyterians. As in Britain, there was little coordination and much friction between them in competition for recruits. In Malaya and Singapore, in the nineteenth century, to take one example from another region within the British sphere of control, Christian mission influence was confined to the English medium schools (Wong and Chang 1975:7-30). Chinese schools imported their trained teachers from mainland China. Tamil schools had no trained teachers until 1937. After

1850, the British authorities attempted to encourage the growth of Malay medium schools and to utilise in them Islamic teachers from Koranic schools. But they received no systematic training. Later, from 1878, when the Malay medium schools required further expansion, the Education Department converted the Singapore Malay High School into a training institution. In Malaya and Singapore at the time, there was no unified national school system and no plan on the part of the authorities to create a national teacher training system.

In the early days, throughout the colonies, it suited the authorities to allow voluntary organisations to provide and carry the financial responsibility for teacher training (Whitehead 1981). Gradually, as in Britain, the government began to provide subsidies and grants-in-aid. Their level and regularity depended largely on the success with which the various missionary societies lobbied in London. In general, as schools expanded, voluntary societies ran their teacher training schemes on increasingly tight budgets. Institutions were under staffed and managerial control was poor. Almost inevitably, state subsidy led to increased state intervention, control over expansion and inspection of standards. Policy was influenced more by the political pressures from the British electorate and parliament than by the educational needs of colonial subjects. Perennial concerns were to keep expenditure on colonial education to a minimum and to contain pressures for rapid educational expansion.

All this led to uneven development in colonial teacher training, as is dramatically illustrated in the case of Guyana (British Guiana) (Bacchus 1980:110-129). The Negro Education Act, 1838, stimulated rapid expansion of primary schooling, largely undertaken by voluntary organisations. There were 100 mission schools by 1841. The first local training centre for teachers, however, was not opened until 1852, 14 years after the expansion began. This typified the low priority given to teacher training by the colonial adminstration over the next 130 years. Early in the 1870s, the training centre was actually closed for lack of funds. The number of trained teachers thereafter fell. There were 200 in 1882 and only 85 in 1928, (six per cent of the total).

Bain Gray, Commissioner for Education in the 1920s, tried to give teacher training more priority. He opened a teacher college in 1928 to provide 30 trained teachers a year and recommended pupil-teacher centres in rural areas where these apprentice-teachers could study for the Teacher's Certificate Examination. But funds were not forthcoming. The intake of the college was cut by half and the proposed rural centres were not set up.

Over the next 30 years, a number of official reports drew attention to the parlous state of the primary teaching force in the colony. The educational level of teachers was poor because secondary graduates would not go into primary teaching. In 1948, the Director of Education pointed out in his Annual Report that the employment of trained teachers would increase the teachers' salary vote by $50,000 per year, 'eventually doubling it; a prospect which cannot be faced' (Bacchus 1980:113). He proposed reducing teacher costs by returning to a monitorial system. But this proposal was not implemented because of public disquiet at the prospect of dilution of the teaching force.

After this, caught between financial pressures and public opposition to cost-cutting, the colonial administration did nothing further for teacher training. There was some improvement in the educational level of primary teachers. But this was because jobs became more difficult to find for secondary graduates and because female civil servants, who had to resign on getting married, turned to primary teaching. But between 1945 and independence in 1966, the proportion of trained teachers fell from 20 to about 16 per cent and the number admitted to training remained at 20 a year. Popularly elected governments in 1953 and 1957 were temporarily successful in raising the number of recruits to the teacher college but in 1959 the course was reduced from two to one year. By 1963 the annual output of one-year trained teachers was 225. On independence in 1966, the government, at the recommendation of UNESCO, diversified both pre- and in service training provision to achieve a fully trained primary teaching force of 2,500 by 1975.

IMPORTED FEATURES

Teacher training in the colonies followed patterns established in metropolitan centres, both in structure and curriculum. Hercik (1976) describes the situation in colonies which inherited other European models. The two features of the British pattern of teacher training which predominated in colonial territories were the monotechnic, residential colleges and the pupil-teacher system.

Colleges

The problem of Guyana in attracting into teaching good secondary graduates was a general one in the colonies wherever better job opportunities in administration and commerce existed. Thus, the qualification level for entry to teacher training remained low in many colonies long after it had been raised in Britain. Secondly, because teacher training college normally required no fee, it attracted recruits from lowly social backgrounds, who could not afford the fee-levying secondary schools. Thirdly, teacher training was regarded as a low preference method of obtaining post-elementary schooling. It thus attracted recruits who failed to gain entry through competitive examinations to the few selective secondary schools. All these factors encouraged the development of a teaching force which had low socio-professional status and commitment and reproduced the divisions between nongraduate primary and graduate secondary teachers which, we have seen, were characteristic in England and Wales.

There, teacher training began as what Lynch (1979) has pejoratively labelled, 'a closed-circuit system'. Trainees were recruited from elementary schools, confined in monotechnic, usually resident-ial, institutions and taught by those who themselves were products of the school-college system. Teacher training was thus cut off from outside academic or vocational influences. It led to in-breeding, professional myopia and lack of academic stimulus for innovation. This situation improved only slowly. As we have seen, the universities gradually came to assume responsibility for teacher education. But not until the 1980s did they take an interest in primary education. In the 1960s, the newly designated colleges of education expanded, raised entry qualifications and improved their staffing. But only in the 1970s were intending teachers able to train in polytechnic institutions where they came into contact with those preparing for other employment. And, even today, despite a change in thinking about induction and in-service professional development, this in-service provision is in fact unevenly funded and very inadequate.

The teacher college model survives today in many countries formerly under British rule. But, as we shall see in Chapter Ten, many adaptations have been undertaken to meet the needs of teachers in developing school systems. However, two general features of the British model tend to persist. One is the isolation of teacher training from the mainstream of academic and professional institutions, especially for non-graduates. Though there are signs of change, teacher training is still treated as a poor relation by universities and professional institutions such as schools of law and business administration. Second, teacher training still tends to be conducted in monotechnic institutions where intending teachers have few opportunities to gain wider experience and to break the school-college-school circuit.

Pupil-Teacher Systems

Pupil-teacher systems paralleled the development of college-based training in Britain and the colonies. The system was widely used because it provided teachers cheaply, despite long and vocal opposition to it from teacher associations and others who feared for the quality of education. In Britain the system came under increasing attack throughout the nineteenth century, notably in the Cross Commission Report in 1888. It was not, however, finally abolished until as late as 1910.

There was similar and persistent condemnation of the system on professional grounds throughout the colonies. But its cheapness, first and foremost, and its attraction to primary school leavers with few other opportunities, enabled it to continue well into the 1930s. In Jamaica, for example, it provided the backbone of the teaching force well into the twentieth century. The teaching certificate examinations were taken by many regular pupil-teachers. In 1899 over 1,100 candidates took the examination. In 1960, there were 15,000 candidates (D'Oyley and Murray 1979:33-34).

Today, many of the training colleges situated in rural areas are the successors of training centres provided for pupil-teachers. Unfortunately, some countries with severe resource constraints, have had to return to a reliance on the pupil-teacher system. If these teachers were given opportunities to upgrade their educational level through in-service courses, such expedients could be accepted as a necessary, though temporary, way of supplying teachers in an emergency situation. However, upgrading increases salary bills, as we have seen in the case of Guyana. It is unlikely, therefore that the weaknesses of the pupil-teacher system can be eradicated in the near

future and it is very probable that the damage to the
teaching profession will be long term.

Teacher Training Curriculum

The curriculum of teacher training in the colonies
was heavily influenced by the metropolitan model.
Though much progress has been made since independence
in devising new curricula to meet contemporary needs,
many countries still rely on material and textbooks
designed for teachers in alien contexts.

The apprenticeship model of training, inherent
both in the college and the pupil-teacher system
still survives. Such a model encourages the view that
teaching is a craft learned merely by imitating
experienced practitioners. It sits uneasily with the
modern idea that teaching skills can be improved by
innovative experiment and problem solving. It does
not allow a role for theoretical understanding, nor
for research and practice based on self-evaluation.
Rote memorisation of subject matter, blind
application of 'tips for teachers' and much
'classroom observation' perpetuates the apprenticeship model of training and inhibits the development
of professionalism. We examine this theme in more
detail in Chapter Eleven.

A second persistent influence of the
metropolitan system has been the style and ethos of
teacher training. The aim of the early voluntary
colleges in England was to mould Christian teachers
to a character and morality appropriate to their role
as teachers of the children of the labouring masses.
Life in the colleges was restrictive. Training was
authoritarian and paternalistic. The curriculum was
narrow. The study of education in its philosophical
and psychological aspects began only late in the
nineteenth century. So too did the ferment of
educational ideas and new practices brought about by
such people as Froebel and Montessori. These
influences, a curriculum and subjects modelled on
English elementary schools, studies of education
derived from a western tradition and educational
ideas and practices generated in Europe and North
America, were imported into colonial teacher
training. Only with the rise of twentieth century
nationalism did attention turn to the development of
indigenous style and content in teacher training. But
even after independence, colonial influences
persisted.

State Intervention

Finally, in this outline of metropolitan influences
in colonial teacher training, we should note the
gradual extension of state financing and consequent
control. In the early days, both in the metropolitan
country and in the colonies, governments took a
laissez faire approach to teacher training. Later,
this evolved into a policy of 'filling in gaps' where
voluntary provision was insufficient. A partnership
between the state and voluntary organisations
developed which, to varying degrees , still exists
today in a number of countries. Zambia, for instance,
was one of the countries which did not extinguish
missionary endeavour at Independence. The first
Minister of Education of an independent Zambia wrote
(Mwanakatwe 1968:35),

> As in many other African countries, the Africans
> in Zambia know and accept willingly that but for
> the pioneer efforts of missionaries education
> would have been late in coming and very slow in
> dispersion to every remote part of the country.

In Britain the gradual increase in governmental
intervention was largely brought about by democratic
pressures. Over nearly 100 years, from 1832, the
electorate expanded and popular pressures forced
governments to assume greater responsibility. In the
colonies, where such pressures were largely absent,
government intervention was on a smaller scale and
generally on an ad hoc and irregular basis.
Systematic government policy on teacher training
began to evolve only in the years prior to
independence.

Increased state financing and increased state
control went hand in hand. The 'payments by results'
system, whereby teachers were paid according to their
pupils' performance on tests administered by
government inspectors, began in England in 1861.
Though it was later abandoned, it heralded the
extension of state regulation of teacher training
standards, teacher certification and conditions of
service. Eventually, both in Britain and in newly
independent countries, governments assumed overall
responsibility for teacher training as an integral
part of national educational systems.

To illustrate some of these points let us trace
briefly the evolution of state control of teacher
training in Zambia (Northern Rhodesia). The first two
teacher training institutions at Kafue and Sefula
were set up by missionaries in the 1920s (Mwanakatwe

1968:33-34). The colonial authorities entered the scene in 1930 with the establishment of a Jeanes School at Mazabuka. Official policy, however, was to encourage voluntary initiative, with the result that by 1939 there were thirteen, mainly missionary, teacher training institutions. But these were already insufficient to meet requirements for new teachers.

After the war, the colonial authorities began to take more control. They centralised teacher training facilities and supervised the upgrading of teaching qualifications. In 1939, the minimum qualification for primary teachers was a full primary education plus two years' professional training. By 1963, a year before independence, the minimum qualification was two years of secondary schooling (though four years was preferred).

The main emphasis of both missionary and official endeavour through the 1920s to 1950s had been in the area of primary teacher training. The development of secondary teacher training in most colonial territories began approximately 50 years later than in Britain. In 1927, the Colonial Department of the London Day Training College, now the University of London Institute of Education, began to train British teachers to work in the colonies (Honeybone 1977). In the years before independence the majority of secondary teachers in Zambia were British. But in 1961, in preparation for independence, the authorities approved a three-year course at Chalimbana Teacher Training College to train indigenous secondary teachers. The entry level was School Certificate with five credits including English Language.

After independence in 1964, the Zambian government strengthened its control over all educational provision in the country. It steadily increased its subsidy to the voluntary sector and required voluntary organisations to submit to its own regulations and standards.

> In an expanding non-static educational system capable of rapid growth, the Ministry of Education has continued to welcome the participation of voluntary agencies, whether, churches, mines , industry, or other recognised groups more particularly in the post primary fields where the need to supplement the Government's effort is considerable. But the basis for continued participation of voluntary agencies in education development must depend

on their willingness to comply with school regulations issued by the Ministry (Mwanakatwe 1968:130-131).

The Zambia National Union of Teachers and the Ministry of Education formed a joint negotiating committee to resolve problems in the teaching service. The legal status of teachers was confirmed under the Ministry of Education and the Teaching Service commission was set up to advise the Ministry on appointments, confirmation of appointments and discipline. After independence, the School Inspectorate was strengthened at Ministry and field levels. Inspectors provided supervision of school administration and professional support to teachers, whether local or foreign, and in government and non-government institutions.

Finally, a comment on the increase in state control of secondary teacher training. Though the proportion of foreign teachers has remained high in independent Zambia, the government has taken steps to diversify away from exclusive reliance on Britons. Also, the Zambian Inspectorate has a responsibility for orienting foreign teachers on recruitment so that they are equipped to serve the needs of the Zambian secondary schools. But, more importantly for the long run, Zambia took immediate steps in 1966 to establish a School and Institute of Education in the new University of Zambia. The school pioneered a four-year B.A. or B.Sc. in Education, in collaboration with Arts and Science departments of the University and took over the postgraduate certificate in education. The Institute was given the responsibility for secondary teacher professional development. In 1967, as a begining, Kabwe Teacher Training College became an associate of the Institute, providing a two-year, non-graduate course of secondary teacher training for Zambians with O level GCE or the Cambridge Overseas School Certificate.

These initiatives in secondary teacher training were characteristic also of other ex-colonies, which, after independence, hastened to make up for the relative neglect of secondary education by the colonial authorities. Schools and Faculties of Education were set up in Universities from Ibadan in Nigeria to Penang in Malaysia. In some countries Institutes of Education were associated with universities as in Makerere for East Africa. In others, they were made directly responsible to the Ministry of Education, as in Sierra Leone, Singapore and Tanzania.

Different Traditions

This brief outline of the origins and evolution in countries which came within the British sphere of influence inevitably glosses over the many local variations and exceptions. Even more important, it must be remembered that other countries inherited entirely different traditions. To illustrate this point briefly, we take the case of the Philippines, whose educational history contrasts in a number of ways with that of countries which came under British influence.

In the latter years of the nineteenth century, the Spanish colonial authorities set up teacher training for both men and women at secondary level in normal schools (Cortes, 1980). This was an initiative to reduce the role of Christian priests in teaching. In the early years of the twentieth century, the Americans established a network of normal schools in Manila and six other provinces. With rapid expansion of elementary education, teacher training also expanded, so that, by 1925, there were 22 secondary level normal schools.

But the financial resources of the government were unable to cope. Therefore, teacher training was gradually taken over by private enterprise. In 1969 there were nearly 400 normal schools of which only ten per cent were government. Educational studies began to be provided also at degree level in colleges and universities. Since the 1950s, all teacher training institutions have become four-year degree granting colleges for primary and secondary teachers. In the 1940s and 1950s rapid expansion of both public and private higher education led to dramatic rises in enrollments in teacher training courses. In 1958, of the 1,642 college courses officially authorised, 32 per cent were in educational studies. However, less than half of those graduating were able to pass the teacher qualifying examinations set by the Department of Education.

In the 1960s the government took steps to regulate the over-supply of education graduates and to improve quality of professional preparation. It laid down national standards for entry to teacher training courses. It issued licences to teachers who passed the Professional Board Examination for Teachers and improved salaries and conditions of service. By 1980, these measures had largely solved the problems of excess supply and improved the quality of teachers.

GLOBAL STATUS OF TEACHER TRAINING

In Chapter Ten and Eleven we examine further some contemporary trends in teacher training. As a prelude to this we turn now from a description of some historical trends to an outline of the status of teacher education and training today. The information derives partly from the ILO/UNESCO Survey (1983) and partly from a survey of industrialised and less developed countries published by UNESCO and relating to the situation in the late 1970s (Gimeno and Ibanez 1981). Readers are referred to these surveys to gain an idea of how fast the scene has been changing and of the tremendous complexity of provision both in individual countries and across the world. Here, we can do no more than provide a bare summary of the global situation for primary and secondary teacher training.

As a framework to this we need to remind ourselves of three important principles laid down as long ago as 1966 in the UNESCO <u>Recommendation concerning the Status of Teachers</u>, which was adopted by a special intergovernmental conference. Principle number 6 stated,

> Teaching should be regarded as a profession; it is a form of public service which requires of teachers expert knowledge and specialised skills, acquired and maintained through rigorous and continuing study.

Principle number 13 stated,

> Completion of an approved course in an appropriate teacher preparation institution should be required of all persons entering the profession.

Principle number 14 stated,

> Admission to teacher preparation should be based on the completion of appropriate secondary education, and the evidence of the possession of personal qualities likely to help the persons concerned to become worthy members of the profession.

Primary Teacher Training

The general tendency is for primary teacher training institutions to be equivalent to upper secondary (second stage, secondary level) or above (Gimeno and Ibanez 1981:104-107). Of the 48 countries surveyed, 44 per cent offered primary training at upper secondary level, 54 per cent at higher education level in the non-university sector, and 20 per cent in universities. There was evidence of a widespread tendency to raise the level of teacher training during the 1970s, as the extension of the period of compulsory education necessitated a higher level of teacher preparation and as governments accepted the case put by teachers' unions for enhanced professional status. The survey suggests, therefore, that most countries are moving towards post-secondary teacher training as laid down in the 1966 UNESCO Recommendation. However, it should be noted that some 'teacher training institutions occupy an intermediate position between secondary education and university. In fact, when teachers trained at such institutions go to university, they have little or no advantage over students coming from secondary schools (Gimeno and Ibanez 1981:104-105).

The situation was very varied in the early 1980s. A few countries, such as Cuba and Indonesia, were still constrained to accept nine or ten years of schooling as a minimum entry level for teacher training (ILO/UNESCO 1983:7). Some of these required only one or two years of professional preparation. Others required three or four. Naturally, there was considerable diversity. To take as an example, countries in the Asian region alone: where length of schooling plus length of professional preparation were concerned, Afghanistan had a 9+3 pattern, Bangladesh 10+1, Burma 10+2, China 10+3, India 11+2, Indonesia 9+3; Lao People's Democratic Republic 8+4, 11+2, Mongolia 8+4, Nepal 9+4, Pakistan 10+2, Philippines 10+4, Republic of Korea 12+2, Singapore 11+3, Socialist Republic of Vietnam 7+4, Sri Lanka 11+2 and Thailand 10+2 (Gimeno and Ibanez 1981:57-59).

Secondary Teacher Training

For secondary teacher training the minimum entry requirements for training tended to be twelve years of general education (Gimeno and Ibanez 1981:137-140). Of 113 countries surveyed, 64 per cent required twelve years, 23 per cent 13 or 14 years and only 13 per cent required 10 or 11 years. Eighty-three per cent of countries accepted intending teachers for training at 18 years of age or above. As far as years of professional training were concerned, 52 per cent of countries required four years, 26 per cent five years and 22 per cent only two or three years.

Global Trends

Gimeno and Ibanez (1981) warn that these quantitative summaries do not adequately convey differences in quality of provision. They also point out that the survey omits a quantitative assessment of in-service training for upgrading and professional development. Nor does it convey an idea of the numbers of untrained and unqualified teachers.

In their summary of trends Gimeno and Ibanez (1981:212-213) demonstrate the world-wide complexity of teacher training arrangements. They point out, however, that there is a trend towards the training of all teachers at post-secondary level and towards a greater similarity in qualifications for teachers of primary, lower and upper secondary levels. In some countries, teachers for all levels are trained in the same institutions and obtain qualifications which allow them to teach from pre-primary to higher secondary level (Japan, United Kingdom and United States). In other countries, pre-primary and primary teachers are trained in teacher training institutions whilst secondary teachers are trained in universities (for example, Egypt, India, Nigeria). In other cases, primary and secondary teachers are trained in separate establishments (for example, Argentina, Cuba, Guatemala). In yet others, lower and upper secondary teachers are trained in separate institutions (for example, Morocco, Socialist Republic of Vietnam).

Finally, the survey points up the need for teachers to combine specialist and general studies in order to match the demands made on them in contemporary educational systems. The trend is for different institutions to cooperate in teacher training. For example, academic studies of specialised subjects are undertaken in university faculties, technical institutes and colleges, whilst professional training is provided by university departments of education, institutes of education or teacher training institutions.

CONCLUSION

In the following chapters we shall examine how countries have attempted to adapt the teacher training arrangements of yesterday to the national needs and the conditions of today. The distinctions between pre-service and in-service training and between initial and continuing teacher education have become blurred with the introduction of work-study schemes, distance training and school-based professional development. Teacher training today is no longer limited to a once-off two- or three-year course of study prior to entering the profession. But prior to examination of some of these trends, Chapter Nine poses the question, 'How worthwhile and necessary is teacher education and training for the development of effective teachers?'

Chapter Nine

IS TEACHER TRAINING WORTHWHILE?

Over the last 25 years a debate has been conducted, first in the USA, then later also in other industrialised and developing countries, about which factors in the home background of pupils and in schools are most important in raising pupil achievement levels (Coleman 1966; Jencks 1972; Dunkin and Biddle 1974; Rutter 1979; Joyce, Hersh and McKibbin 1983). Some of this research cast doubts on the importance of teachers for educational outcomes. A review of studies from Chile, the Congo, India, Iran, Kenya, Malaysia, Puerto Rico, Thailand and Tunisia, concluded that the educational and professional qualifications of teachers are not important for pupil achievement at primary and lower secondary levels, though they are somewhat important at upper secondary level in certain subjects such as Science (Simmons and Alexander 1980; Heyneman 1980).
   Such disturbing conclusions were put forward at a time of world-wide recession and in the midst of fears that high expenditure on education was producing low social and economic returns. The question which was inevitably raised, therefore, was whether high levels of spending on teachers' salaries and, in particular, teacher education and training, were justified. In this chapter we review the evidence for and against the proposition that investment in teacher training is worthwhile and suggest ways in which research can continue to inform policy makers on such issues. First we turn to what is commonly labelled 'teacher effectiveness' research to discuss whether recent findings support the conclusion that teacher training makes little difference to pupil achievement.

TEACHER EFFECTIVENESS RESEARCH

The notion that teachers make little impact challenged commonsense assumptions about their importance and had major implications for teacher professionalisation. They prompted two large policy-oriented studies into the issues of teacher effectiveness in developing countries. Both of them were reviews and re-analyses of existing research. The World Bank, seeking a sound basis for its priorities in educational investment, particularly teacher training, commissioned the Institute of International Education at the University of Stockholm to assess the evidence on teacher effects on pupil achievement (Husen, Saha and Noonan 1978). By 1983, 37 studies of 230 independent research findings in 21 countries had been analysed (Fagerlind and Saha 1983: 181-185).

Broadly, the findings can be grouped in four categories:
1. <u>Demographic and background variables</u>: the teacher's age, sex, and socio-economic status do not have any consistent effects. But there is some evidence that male teachers are more effective in Science and Mathematics and older teachers with secondary pupils.
2. <u>Teacher qualifications and experience</u>: qualifications, length of experience, amount of education and verbal knowledge of teachers do have a positive effect on pupil achievement.
3. <u>Teacher attitudes</u>: attitudes prove important, particularly the extent to which teachers hold positive expectations of pupils. These appear to improve pupil motivation and achievement.
4. <u>Teacher behaviour and school effects</u>: increasing homework or spending more time on lessons have a moderate positive effect.

The second study was sponsored and organised by the International Development Research Centre (IDRC) (Avalos and Haddad 1979). It was based on work carried out by local researchers in Latin America, Sub-Saharan Africa, the Arab Middle East and North Africa, India, Thailand, Malaysia and the Philippines. The findings are not strictly comparable with those of World Bank study since teacher effectiveness is defined more broadly to include teacher attitudes and behaviour as well as their effects on pupil achievement. However, results were broadly similar with respect to teacher age, sex, experience, socio-economic status, ability, knowledge of subject matter and pupil expectations.

The main results of interest here concern the impact of teachers' education and training on their effectiveness. Avalos (1980) summarises the findings.

1. Trained teachers have better professional attitudes and relationships and are less authoritarian and make better lesson preparations than untrained teachers (especially India, Iraq and Sierra Leone).

2. Trained teachers have more positive effects on pupil achievement than untrained teachers, at both primary and secondary levels (Malaysia and India).

3. However, youths or peers with rudimentary teacher training and good teaching materials have positive effects on pupil achievement at lower levels of the primary school (Philippines and Mexico).

4. The level of teachers' qualifications (years of schooling, graduate/non-graduate) has inconsisent relationships with teacher attitudes and behaviour. In Jordan, Thailand, Egypt and India positive attitudes to teaching correlate with higher qualifications. But other studies showed less job satisfaction amongst highly qualified teachers. In Latin American countries and Thailand, teachers with higher qualifications tend to be more participatory, use modern aids and inquiry methods of teaching. But studies in Jordan and India show no such relationship.

The findings of these two studies were sufficiently convincing for the World Bank to give teacher training a higher priority in its outline of future policy in the Education Policy Review (World Bank 1980). However, like all good research, the studies raised more interesting questions than they answered. Here, we examine two aspects which appear to have direct implications for educational investment.

One question was why home background factors seem to be relatively more important to pupil achievement in the USA whilst school- and teacher-related factors are more important in the context of developing countries (Heyneman 1976; Husen 1977). This is a complicated issue but one strong possibility has to do with the congruence or lack of congruence between home and school culture (Saha 1983). In many developing countries, especially in rural areas, teachers represent almost the only source of knowledge as prescribed in the school curriculum. In more developed contexts, in contrast, there are alternative and supplementary sources of school knowledge. In developing countries home-study

197

facilities may be limited, libraries, books, radio and television may not be available. Learners are more dependent on the school and teacher. One implication of this line of reasoning is that complementary investment in social infrastructure and communications, and adult education may well have indirect positive effects on the quality of schooling (Fitzsimmons and Freedman 1981).

School Effectiveness

Another issue highlighted by the studies was the fact that <u>teacher</u> effectiveness cannot sensibly be separated from <u>school</u> effectiveness. One aspect of this which is beginning to receive the attention of researchers and policy-makers in developing countries is the level of school resources. Commonsense suggests that teachers, however well-educated and trained, are rendered less effective if schools lack the basic facilities, equipment and materials necessary for teaching and learning. Only too often teachers in training learn how to use overhead projectors only to be posted to schools where seating, blackboards and chalk are lacking.

Heyneman (1983) points out that in industrial-ised countries 14 per cent of the recurrent costs of primary schools are allocated to classroom resources - books, maps, visual aids, furniture - and 86 per cent to salaries. In contrast, in the developing world, schools are grossly under-resourced. In Asia the average is 9 per cent on material resources and 91 per cent on salaries and in Africa, 4 per cent and 96 per cent. He alludes to research which 'shows conclusively that better quality teaching and teaching tools - particularly more and better textbooks - have a substantial effect' on pupils' achievement.

In fact, this message has had an impact on the lending pattern of the World Bank and the willingness of countries to invest in a higher level of textbook provision. However, if the absolute level of educational expenditure is not to rise, higher expenditure on textbooks must mean economies elsewhere. The temptation for the authorities is to cut back on teachers, either by hiring fewer of them or recruiting cheaper, less qualified ones. But the experience of curriculum development two decades ago showed clearly that teaching materials (teacher-proof packages) are not <u>substitutes</u> for teachers. Rather, investments in textbooks and in teachers (trained to use them well) must be seen as complementary, not competitive (Schiefelbein, Farrell, Sepulveda-Stuardo 1983).

Moreover, in some contexts, especially at primary level, textbooks are not the only resource constraint. Classrooms lack consumable materials such as paper, pencils, chalk, and exercise books. Some lack running water, sanitation, and facilities to provide school meals. In order to improve the overall quality of schooling, expenditure on such items must be complementary to investment in teachers. Meanwhile, further research is needed to indicate the optimal mix of investments in teacher and non-teacher school resources to improve the environment in which teachers and learners operate.

And Effective Schools

In the 1970s and 1980s, research in industrialised countries has paid attention to both teacher effectiveness issues and to other in-school factors which may be crucial to pupil achievement. One study, based on empirical research, (Joyce, Hersh and McKibbin 1983) identifies two broad categories of attributes which, they suggest, are characteristic of effective schools. These are Social Organisation and Instruction and Curriculum. Table 9.1 lists the different attributes under these two heads.

Figure 9.1: Attributes of Effective Schools

Social Organisation	Instruction and Curriculum
Clear academic and social behaviour goals	High academic learning time (ALT)
Order and discipline	Frequent and monitored homework
High expectations	Frequent monitoring of student progress
Teacher efficacy	
Pervasive caring	Coherently organized curriculum
Public rewards and incentives	Variety of teaching strategies
Administrative leadership	Opportunities for student responsibility
Community support	

Source: Joyce, B.R., Hersh, R.H. and McKibbin, M. (1983) The Structure of School Improvement, (Longman, New York) p. 25.

On the face of it, these attributes would appear to be important in any context, though the empirical research has not yet been attempted in developing countries. But the important point for our purposes here is that almost all, if not all, the attributes of effective <u>schools</u> seem to depend on the way <u>teachers</u> conduct themselves. Perhaps only 'community support' is relatively independent of teacher initiative, and even here, as we saw in Chapter Four, teachers can do much to affect community support for the school. All the other attributes depend on teachers. Five or six of them – clear academic and social behaviour goals, order and discipline, public rewards and incentives, administrative leadership, coherently organised curriculum and opportunities for student responsibility – also depend crucially on the quality of school leadership by principals and supervisors.

This brings us back to the issue of teacher effectiveness because, ultimately, it is the quality of the <u>people</u> who operate and manage institutions who largely determine their effectiveness, given, of course, a certain minimal level of basic resources. At the same time, it should also highlight the importance of research which examines not merely the individual teacher's quality, but the effectiveness of teachers working <u>as a team</u> in the school. This would include their management of school resources to enhance pupil achievement, their liaison with authorities who supply resources and the community who may contribute a variety of different types of support.

ISSUES FOR TEACHER EDUCATION AND TRAINING

What, then, are the significant issues for teacher education and training raised by the teacher effectiveness studies?

Teacher Qualifications

The research evidence on the effect of the length and level of teachers' educational qualifications on pupil achievement is inconclusive. Perhaps future research should ask somewhat different questions, crucial to policy on teacher professionalisation. The important issue is the optimal level and type of general education teachers require in order to gain maximum benefit from teacher training. Currently, we do not know whether it is the length of schooling or the level of subject matter competency or both, which make for a good teacher. It cannot be assumed that just because people go through secondary school or university, they thereby acquire the potential to become good teachers. Indeed, there are some who have argued that formal schooling inhibits creativity, resourcefulness and imagination, attributes which it would be difficult to deny the best teachers need (Reimer 1971; Persaud 1976).

Length of Experience
In neither the developed nor the developing world has the voluminous research on teacher characteristics - sex, social background, ethnic group, personality type and so on - produced evidence to show that teacher effectiveness depends on any of these factors. One factor, however, the length of teaching experience, does seem to warrant further investigation because, it seems, the more experienced teachers are, the more pupils learn (Simmons 1980:90-91). Interestingly, there is an optimum level of experience, between 10 and 20 years, when the effects of experience are more evident. Further research should be directed to investigating why and how experienced teachers are more effective. Is it mainly because of personal maturation, the lessons of experience or because they have benefitted from more training and professional guidance than less experienced teachers. Are they more effective in managing the curriculum, in communication, in classroom organisation or some other factors?

A second area for investigation is to discover at what points in teachers' careers, training or specific types of professional development would produce maximal gains. For instance, would in-service training after five years speed up the period in which a teacher becomes effective? Would training after 20 years prolong a teacher's effective years? Such questions and their answers would do much to inform planners and managers of the teaching force on issues such as teacher wastage, deployment and retirement. For instance, the wastage of female teachers through marriage in the most productive teaching years would become a matter of concern. The deployment to schools of an appropriate mix of experienced and inexperienced teachers would also become of prime importance.

Teacher Attitudes

It has long been known that attitudes affect behaviour. Presumably, this is one reason why so much research all over the world has focussed on teachers' attitudes, their self-concepts, their job satisfaction, their political views and their commitment to teaching. (Another reason is possibly because attitude surveys are technically much simpler to mount than experimental or ethnographic research). Not surprisingly, no consistent results emerge from such studies, which would link teacher attitudes to pupil outcomes.

But one line of research appears to be full of potential. This is the finding that teacher expectations of pupils, with respect to pupil motivation and achievement, are as powerful in the developing world as they have been proved to be in the developed countries. Now that this is firmly established, further research needs to be done on training teachers how to develop positive attitudes towards pupils and how to give them accurate, helpful and positive feedback.

Pupil Outcomes

At this point it is important to note that research into what makes a good teacher advanced considerably when it began to study the effects of teachers on pupil achievement. Previously the good teacher has been defined according to his or her classroom behaviour. Teacher effectiveness depended on the value judgements of researchers about what modes of behaviour they favoured. For instance, teachers were judged according to whether they were democratic/authoritarian or by the degree of 'pupil talk' in relation to 'teacher talk'. Pupil achievement, in contrast, is a universally accepted, empirical and measurable standard for teacher effectiveness. Generally, researchers use language and numeracy tests and subject-based achievement tests for higher levels. In future, research should also be directed at some of the important non-cognitive aspects of pupils' development for which schools have responsibility. These would include their regular attendance at school and their social values.

Research Methodology

This calls for a change of research orientation and methodology. Much recent research has been of the survey type which correlates <u>on the macro-level</u>

teacher characteristics with pupil outcomes (achievement). This approach fails to take account of the real situation where specific teachers interact with specific pupils for a specific period of time and, at higher levels, for specific subjects. Research has in future to examine through observational and ethnographic techniques the unique relationships which teachers have with specific pupils and classes. Examination is needed of not just individual teachers but the group or team of teachers in a particular school. The particular mix of teachers in a school, new recruits, experienced teachers, trained and untrained, well-educated and poorly educated, may reasonably make all the difference to high or low levels of pupil achievement and to attitudes and values. If there is frequent turnover of teachers, through wastage or transfer, it may make sense for the unit of analysis to be the school district within which recruitment and transfer take place. Such changes in research direction towards small scale case studies would accord more with reality than large scale survey, or even experimental types of research.

TEACHER TRAINING RESEARCH : THE FUTURE

Research has confirmed what commonsense suggested, that teacher training is indeed worthwhile. But it tells us very little else about what structures, patterns and processes of training are most useful for producing effective teachers, defined in terms of pupil outcomes. It is a sad fact that at the moment much training is a ritual, necessary for the certificate to which it entitles the teacher, but worth very little more than that. Whilst it may satisfy political and professional sensitivities to claim that a high proportion of the teaching force is certificated, in the long run this is an expensive effort unless real gains in teacher effectiveness are achieved.

Pattern and Structure of Training

Most of the research so far has concentrated on the relationship of pre-service training to teacher effectiveness (Avalos 1980). In-service training has received very little attention (Thompson 1982). The fact is that over the years of rapid school expansion, many teachers have never had pre-service training and some have not had any form of in-service

203

training. Current orthodoxy is that pre-service, however long or short, should be followed by further in-service training for induction, for up-grading and professional and career development. Many countries are putting resources into lengthening and up-grading pre-service provision, as we saw in Chapter Eight. Others are experimenting with different forms of in-service training for both new and serving teachers. Yet there is no sound basis in research for these investments. We need to know what particular patterns and mixes of pre- and in-service provision are most conducive to enhancing teacher effectiveness. Countries introducing new patterns and structures of training should build into their pilot schemes systematic evaluations of the comparative utility and cost of both existing and innovative systems of training.

The Training Process

Much research in developing country contexts has understandably been concerned with the relative effectiveness of trained and untrained teachers. We now know that training makes a difference but we do not know which particular processes of training are crucial. Currently, many pre-service courses are based on conventions, their curricula and examinations hallowed by traditions (Chapter Eleven). Many in-service courses are 'crash' programmes designed of necessity to cater to the needs of underqualified and untrained teachers for up-grading in subject matter and pedagogy (Chapter Ten). What little evidence there is suggests that such courses may be an expensive waste of time and resources (Schiefelbein and Simmons 1981; Thompson 1982).

The potential of even the best research to influence policy decisions should not be over-estimated, since policy is subject to political as well as professional factors (Husen and Kogan 1984). Nevertheless, those who have responsibility for guiding the development of teacher training and for the design and content of courses would benefit immensely from research on effective training processes.

Much of the research reviewed in the IDRC (Avalos and Haddad 1979) study examines the effect of training on teacher behaviour. It shows that particular training processes do influence how teachers teach, though this influence may be diluted through peer pressure the longer teachers have been away from training (Schiefelbein and Simmons 1981). In Thailand, India and Nigeria, for instance, active training methods such as microteaching and simulation, role-play and case study discussion result in 'participatory' and 'discovery' teaching behaviour. But such research suffers from the weakness that an inferential leap has to be made between what constitutes desirable teaching behaviour and actual pupil achievement.

There have been three main approaches to the study of teachers' classroom behaviour, all of them initiated in developed countries. Investigation of teaching styles (progressive/traditional, demo-cratic/authoritarian; direct/indirect) has largely foundered because little empirical basis for these dichotomised styles exists and because teachers' behaviour has often varied widely from their conceptions of what they do (for example, Bennett 1976; Galton and Simon 1980).

Research into training based on particular teaching models has likewise produced little of use. Models may be derived from learning theory, for example, Skinnerian behaviourism or Brunerian cognitive psychology (Weil and Joyce 1978). Desirable teaching behaviour is inferred from the relevant learning theory. But there is no consensus about the validity or compatibility of the many different models, and there are few adequately field-tested training programmes which rely exclusively on the insights of one model. Research is rarely able to identify actual instances of teachers' classroom behaviour which typify one model in pure form, let alone relate them to pupil outcomes.

Skills Training. The third approach has been to base training processes on skills which are thought to be, or better, which empirical research has shown to be useful. The Competency/Performance Based Teacher Education (C/PBTE) movement is an example which has been influential particularly in the USA (Magoon 1976). Its inspiration is the mastery learning model. It sets targets (and, ideally, levels of mastery) for specific teaching, classroom management and communication skills which trainees must observe, practise and master. They are assessed according to what they do as teachers rather than, as in conventional training, what they know about education.

Another influential skills-oriented approach is 'direct instruction' (Rosenshine 1979; Peterson

1979). It is based on research which shows that pupil achievement is related to the amount of time teachers use in direct interaction with pupils on learning tasks. It is also related to the 'academic engaged time' at school and in homework which pupils spend on learning tasks (Rosenshine and Berliner 1978). Training emphasises skills of questioning, cueing, feedback and helping trainees select and manage learning tasks.

Both these approaches have their critics. Their rather weak empirical bases are at the core of the problem of deriving any one comprehensive model of teaching from empirical research (Winter 1982). They are also criticised because they pre-determine the discrete skills which trainees should acquire and potentially neglect the autonomous, personal and holistic aspects of professional developments. C/PBTE is criticised because, in practice, many schedules for skills development are not adequately prepared with measurable criteria for mastery. The 'direct instruction' approach is critised because it appears to neglect higher order intellectual skills in favour of the 'basics' (Peterson 1979). Both approaches are also criticised by those who believe that the personal judgement and attitudes of teachers must be developed in training; that teaching is more than the exercise of a number of specific skills (Anderson 1984).

This criticism would be understood by those who have utilised an approach to training which derives its philosophy from the humanistic psychology of Carl Rogers. Such training uses group counselling techniques to encourage trainees to gain deeper personal knowledge; by understanding their own attitudes and behaviour they are better able, so it is assumed, to undertake their own professional development. Such 'teacher perspectives' are the focus also of approaches which emphasise that teachers must engage in their own classroom research because, it is believed the key to change lies in their personal observation and analysis and evaluation of their own teaching. (Hammersley 1977, Woods 1983).

A Training Model
None of these skills-oriented approaches to training are as yet firmly based on empirical research about what attributes effective teachers actually have and what they actually do, which improves pupil outcomes. Nevertheless, they all possibly have potential

Figure 9.1: Internal Structure of the Teacher Training Process: Components and Outcomes.

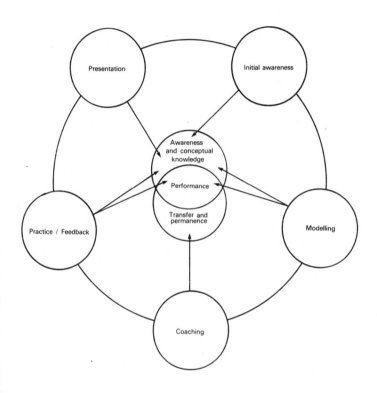

Source: Avalos, B. (1985) <u>Teacher Effectiveness and Teacher Training</u> (unpublished paper)

207

contributions to make to teacher training. Research in Bolivia, Columbia, India, Kenya, Malaysia and Thailand (Avalos 1985) is currently showing promise in utilising skills-training techniques such as microteaching, teachers' diaries for self evaluation, role-play, simulation, workshops and discussion groups. Avalos (1985) has imposed an organising framework on her description of these rather fragmented action-research efforts, by adapting a model of the teacher training process from Joyce and Showers (1981).

The model (Figure 9.2) emphasises processes by which trainees can examine and change their own 'interpretative frameworks' by self- and peer-observation and by the coaching of supervisors. With self-knowledge and information about alternative modes of behaviour trainees can, it is suggested, change or add to their teaching skills. Opportunities for self-examination, practice and the support of peers and supervisors is intended to ensure that improved teaching behaviour will be long-lasting.

1. <u>Stimulation of initial teacher awareness</u>: teachers' awareness about their own views, philosophies of education and teaching, their teaching behaviours and the teaching context. <u>Training methods</u>: analysis of live or video lessons, diaries and discussion, analysis of pupil and community records, community interaction.

2. <u>Presentation of information</u>: about selection of teaching approaches and skills and feedback on performance. <u>Training methods</u>: lectures, group discussion, structured and programmed materials, individual and group assignments.

3. <u>Demonstration and modelling of the teaching pattern or skill</u>: observation of live or videoed teaching, simulation, role-play and games.

4. <u>Practice and Feedback</u>: practice of a teaching model or skill by trainees, with teachers and supervisors analysing the practice, identifying problems and deciding on changes for future practice: <u>Training methods</u>: microteaching workshops with peer observation, rating by feedback from peers or pupils or teachers' self-rating.

5. <u>Coaching</u>: provision of a means of analysing the teaching situation, determining the appropriateness of the skill, the adaptation of it to learners and the adjustment of to a variety of situations. This process is intended to encourage skill transfer. <u>Training methods</u>: regular contact with trainees by supervisors and teacher-tutors to enable them to reflect on their experiences, assess their own

progress and be offered alternative strategies where necessary.

Avalos (1985:21) comments:

> Perhaps one of the unfortunate elements of the available research on training that comes from developing countries is that projects have concentrated for the most part on particular aspects of training rather than evaluating comprehensively a training process ... Thus, they are unable to sustain that their methods improve practice in all its aspects. (Also if) training is pursued in a mechanical form that does not stimulate teacher awareness and creativity, what they may learn may become a caricature of what might be a sound teaching practice.

CONCLUSION

The training model described above avoids the pitfall involved in the tackling of skills' training in a piecemeal way. It is a continuous training <u>process</u> model. Similar models (Cogan 1973; Stones 1984) have been derived from working practice in the USA where resources should be available to implement them. As a minimum there must be adequate time for the lengthy processes of observation, modelling, practice and coaching. Training institutions must have regular, cooperative and close contact with practice schools and teachers. Supervisory trainers and teacher-tutors must be available and able to spend a great deal of time in classrooms with trainees. In addition, trainees must have the autonomy necessary to develop their own teaching philosophies and practices. Thus, the institutionalisation of skills-oriented training, whether for pre-service trainees or serving teachers, depends not only on curriculum changes but on managerial capacity and additional resources.

It should be noted that the model described above is a model of training rather than a model of teaching. It is not prescriptive about how teachers should teach. Rather, it challenges them to generate their own models of teaching based on personal experience, self-evaluation and expert supervision. For those who believe that teaching is ultimately a unique personal interaction between teacher and learner, and that theories of teaching can only be validly derived by practitioners, such an approach presents a challenge full of promise.

The use of a training model has the advantage that it may persuade those who plan teacher training curricula to re-think content and to re-structure programmes away from didactic, over-academic and passive 'courses' towards more practical, skills-oriented approaches. The training model described above lends itself easily to active methods of training for classroom skills. But attention must also go to ways of invigorating the traditional 'academic' components of teacher training, including subject-matter upgrading, child development, and the 'disciplines' of education such as psychology and philosophy. We turn to these issues in more detail in Chapter Eleven. In Chapter Ten, first, we survey recent trends in teacher training provision and changing structures and patterns of teacher education and training.

Chapter Ten

TEACHER TRAINING: NEEDS AND RESPONSES

Chapter Nine reviewed the evidence which suggests that investment in teacher training is worthwhile. But what sort of teacher training? How should it be organised and what should be the curriculum? These are the questions which we raise in this chapter. We suggest here that spending more on the types of teacher training which served the needs of yesterday may not necessarily pay off and that conventional approaches to teacher training may no longer be adequate to meet the growing and diverse needs of schools.

It would not be a gross overstatement to suggest that the key to real improvements in the quality of future educational provision lies in the capacity of the authorities to make substantial improvements in pre-service and in-service teacher training. Therefore, these final chapters are devoted to examination of current issues and problems in teacher training. In this chapter there is an overview of the main training needs to which attention must be directed if teachers are to operate effectively in development-oriented schools. Some of the organisational strategies currently in use to respond to these needs are described. In Chapter Eleven selected issues for the curriculum and process of teacher training are examined. Brief reference is made to relevant innovations and case studies from a variety of countries. The aim is to highlight issues of fairly general concern in countries attempting to develop their school systems.

There is no suggestion here, however, that an innovation which works in one context would automatically suit another (Raggatt 1983; Perrin 1984). Although international sharing of ideas and experience is helpful, the transfer of educational practices is fraught with dangers. Workable solutions to particular problems in teacher education and training must be indigenous, taking account of the unique socio-economic, political and cultural context to which they apply.

CONVENTIONAL TEACHER EDUCATION AND TRAINING

As noted in Chapter Eight, it appears that initial teacher preparation programmes have, in general, increased in duration. Ranging from one to five years, they comprise academic and professional components, taken consecutively, as in postgraduate education courses, or concurrently, as in education degrees or teacher training certificates or diplomas. The ILO/UNESCO survey (1983:137-138) found that there is a strong trend towards the training of all types of teacher in organically related or geographically adjacent centres. This involves training primary and secondary teachers in the same type of institution, training pre-primary, primary and lower secondary teachers together, promoting a uniform level of professional training for all age levels, raising primary teacher training to university level, coordinating college training of primary teachers and university training of secondary teachers and, finally, transferring teacher education to universities. The advantages of this integration are significant. It helps to reduce differences in status associated with different levels of schooling and encourages greater mobility within the profession. In addition, there is a potential for close links between teacher education and training and research.

There is widespread agreement today that in-service education and training for professional development is an important ingredient in the process of teacher professionalisation. In-service provision has certainly become more diversified in recent decades, much of it devoted to the upgrading of underqualified teachers. However, it is not possible to quantify precisely how resources are allocated on a global basis because the data have not yet been put together systematically. Nor is it possible to estimate accurately the proportion of education budget allocations which go to teacher training in general, though they tend to range between five and 15 per cent. It is probably true to suggest, however, that conventional teacher training receives regular budgetary allowances whilst in-service programmes are sometimes financed ad hoc and on a shoe-string.

INITIAL EDUCATION AND TRAINING

Teacher colleges, normal schools and university departments of education have long been centrally concerned with the initial, pre-service preparation of teachers. As large numbers of untrained and unqualified teachers have been recruited at various times to meet expanding requirements, so these institutions have found themselves increasingly involved in the initial training of serving teachers. But in some situations training needs have been too great to be met by existing institutions and new strategies have had to be sought.

In this section the focus is on the contemporary diversity of teacher training provision to cater to the needs of untrained and unqualified serving teachers. The presence of untrained teachers has been and will continue to be a problem in different countries at different times. As we have seen in Chapter Six, policies for rapid universalisation of schooling in countries like Ghana, Nigeria and Bangladesh have led to chronic, absolute teacher shortages and recruitment of large numbers of

Table 10.1: % Underqualified Teachers, 1980-1981

	Primary	Secondary	Primary & Secondary
Bangladesh			46
Barbados	15		
Cameroon	48		
Chile			20
Cuba			40
Ecuador	3	1	
Guyana			30
India	37	20	
Jamaica			23
Madagascar	0	0	
Mauritius			3
Nicaragua			70
Peru			22
Sri Lanka	0	0	
Tunisia	1		
Venezuela	22	27	

Source: ILO/UNESCO (1983) Report of Joint ILO/UNESCO Committee of Experts on the Application of the Recommendation Concerning the Status of Teachers (ILO, Geneva), p. 126

untrained teachers. Other countries no longer have overall shortages but many teachers are teaching in subjects or at levels for which they are not qualified. Malawi, for example, does not lack lower secondary teachers but requires many more Science specialists. Similarly, Sri Lanka lacks adequately qualified teachers of English to support recent initiatives in the teaching of English as a foreign language from grade 3 primary.

A global survey of in-service provision for untrained and unqualified teachers is needed. There are few reliable and comparable statistics, country by country, on the size of the untrained and unqualified teacher problem. This is partly because what counts as 'trained' and 'qualified' varies from place to place. The ILO/UNESCO (1983) survey provides some very limited information culled from the replies of 40 countries, both industrialised and developing, to a question on underqualified teachers. Also, a recent and important survey of thirteen English-speaking sub-Saharan African countries exists (Greenland 1983, hereafter referred to as the Africa Survey). It provides a detailed picture of the problem in one part of the developing world and the diverse ways in which the authorities are responding to it. Table 10.2 gives an idea of the size of the problem of untrained and unqualified primary teachers in the thirteen countries surveyed. In five of the countries the situation has deteriorated since 1965-6 and only in one country, Malawi, has the situation markedly improved.

The survey differentiates between different categories of untrained and unqualified primary teachers in need of initial training. Ghana, for example, uses many pupil-teachers who are neither qualified nor trained but are relatively inexpensive. In Swaziland a qualified primary teacher has two years of secondary schooling, a Junior Certificate and two years of college training. In Nigeria the preferred route to a Grade Two teaching qualification is three years of lower secondary schooling and three years of college training. In Nigeria also, 90 per cent of teachers are categorised as trained but unqualified because they fail to pass all subjects for the Grade Two Certificate.

The Africa Survey details two types of in-service training for untrained and unqualified teachers, longer training and education leading to certification and short 'emergency' orientation courses which rarely lead to full certification.

Table 10.2: Thirteen Countries in English-speaking Africa: Size of Primary Teacher Force and Percentage of Teachers Unqualified: a Comparison between Trevaskis' Figures (1965-1966) and the Most Recent Available

	Size of primary teacher force		% primary teachers unqualified	
	Trevaskis (a)	This report	Trevaskis (a)	This report
Botswana	811	4,870	36	36
Gambia	393	1,370	33	68
Ghana	50,950	48,400	71	36
Kenya	33,522	98,000	36	31
Lesotho	2,799	5,090	38	36
Liberia	n.a. (b)	7,182	n.a.(b)	71
Malawi	8,735	11,552	32	19
Nigeria	3,860L(c) 23,480W 15,312N	256,979	26L(c) 47W 23N	57
Sierra Leone	3,729	7,088	54	61
Swaziland	1,486	3,016	28	23
Uganda	17,848	36,442	12	50
Zambia	8,716	19,868	4	25
Zimbabwe	19,355(d)	36,400	20(d)	40

Notes: (a) Trevaskis' figures are taken from Trevaskis (1969) pp. 104 and 100.
(b) The Trevaskis Report did not include Liberia
(c) In Nigeria, Trevaskis' data are for Lagos State, Western State and Northern States only.
(d) Trevaskis' figures for Zimbabwe are for what was then called the African division in Rhodesia.

Source: Greenland, J. (ed). In-Service Training of Primary Teachers in Africa (Macamillan, London) 1983, p.7.

Certification

In Kenya, Zambia and Botswana the official strategy is to reduce the proportion of untrained and unqualified teachers in the system, at least as far as government schools are concerned. They are trained alongside pre-service trainees in colleges. In Kenya and Zambia serving teachers have, in recent years, been given time-limits to get themselves into training. Kenya and Botswana have plans to phase out pre-service training by requiring everyone to teach for one year prior to entering college.

Lesotho, Liberia, Nigeria, Sierra Leone, Swaziland and Zimbabwe mount special in-service programmes, distinct from pre-service courses for school leavers. In Lesotho, Liberia and Zimbabwe conventional pre-service residential training for two or three years has been phased out and all trainees participate in 'sandwich' courses, partly college-based and partly school-based.

Short Orientation

Short orientation courses for untrained teachers, often recent school leavers, exist in Gambia, Ghana, Malawi, Nigeria and Zambia. They are organised by a variety of bodies, including the teacher unions in Gambia and Ghana, the Local Government Authority in Nigeria, the Institute of Education in Sierra Leone, the Provincial Inspectorate in Zambia and the In-service Centre in Malawi. At one end of the scale, in Sierra Leone, they last for one week and reach about one in three untrained teachers a year; at the other end, in Malawi, they last about six weeks and reach about one in eleven teachers. In Ghana and Nigeria they probably reach fewer teachers. None of these courses leads to qualified teacher status.

UPGRADING SUBQUALIFIED TEACHERS

Although courses for upgrading teachers with low educational or professional qualifications are not necessarily initial training, they are described here because they are important elements in training provision in the Africa Survey countries. They cater to teachers who have had their qualifications undermined by higher standards set more recently, particularly after countries had attained independence. Subqualified teachers are often experienced and committed yet they cannot claim the salary, status or promotion available to less experienced but more highly qualified teachers. In Swaziland they are trained alongside unqualified teachers. In Malawi, Nigeria, Uganda and Zimbabwe separate provision is made. In the majority of instances teacher colleges play a major role. In Zimbabwe, for instance, Umtali College was designated to train all the subqualified teachers. In Uganda two colleges have been involved exclusively in such work.

Greenland (1983:39-42) suggests that govern- ments are undecided about the priority to be given to this type of training and that this is reflected in the relatively small scale and probable low impact of such programmes. Governments do not have follow-up data which show conclusively that upgrading does improve teacher effectiveness; on the other hand, they are clear that it is costly both in terms of the time spent in training out of the classroom and in terms of inflationary pressures on the salary bill.

Distance Teacher Upgrading in Kenya
Kenya's distance teacher upgrading strategy provides one example of a thorough-going attempt to find alternative means of preparing serving teachers to meet the demands of an expanding school system. In 1967 the Correspondence Course Unit was set up within the Institute of Adult Studies of the University College of Nairobi (Hawkridge, Kinyanjui, Nkinyangi and Orivel 1979). The main focus of the unit's work was the upgrading of teachers' academic qualificat- ions, in particular the upgrading of primary P3 teachers to P2 through the Kenya Junior Secondary Examination (KJSE). P3 teachers were allowed to take two subjects a year, accumulating credits till they had five passes. The course gave instruction for two years in each subject and allowed teachers flexibility in the time within which they had to present themselves for examination.

The course consisted mainly of correspondence material with radio programmes broadcast on national networks in the late afternoons on weekdays. It gradually gained in reputation and by 1977 had attracted substantial enrollments of over 4,000 teachers.

In 1969, at the request of the Ministry of Education, the unit began to cooperate with the Kenya Institute of Education (KIE) to provide upgrading to P3 level for unqualified teachers. The first phase of training was in methodology, through three short residential courses over one year, supplemented by radio lectures in term time. Phase two was for academic upgrading in three subjects using first-year KJSE correspondence materials and radio. By 1974 nearly 8,500 teachers had participated in the course. It was then phased out because few teachers remained who wished to gain P3 status.

In 1977 a further upgrading course in seven subjects was begun for the East African Certificate of Education, normally taken after four years in secondary school and two years after the KJSE. Again the course was by correspondence and radio.

Details of the achievements, organisation and cost of Kenya's distance teaching upgrading programmes are in Hawkridge et al. (1979). The points to note here are, firstly, that such upgrading programmes are likely to be universally popular with teachers and that the main constraint on provision is likely to be the inability of the public purse to finance increases in salary of upgraded teachers. Secondly, upgrading, and particularly academic upgrading, can be achieved without the substantial involvement of college personnel in traditional face-to-face training: it need not be labour-intensive. Thirdly, such innovations, although not necessarily cheaper than conventional training, unless there are very great economies of scale, do release college trainers for other tasks and do keep teachers in the classrooms whilst they study (Taylor 1983). Finally, training which involves a number of different media, in this case print and radio, (but television, video, audio-tape and telephone may also be used), involve the cooperation of a number of different agencies and institutions, some of them not under the Ministry of Education (Welsh 1979). In the Kenyan case there existed vital political will and the crucial cooperation of the Ministry of Education, the Ministry of Information and Broadcasting, the University College and the KIE.

The Africa Survey shows that a substantial majority of the countries represented provide upgrading for untrained/unqualified and subqualified teachers. In 1983, six countries, Lesotho, Malawi, northern Nigeria, Swaziland Zambia and Zimbabwe were using programmes which include a distance teaching, usually correspondence, element. Five countries, Ghana, eastern Nigeria, Liberia, Sierra Leone and Uganda, ran short courses of a conventional kind (Greenland 1983:127-128). But teacher training by distance education, and using a variety of media, is increasingly practised in other regions also (Brophy and Dudley 1982). Table 10.3 shows the position in eight Asian countries in 1984.

Table 10.3: Distance Education in Selected Asian Countries

SN	Countries	School Education		Teacher Education		Functional Education	Parent Education
		Primary	Secondary	Primary	Secondary		
1	India		A 1,6 C 2,3 C 1,2,4		C 1,2,6	1,2	
2	Indonesia	A 1	C 1,2,4	C 1,2	C 1,4		
3	Malaysia	C 1,2,3	C 1,2,3	A 1,2,6		2,3	
4	Nepal	C 2		A 1,2,6			
5	Pakistan		A 1,2,3 4,6	A 1,2,6	A 1,2,6	1,2,3,6	
6	Philippines		C 1,6 A 1,6	A 1,4,6	A 1,4,6	1,6	1,6
7	Republic of Korea	C 2,3	C 2,3	A 1,2,6			3
8	Sri Lanka		A 1,2, 4,6	A 1,2,3	A 1,2,3	1,2	

Note: Media used: 1 = print, 2 = radio, 3 = TV, 4 = audio tapes, 5 = video tapes, 6 = tutor (face to face teaching)
A = independent structure
C = Complementary system to formal system

Source: APEID (1984) <u>Training Personnel for Distance Education</u> (UNESCO Regional Office for Education in Asia and the Pacific, Bangkok) p. 27

Distance Teacher Training in Sri Lanka

The Sri Lankan programme provides just one Asian example of a multi-media approach to upgrading untrained teachers. In the early 1970s a 'postal training scheme' was launched to train all the teachers who could not be absorbed into training colleges. They were given three years' training whilst they were in the schools. Materials and assignments were sent to them by post. Contact lessons were organised during holidays and weekends. Those who passed a written examination and teaching practice were awarded the trained teachers' certificate. During the same period a similar scheme was organised for graduate teachers. This has now been taken over by the Open University of Sri Lanka.

In the early 1980s the authorities decided to develop the distance training scheme for untrained non-graduate teachers. Since 1979, 20,000 additional teachers have been recruited (APEID 1984a:24-25). There are approximately 35,000 untrained teachers out of a total of 140,000, according to the School Census, 1982. There are 24,000 untrained teachers with only O or A Level qualifications and it is these teachers at whom the distance training opportunities are currently targetted. The colleges have the capacity to train 5,000 teachers per year on a two-year residential course. This has traditionally been an in-service programme only but from 1986 the colleges will be rationalised and many will become specialist pre-service institutions. Overall training capacity is adequate to produce replacements for the existing stock of teachers but cannot cope with the backlog of untrained teachers in the system.

In 1982 a pilot distance training programme was launched. Course writers were trained and courses were prepared in primary teaching methods and in Mathematics and Science at secondary level. The course components include printed materials, audio-visual aids, written assignments, practice lessons and practical training with access to local facilities and tutors.

RECURRENT TRAINING AND CONTINUING PROFESSIONAL DEVELOPMENT

Until recently in-service training was conceived as a means of imparting to teachers new information, ideas or skills necessary for them to implement new curricula or utilise new materials designed by non-teacher experts and specialists. Over the last twenty

years the notion of teachers as professionals has led
to a different concept of in-service training,
whereby teachers are not merely passive recipients of
training but active participants in the planning,
implementation and evaluation of their own
professional development throughout their teaching
careers (Lynch 1977; Cropley and Dave 1978; Hoyle and
Megarry 1980; Goad 1984).
In 1975 the 35th International Conference on
Education (UNESCO 1975:24-25) spelled out the goals
and approaches at that time rapidly becoming orthodox
about in-service teacher training.

In-service Education

Continuing education should be an integral part
of the teacher education process and should
therefore be arranged on a regular basis for all
categories of educational personnel. Procedures
should be as flexible as possible and adaptable
to teachers' individual needs and to the special
features of each region, taking into account
developments in the different specialities and
the extension of knowledge.
The functions of teacher education
institutions should be extended not only to
provide for the pre-service education of
teachers but also to contribute substantially
towards their further education; it is thus
desirable that these institutions provide pre-
service education and continuing education.
Special regional centres should also be
developed for this purpose and also to provide
initial in-service education for those
teachers, particularly in developing countries,
who did not receive adequate preparation before
starting teaching.
Teachers' organizations should be encouraged to contribute to the continuing education
of teachers by initiating opportunities for
teachers to meet and work together on common
problems. Conferences, seminars and courses
organized by teachers' organizations may
represent a significant measure in encouraging
teacher development by the profession itself.
Self-education of teachers should be
considered as an important element in their
continuing education. The educational authorities and educational research and document-
ation centres should help the teachers to
organize their individual in-service education

by providing guidance, the necessary document-ation and literature, library facilities, etc., and by making the necessary time available.

In order to make continuing education more effective and to reach educators in remote regions, extensive use should be made of radio, TV and correspondence courses. The combination of short full-time courses with long periods of multi-media programmes, including radio, TV and correspondence courses may provide one immediate solution of in-service education of the broad mass of teachers.

The strengthening of the continuing education of teachers as required at all levels of the system, from early childhood education to the tertiary level and adult education, will require considerable efforts on the part of education authorities. Such efforts include the quantitative analysis of teacher supply and demand in the country and the working out of national or regional plans for the continuing education of teachers.

Present rules, regulations and statutes should be so modified as to recognize the importance, necessity and effect of in-service education, to take into account the developments in its organization which have already occurred and to provide a legal right for all educational personnel to take part in continuing education.

Measures should be taken to give all full-time or part-time specialists working in education the opportunity for in-service education and at the same time to ensure that their professional experience benefits other teachers.

These ideals are largely unchanged today but they are far from being realised, partly because resources for comprehensive in-service training are severely limited by economic depression and partly because the demands they make on managerial capacity and on hard-pressed personnel and institutions are great. However, much experience has been gained from efforts to develop in-service training to cater to a variety of needs. First, we look briefly at some of these needs. Then, we examine some of the strategies and approaches which have been utilised in recent years.

Needs
We have seen how the task of upgrading untrained, unqualified and subqualified teachers has absorbed resources in in-service training during periods of rapid educational expansion. But some countries have now largely upgraded the backlog of these teachers and have been able to turn attention to providing in-service training for other categories of teachers.

Induction. Induction, in the sense of planned and systematic support to new teachers in schools, is widely acknowledged to be an important type of in-service provision (Tisher 1980; Bolam 1984; Griffin 1985). It can help to consolidate and make good deficiencies in initial training, assist new teachers overcome unfamiliar teaching and classroom management problems and reduce feelings of isolation and frustration. Done well, it might make a substantial contribution to reducing teacher wastage. Nevertheless, it is a neglected aspect of training, possibly because there are problems of a practical nature involved in organising and financing training for a particular category of teachers who may be widely dispersed and who face different problems.

There is very little information about induction schemes in developing countries, possibly because very little is actually being done. But there are a number of potential sources of support for new teachers. For instance, personnel from teacher training institutions may follow up the progress of ex-trainees in schools. For this to be feasible and effective, however, there needs to be coordination between the recruiting and deploying authorities and teacher training institutions. Also, some additional resources have to be found in the training institutions since induction responsibilities are labour-intensive and time-consuming. Existing trainers have to be retrained in supervision techniques or else new categories of specially trained personnel have to be created, as was the case in Lesotho (Mathot 1983).

Another source of support is the inspectorate and supervisory service. Such personnel are accustomed to visiting schools and can combine induction tasks with their other duties, as long as they are not over-stretched. But this in itself may cause tensions unless the possible conflict of duties between the evaluation and support of new teachers can be avoided.

Alternatively, personnel in teacher centres and resource units may take on special responsibilities for mounting short programmes of a social or professional nature and for individual counselling. One advantage of this approach is, again, that it utilises existing resources. Another is that it provides support to teachers in a neutral and stress-free environment, which is relatively independent of the authority structure of the school and inspectorate. A disadvantage is that it is costly to take teachers away from school during the working hours but reduces their personal time otherwise. Travel expenses, unless subsidised, could well deter them from utilising the service.

Perhaps the least costly strategy is for principals or other senior teachers to make provision for induction in their own schools or for a group of neighbouring schools. In Papua New Guinea, for instance, senior subject teachers in high schools are responsible for checking the lesson plans of all new teachers. They visit their classrooms, give demonstration lessons and encourage new and experienced teachers to share experience.

New Curricula. Training to introduce teachers to new curricula, textbooks and materials has traditionally been one of the most widespread purposes of in-service provision (Greenland 1983:84-90). The customary format has been the short course run by college trainers, inspectors and advisers. Sometimes secondary teachers have been utilised to train primary teachers. The courses are held during holidays in a major centre on a residential basis or for a day at a time in local facilities.

Such updating and refresher courses can be criticised on many grounds. They can be costly in travel and subsistence. They may take teachers away from the classrooms. Unless there is careful selection and direction, teachers for whom they would be most helpful often do not attend. They are frequently too short, overloaded, irrelevant to the classroom situations and resources of teachers and formal and over-didactic in style. Although follow-up studies are rarely done, it is likely that individual teachers, trained in isolation from others in their schools, are unable to use and disseminate new ideas and practices against the likely tide of institutional conservatism of their schools.

224

Curriculum Development. In Chapter Three we examined
the core roles of teachers in curriculum development,
assessment and examinations. The short course
strategy outlined above can achieve little more than
make teachers aware that new curricula exist.
Alternatively, this can be done, as in Korea, through
newsletters, radio and television (APEID 1984a:20-
23). But genuine involvement of teachers in
curriculum development has to be stimulated through
participatory forms of in-service training, with
teachers planning their own activities and
evaluating their own achievements.

The re-training of teachers to handle new groups
of pupils or new specialisms is likely to be an
increasing need as school systems expand and
pressures to cut costs through more intensive
utilisation of personnel increases. For instance,
more attention is nowadays being paid to the
integration of handicapped children in ordinary
schools. Remote and sparsely populated rural areas
are gradually being provided with schools where one
or two teachers may have to cope with pupils of a
wide range of ages and abilities over a number of
specialist areas. In school systems where
expansionary pressures have now reached the
secondary level, teachers trained at lower levels
need retraining to cope with their redeployment to
vacant posts at higher levels. In the interests of
efficiency many countries are discouraging
repetition and dropout. With more pupils of all
abilities passing up the school system, teachers have
needs for training in diagnostic testing and remedial
teaching. Teachers specialised in guidance and
counselling will be needed to help pupils to make
informed choices of further study and work
opportunities.

Community Development and Non-Formal Education. In
Chapter Four we examined the potential roles of
teachers in a variety of community-oriented
educational activities. All teachers are benefitted
by being trained to work with parents and members of
the community in the interests of pupils and to
familiarise themselves with the life of the
community. In some countries, as we have seen, policy
may also require them to take on roles as animateurs,
community development agents or adult educators.
These are challenging and skilled responsibilities,
yet, despite the rhetoric on the teacher-community
theme, this is a neglected aspect of both pre-service

and in-service training (Dove 1982b:77-121; Dove 1982c). In the Africa Survey there is not one report of any such training in any of the thirteen countries. (Botswana, however, has, in fact, held a series of conferences on the theme for educational personnel from the ministry, the university, the inspectorate, colleges and schools). Martin (1984) examined training for community roles in a number of countries. He found provision seriously inadequate though there have been some promising experiments, often with limited life and impact, in Peru, Ecuador and North-east Thailand.

Principals or Headteachers. The in-service training of school principals or headteachers is more important today, perhaps, than ever before. The responsibilities of schools towards their pupils and the community are greater and more complex than in the past. In countries where management is being decentralised to local level, principals are required to learn new skills (Akube 1983). The ideology of professionalism endows the principal with greater autonomy to take the lead in school-based curriculum activities and professional development for teachers. The same philosophy also places greater reliance on principals' reports on teacher performance for promotion purposes and creates a need for principals to be trained in evaluation techniques. The Africa Survey (1983:53-61) noted that training for principals tends to be provided for those already in post rather than for those being groomed for them. Programmes range from one-day sessions with limited objectives such as managing a filing system, to one-year programmes such as a Benin course which equips principals to train other teachers in classroom management.

Retirement. According to UNESCO, between 1970 and 1975, the growth of the teaching force in developing countries rose by over seven per cent; between 1975 and 1982, the annual growth was nearly three per cent at primary and over five per cent at secondary levels (Table 6.3). This means that many of the teachers recruited in large numbers in expansionary periods will reach the age of retirement by the year 2000. These retired teachers represent a sizeable proportion of experienced, educated manpower in many countries. Very few countries are so replete with educated people that they can afford to ignore the

potential contribution of retired teachers in
development work, both educational and non-
educational. In-service programmes could encourage
retiring teachers to seek out ways in which they
could continue to offer their services in part-time,
paid and voluntary work. This would, of course, need
to be done within the framework of national policy
and agreement with teachers' organisations.

Teacher Trainers. The Africa Survey (1983:61-68)
suggests that, in six of the countries surveyed,
serious attention is being given to the task of
equipping primary teachers to become teacher
trainers. In Botswana, Lesotho, Malawi, Nigeria and
Zambia, primary teachers with long experience and
appropriate qualifications follow programmes of full
time study from between one and four years, leading
to diplomas, B. Eds or M. Eds. In India, the State
Councils of Educational Research and Training, the
State Institutes of Education and the State
Institutes of Science Education organise courses for
resource personnel who train teachers on in-service
programmes at district and block levels.

In general, however, there is a dearth of
information about the characteristics and the
training of teacher trainers, for both college and
university personnel. The ILO/UNESCO Survey (1983:13
and 138) stated that more training of trainers is now
available than formerly. Most countries require
teacher trainers to have at least five years'
previous teaching experience. But this experience is
not always at the level of schooling for which the
trainers are preparing teachers. In addition, it is a
problem how to broaden the conception of their role
from mere lecturing to practical training and applied
research. Teacher trainers often find themselves out
of the mainstream of educational developments and
with few opportunities for career mobility. In
addition, they are sometimes passed over for foreign
refresher training in favour of more prominently
placed planners and administrators. Yet, in the
opinion of the author, the preparation and
professional enrichment of teacher trainers at all
levels is one of the potentially most powerful ways
of introducing innovations in school teaching and
should not continue to be neglected.

ORGANISATION OF TRAINING

Much teacher education and training will continue to be organised at colleges and universities on conventional lines. But long courses at institutions take time to produce teachers for the classrooms; they can be very costly especially if they are residential; and they are sometimes criticised for their isolation from the schools. Alongside conventional training there is much organisational diversification taking place today, as countries search for new approaches which are both low cost and appropriate to the expanding training needs of teachers.

Here we describe some of the organisational models which have been used in recent years and have the advantage that they can be easily adapted to serve a variety of different categories of teachers and training needs. Unfortunately, very few thorough evaluations of cost and effectiveness have been carried out which would permit an analysis of their comparative advantages and disadvantages. In any case, much depends on unique contextual factors. However, where possible, some comments are made on their obvious strengths and weaknesses.

ZINTEC in Zimbabwe

The Zimbabwe Integrated National Teacher Education Course (ZINTEC) is an initial teacher training programme for primary teachers. It exemplifies a multi-media approach to teacher training which aims to be professionally equivalent to the conventional training course and efficient in its use of scarce educated manpower (Ncube 1983; Sibanda 1983). At independence in 1980 there were in Zimbabwe approximately 22,000 trained and 15,000 untrained primary teachers. The existing seven primary teacher colleges had a combined annual intake of 1,500 trainees on a full time three-year course. The new national government declared education for all a right and began a rapid primary school building programme. It became clear to the authorities that the problem of teacher shortage and of untrained teachers could not be solved through the conventional training courses and that new approaches were essential.

The ZINTEC strategy was devised to overcome existing teacher shortages, especially in rural areas, and to provide more trained teachers to keep abreast with school expansion (Gatawa 1985). ZINTEC is a four-year training which combines face-to-face contact and distance teaching. The curriculum is similar to the conventional training course. Phase One is a four-month, college-based, residential programme, intended to give trainees a basic training in classroom skills. Trainees are assessed at the end of this initial phase. Phase Two is school-based. Trainees are placed in schools in rural areas with full teaching responsibilities. During the ten terms of this phase, trainees receive four correspondence modules per term and write two assignments. After every two terms they attend two-week vacation courses. In addition, they attend Saturday seminars every two weeks. At school level, there are school tutorials and lesson supervisions by field staff, education officers and principals. There are also weekly radio broadcasts intended to complement the correspondence materials. In the last two terms of Phase Two, trainees are examined in Teaching Practice. Phase Three comprises a consolidation of the programme in a college-based, residential course and a final written examination which leads to certification by the University of Zimbabwe.

ZINTEC can accommodate three intakes of trainees at four-monthly intervals. The total intake per year is 2,430. Trainees receive a salary which rises, by the end of the course, to the starting salary of a qualified non-graduate teacher. The conditions of service during training are the same as for qualified teachers except for retirement benefit. Teachers are bonded for three years after qualifying. The dropout rate is insignificant and it is claimed that the programme is sufficiently attractive to draw trainees away from the conventional three-year course (Gatawa 1985:8).

ZINTEC is organised in the Ministry of Education and headed by a Director. He manages the ZINTEC National Centre which produces distance correspondence materials and coordinates the activities of the four ZINTEC colleges. The National Centre has two units and 15 professional staff. The Professional Unit is responsible for course development and course editing, course implementation, through the college staff, and evaluation. The Administrative Unit provides the support services including secretarial, accounting, printing and despatch. In addition, ZINTEC calls upon the National Radio Service and the Department of Audio-Visual Services.

There are approximately 335 college staff. College-based lecturers are recruited on a staff-trainee ratio of 20, whilst for field staff the ratio is 50. The staff are recruited from among secondary school teachers who join the programme on promotion. There are also some experienced primary trained teachers in Art and Craft, Physical Education and Music. (The 1982 evaluation of ZINTEC exposed a need for staff development for teacher trainers, most of whom had school experience but little training experience.) There is mobility between staff of ZINTEC colleges and conventional colleges. 'This has facilitated cross-fertilisation of ideas and encouraged the development of a community of interest among all teacher educators in the country' (Gatawa 1985:9).

By 1985, 8,000 teachers have graduated from the programme and been posted in rural areas. The conventional three-year programme has now been abolished and a secondary teacher training programme which builds on the experience of ZINTEC has been initiated (Chivore 1985).

Cascade Training

In essence cascade training means that training 'messages' 'flow down' from experts and specialists, through several layers of personnel and eventually to the teachers. A small group of specialists are brought together to train larger numbers of middle level personnel such as college lecturers or school inspectors. They, in turn, train larger numbers of principals and other selected teachers who, in turn, train all the teachers at local level.

The strategy is widely used, particularly in Asia. It has the advantage that it can reach large numbers of teachers fairly quickly, without the costs associated with teachers being brought to training centres far from their homes and schools. It is essentially a 'top down' approach and lends itself best to training in which the message is relatively simple or informational and for which a formal, didactic style is appropriate. For instance, it may work well for a once-off campaign directed at teachers to 'Save Water' or to alert them to a major change in educational policy.

In Malaysia the strategy has been used to improve teaching methods and curriculum implementation. Key personnel selected from inspectors, teacher trainers and senior teachers are prepared with the cooperation of the Curriculum Development Centre. The key personnel then train teachers at both state and district level. An important feature is the provision for follow-up training at school level to enable teachers to find support in solving implementation problems. One lesson learned from the Malaysian experience is that training for curriculum implementation cannot be rushed and that carefully prepared and tested materials are essential to the process (Mukerjhee and Singh 1982).

The Indian State of Andhra Pradesh is currently experimenting with a cascade approach to improving the quality of teaching in primary schools. If it is successful other states may take up the programme. In this case the top level resource group is composed of Education Officers who manage and supervise the schools and teacher trainers from the colleges. A selected number of these are trained overseas in supervision, teaching methods, curriculum and materials design. They then return home and organise workshops for other personnel, successively at state, district and block, or school, level. The crucial question in this case is whether the overseas trained people can successfully adapt what they learned to their own environment in such a way that those who have not had such exposure can benefit from the training.

A recent survey of cascade operations in Asia indicated that the main weakness is the dilution effect, as the training is passed down the various levels of personnel (APEID 1984b:6). This is why it may be suited to relatively simple messages involving no radical innovations in ideas or working practice. Otherwise there is a danger that innovations imperfectly adopted at one level may be contorted or ignored at the next lower level, and so on down the system.

One way in which this danger may be reduced is if the top level group of trainers is given a long term responsibility for follow-up training to reinforce the initial effort. If the top group disperses after the initial effort it is more difficult to build in such reinforcement. One way of institutionalising such follow-up is to base the training on an established institution. As described in Chapter Five, Bangladesh set up its National Academy for Primary Education, to spearhead the development of the Universal Primary Education policy. In 1981 its staff participated in overseas training in preparation for their work in developing training programmes for the teacher trainers at the country's 47 Primary Training Institutes (Dove 1983b). By 1983 the first groups of PTI staff had received a three-week orientation to their new responsibilities under the UPE programme. The major

231

problem for the Academy now is that, as a new institution with many responsibilities, it faces a challenge in establishing itself at the same time as setting up entirely new training schemes. Secondly, many of its staff themselves, though highly qualified, lack experience in primary teaching and require sustained support in implementing innovations inspired by their overseas training.

Mobile Teacher Trainers

The aim in Bangladesh is that the Academy should also eventually undertake the training of a new category of mobile teacher trainers, the Assistant Upazilla Education Officers. Currently these are trained by an ad hoc group of key personnel drawn from a number of institutions including the Academy. The mobile teacher trainers each supervise approximately 20 schools (Dove 1985). They have a monthly schedule of visits at each school during which they bring the teachers together to work on training topics set out for them in specially prepared Teachers Leaflets captioned, 'What shall we do? How shall we do it?' Topics range from methods of encouraging school enrollment and attendance to active learning methods for environmental studies (APEID 1984b:55-70). The leaflets support the mobile teacher trainers in encouraging participatory modes of learning in their small teacher groups and are left with the teachers for follow-up under the leadership of the school principal. The strength of the strategy is that regular, recurrent in-service training is available for all the 156,000 primary teachers in their own environment and at low cost.

The mobile teacher training strategy has been used in many different countries and contexts with mixed results. In Botswana, for instance, mobile teacher trainers from the colleges were brought into an in-service support team in 1974 (Molomo 1983). The team worked through Local Curriculum Committees to plan and implement in-service activities such as testing children's stages of development and introducing new teaching methods. A positive element of this approach was that the trainers were able to integrate pre-service and in-service teacher training.

The Primary Education Improvement Project in Northern Nigeria started in 1970 utilised curriculum development specialists to develop materials and support teachers in their schools. (Hawes 1979:57-58 and 127-128). Some of the materials proved excellent and were enthusiastically taken up by teachers but the project did not achieve its ambitious goals of transforming teaching in primary schools. For this, much more intensive effort over a longer time was needed and more trainers with a greater capacity to move easily from centre to centre were a necessity. But this would have been very costly.

The major arguments in favour of some variant on the mobile teacher trainer strategy are two. It is relatively low cost because a few trainers move from place to place instead of large numbers of teachers moving to distant training centres. Training can, therefore, be frequent and regular. It also has potential, if well done, to engage teachers in gearing the training to their own context and problems.

But there are still some unresolved issues evident from the experience of many mobile teacher trainer schemes. One concerns the trainers themselves. Very few countries can create an entirely new cadre of mobile teacher trainers specialising in in-service training. This would be costly and, in any case, people with relevant skills are scarce and would have to be trained. Lesotho is one of the few exceptions, having created a cadre of field staff for its Lesotho In-Service Education for Teachers (LIET) programme, a correspondence-with-contact method of training unqualified primary teachers (Mathot 1983). Significantly, the Lesotho authorities adopted this approach because teacher college personnel proved unsuited and reluctant.

The mobile teacher training strategy can be kept low cost if <u>existing</u> personnel can be utilised. Many countries, Lesotho, Zimbabwe and Tanzania (Mrutu 1979) among them, have looked to college trainers to provide in-service support in schools. But, as Kurrien (1983:202) suggests in the case of India, few pre-service colleges have extension units or seem to give importance to in-service work; trainers lack the interest and competence to do the job properly. 'There are few who know, for example, the organisation and practical problems in introducing ... reading readiness programmes in our primary schools and can demonstrate the appropriate teaching methods to be used.' Another problem, of course, is that college personnel often lack means of travelling easily to outlying schools and, without additional resources (which again add to costs) have difficulty in sharing their time between college and schools.

An alternative approach utilised in Bangladesh, Botswana, Indonesia, Malaysia and Nepal (Hawes 1982;

Wheeler 1980) is to utilise existing inspectors and supervisors. But a major problem with this, as suggested above, is that there is an inherent conflict between their inspectorial and advisory roles. Teachers, understandably, tend to be circumspect in their relations with support personnel who may also have powers to promote or transfer them. Without careful training inspectors find it difficult to adjust their behaviour to advisory roles. In some countries where this problem has been recognised, inspectors have been redesignated as advisers and training in their new tasks has been provided. But until the inherent conflict of duties is resolved, the problem is unlikely to disappear and inspector-trainers will be limited in their effectiveness.

Master Teachers

The master teacher strategy does not suffer so severely from a problem of inherent role conflict and has a number of strengths. Henry (1983), describing a combined cascade and master teacher strategy in Papua New Guinea comments positively on schemes where local teachers, selected for their good classroom teaching, are trained to work with the other teachers in their schools on an in-service programme which they themselves have devised during training. Master teachers are in a pre-eminent position to adapt in-service training to the needs of teachers in their own schools or locality. They may share their time between regular teaching and training. They may form a corps of local in-service training specialists which may be re-activated as required. The strategy also provides an avenue of promotion for good classroom teachers. Thompson (1982:126), commenting on experience in Sri Lanka, Malaysia and Singapore, suggests that intensive training, follow-up and support to master teachers is needed if authoritarian modes of training are to be avoided, and if they are to maintain their expertise and generate commitment to innovation amongst other teachers.

Principals and Staff Development

There is, sadly, a certain amount of rhetoric, unsupported by positive action, about the role of school principals in in-service, school-based training. The idea is not that they themselves should train other teachers but that they should develop school-based in-service training as part of an overall strategy for staff development. These ideas may be sound enough in themselves but they are only workable in an environment where real responsibility and resources are devolved to principals and where they have managerial autonomy. Where this is not the case, no amount of training by principals through in-service strategies can produce substantial results.

In the 1980s the Papua New Guinean authorities have mounted in-service training at national, provincial and school level in an effort to maintain standards at a time of rapid localisation of the teaching force and changing curriculum. Many of the provincial high schools are in remote and inaccessible areas thus making devolution of authority to school principals a practical necessity. Under the direction of the principal a senior teacher in each school is responsible for carrying out an in-service training programme. In one school described to the author by the former principal, general in-service sessions are held fortnightly. The sessions are planned to create a <u>corps d'esprit</u> amongst all teachers, to share <u>problems, ideas</u> and expertise and as a vehicle for change. Over a two-year period many themes were covered, ranging from testing and report cards, motivating students, planning lessons, to use of equipment and the library, medical emergencies, personal filing systems and the inspection systems. Teachers also held debates on general topics such as the qualities of a good teacher and made visits to local primary and community schools.

Teacher Centres and Groups

Local teacher centres have been a part of in-service training provision since the 1960s. They have served a variety of purposes in many countries from Asia to the Caribbean (Thompson 1982:127). Ayot (1983) provides a detailed account of Teachers Advisory Centres in Kenya. He lists a number of broad functions which they are intended to serve including feedback and dissemination for curriculum projects, research into teaching methods, local curriculum development, counselling, receiving centres for materials, contact points with teacher colleges, and, lastly, community service centre.

The purpose for which most teacher centres are set up is as what Ayot (1983:157) calls a resource centre, a centre which helps teachers solve their day to day teaching problems. 'Tutors may help teachers by giving appropriate support materials and advice in new ideas, skills and teaching methods which have proved successful in other schools ... Apart from the use of the library at the centre, teachers may make use of reprographic facilities such as duplicators, photocopiers and typewriters ...'

Some teacher centres have been purpose-built and expensively equipped. But this itself is no condition for success. Indeed, centres which are inaccessibly located or do not fulfil the needs of teachers may be under-utilised. The Calcutta Teacher Centre, set up in 1969, was a sparsely equipped centre which nevertheless attracted considerable participation from local teachers (Blackwell 1977). It began as a single-purpose centre to develop an Environmental Studies Pilot Project. Through the dynamism of its director and the enthusiasm of its committee, mainly teachers, it became a multi-purpose centre. It ran short, full-time in-service courses, part-time evening courses, study conferences for principals, workshops for making teaching aids in Science and Mathematics, informal seminars and social events such as film shows and exhibitions. Its success can be put down to a number of factors. First, it was in a city and easily accessible to large numbers of teachers. Second, it was initiated in response to a need of teachers for materials and around a specific, focussed activity based on the Environmental Studies Pilot Project. Third, the direction and organisation of the Centre depended on active teacher representation on the committee. They were able to assess the needs of local teachers and encourage their participation.

A variation on the Teacher Centre strategy utilises the concept of training through the interaction of teachers in informal groups. The Cianjur district of Indonesia houses the national centre for the training of 'master teachers'. It is also the focus for a project to develop in-service training in 60 model schools (Hawes 1982). Inspectors and principals are trained and a teacher college is designated as a professional centre. At the sub-district level some model schools have resource centres and others have rooms where teachers can meet in Teachers Clubs to work on materials and develop teaching methods. Meetings are held regularly in schools for teachers to report back from their clubs. At a preliminary stage in the development of the project much of its success was due, significantly, to the enthusiasm of school principals.

In the early days, support for teacher centres was generated by their apparent success in some western countries where teachers generally were somewhat more accustomed at that time to the idea of professional self-development. But even in these more favourable climates, not all teachers, by any means, accepted and used available teacher centres for professional improvement. In countries where a culture of autonomous professionalism does not exist or where teachers are restricted by bureaucratic regulations from gathering together informally, teacher centres are probably not an appropriate strategy for in-service training (Dove 1977).

Teacher Associations

Teacher centres are usually more attractive to primary teachers. Teachers with a subject specialism at secondary level normally prefer to search out a subject association if they wish to keep themselves abreast of developments in their field. Of course, subject associations tend to be physically located in urban centres and are not easily accessible to teachers in rural areas. Being, for the most part, voluntary groups, they do not often receive official backing, though their representatives may play an active part in official curriculum development activities.

The types and ranges of teacher participation in subject associations are not in general well documented and the theme deserves further investigation. Subject associations have been responsible, in countries as far apart as Nigeria and Hong Kong, for promoting new Science curricula. But the Ghana National Association of Teachers is, perhaps, typical in that it is a teacher union responsible for representing teachers in their campaigns for improved salaries and conditions of service and for professional development (Asiedu-Akrofi 1983). It has a Professional Development Division responsible for improving the skills and competency of teachers. There are five Units. The Course Unit is responsible for courses for final-year trainees in colleges and also organises promotion courses for serving teachers. The Leadership Seminar Unit organises courses to improve academic and administrative standards and international cooperation. The Book Development Unit makes recommendations on textbook suitability and trials newly developed materials in selected schools. The Coordinating Unit brings together the activities of different subject associations. The Library Unit and Research Centre provides books and visual aids for teachers. The

Ghana teacher association is remarkable for the energy with which it has pursued its twin strategy of supporting teachers in improving their conditions of service and in improving standards of professionalism.

Workshops

The terms 'course' and 'seminar' connote rather formal, didactic approaches to training, whereas 'workshop' implies a concept of training which is active, participatory and likely to produce tangible outputs such as teaching materials or aids. For training which aims to equip teachers with new skills rather than book learning, the workshop approach is obviously more appropriate. It is also adaptable to any of the broad strategies described above.

Sadly, however, much teacher training now poses as workshop activity when it falls far short of the ideal. Changing the name of a course to a workshop is not sufficient. Workshops are very demanding of preparation time and organisational skills. Workshop resource persons and facilitators require a high level of skill in order to motivate and sustain the efforts of teachers to produce good results from training activities. Only too frequently trainers themselves lack these skills and fall back on the traditional lecture and chalk-and-talk approaches. Or the workshop format is reduced to a ritual with papers being delivered and questions or problems being artificially produced for teachers to discuss and 'report back' at the end of the session. Evaluation is similarly ritualistic with, typically, an opinion questionnaire handed out at the end of the programme for 'participants' to check which aspects they found 'interesting', 'valuable' or the opposite. There is rarely much effort to assess the longer term effect of training on improving teachers' performance. And until there is, no sound judgements can be made between one type of training and another, nor on their relative cost-benefits.

Workshop activities predominated in two initiatives under the Sri Lanka Small School Development Project and spearheaded by the Hinguakgoda Teacher College. In 1982 nearly 2,300, or 25 per cent, of all schools in Sri Lanka had 100 pupils or less and one or two teachers only. Many have primary grades only and secondary schools may be some distance away (Perera and Wijedasa 1984; UNESCO-UNICEF 1978). In an effort to improve the quality of these small, mostly rural schools, the Small School

Development Project was launched. The in-service training focussed on enabling teachers to acquire skills in activity methods and multi-grade, mixed ability teaching. Workshops were held at weekends in local schools selected by rotation to encourage participation, local relevance and cooperation with the community. In another series of workshops teachers learned more about the local community (Dove 1982:102-111 and 136-146; Ekanayake 1982). They surveyed local people, held discussions with villagers and representatives of the health and agricultural services. Together they identified joint projects which would benefit school and villagers. With community contributions, teachers organised a plot of agricultural land for school use and a sewing class for out-of-school children. In the workshops the teachers developed curricula and materials which drew on community resources.

CONCLUSION

All of the strategies described above, distance techniques, cascade training, mobile teacher trainers, master teachers, teacher centres and groups, as well as established teacher colleges, are capable of being combined and adapted to serve a variety of purposes and contexts. But whilst such structures and organisational strategies provide the framework for training, ultimately it is what goes on in the process of training itself which determines its quality. This is the theme of the next chapter.

Chapter Eleven

THE CURRICULUM OF TEACHER EDUCATION AND TRAINING

Chapter Ten outlined some of the ways in which Ministries of Education have been adapting the organisational structure of teacher training to meet contemporary needs. Possibly, the main efforts have gone into diversifying provision for the initial training of new recruits and untrained serving teachers. At the same time there has been some action to provide in-service training for the professional development of some categories of teachers. But these remarks are based on impression rather than hard fact because no comprehensive, global surveys exist which detail the type, range and extent of teacher training provision, nor, importantly, the balance of expenditure on initial and recurrent training.

What is certain is that the professional literature on teacher training over the last twenty years has focused on organisation and structure whilst serious study of the curriculum and process of training has been neglected. In one way this is understandable because to find out what actually goes on during the process of training takes a great deal of time and patience. Moreover, official syllabuses may give some guide about the intentions of those who constructed them but only actual observation and analysis of the interaction of trainers with trainees can illuminate whether intentions are translated into practice in one place and another. Whilst organisation obviously affects curriculum, it is, ultimately, the process of training which determines quality and it is to this important and complex theme we turn here.

LESSONS OF RESEARCH

One of the few firm conclusions of the teacher

240

effectiveness studies reviewed in Chapter Nine was that teacher training does improve teacher performance and pupil achievement. More precisely, effective teachers are those with a high level of cognitive ability, higher educational levels and teacher training. The policy implications of this are clear. Selection criteria for direct entry to teaching and to initial training should emphasise good educational qualifications. Selective entry tests should focus on higher level cognitive skills such as analysis, synthesis, problem solving and evaluation. All teachers should have initial teaching, whether pre- or post-experience. All teachers with low educational qualifications should have access to in-service up-grading programmes. The research offers no specific guidelines about the worthwhileness of in-service provision for professional development but there are no sound reasons why it should not be valuable and many why it should.

Unfortunately, of course, even if all Ministries of Education were anxious to take action on these lines, the research does not give guidelines as to which aspects should have priority. In addition, absolute shortages of teachers in some areas and the cost implications of a better qualified teaching force militate against governments going all out to upgrade teachers. Yet if teachers really are the most important ingredient in the schooling process, and there is plenty of evidence that they are, real efforts to improve the quality of teachers would have a multiplier effect through the education system and on human resource development.

General Education

A basic implication of research is that the foundation on which sound teacher training can be laid is a good general education. This should help develop cognitive skills and enable learners to familiarise themselves with the internal structure, norms and content of the various disciplines and subjects of the school curriculum.

There is ample evidence that many school systems fail their clients in these ways. The number of years people spend in formal schooling and the level of examinations they have passed is used in research as a proxy for their educational level. But, in reality, passing higher level examinations is sometimes little guarantee of progress beyond rote learning or of a deep understanding of subject specialisms. For

241

this reason, much of what passes for teacher training, especially for non-graduate teachers, is no more than supplementary general education with some additional elements such as Principles of Education, Child Development and practical experience of teaching.

Improvements in the quality of general education depend largely on the efforts of teachers already in the schools. Improvements in the quality of the teaching force depend largely on teachers' general education. The vicious circle of low quality has to be broken. For this reason alone, if for no other, there is a strong case for countries to devote a larger share of their resources to the initial and in-service educational upgrading of teachers.

TRAINING

Throughout this book no rigid distinction has been made between the education and training of teachers. Here, for the first time, teacher education has been differentiated in terms of an emphasis on cognitive development and specialist understanding of the subject teachers teach. It also makes sense to suggest that teacher education comprises wider perspectives including an understanding of the social, economic and professional aspects of education, psychological and social theories underpinning pedagogical practice and knowledge of teachers' roles and responsibilities.

However, the fact that teacher education and teacher training are terms which can be interchanged with ease for many purposes reflects the lack of a hard distinction between them. In general, teacher education refers to the knowledge aspect and teacher training to the acquisition of pedagogical skills. Both education and training should contribute to the development of professional attitudes and roles. In addition, if teachers are to claim to be professionals rather than semi-professionals, training in specific skills must be supported by a general education which enables them to apply and adapt their knowledge and skills in all the varied conditions of teaching and learning which they meet.

The Training Process
Teacher effectiveness research has, on the whole, concentrated on evaluating whether <u>having been trained</u> makes a difference to teachers' performance

or pupil achievement. Only recently has the deeper question also been asked of <u>how the training process</u> makes a difference. Specifically, <u>how</u> is an effective teacher trained?

Very few general answers have so far emerged. This is partly due to the difficult methodological problems for research on process issues. Also, research findings have meaning in the cultures to which they relate but cannot be universalised easily. For instance, what counts as democratic or authoritarian training in one context may not count the same in another. Likewise, training teachers to set and mark homework in one culture, where parents perceive themselves as partners with the schools in the education of their children, may positively affect pupil achievement; but it may be detrimental in a culture where parents perceive homework as a sign that teachers are neglecting their responsibility to teach in school hours. Even the research which shows that textbooks are important inputs to education allows that their utility depends on a host of factors, including the subject matter, the level of schooling, their content and the way teachers and pupils use them (Heyneman 1983; Schefelbein, Farrell and Sepulveda-Stuardo 1983; Gardner 1982; Kajubi 1982).

As it stands currently, the research can be used to support claims for training teachers according to almost <u>any</u> method or style of teaching, formal or informal, in large groups, small groups or by individual instruction, with or without the use of various audio-visual aids, radio or television (Avalos and Haddad 1979:60-63). The only fairly universal finding is that formal, didactic methods of teaching are adequate for teaching low level cognitive skills such as memorisation, but discovery methods or problem solving techniques are more appropriate to the development of higher level cognitive skills (Guthrie 1982:303). As Avalos and Haddad (1979:73) comment, this finding is 'particularly interesting as surveys of existing practices in many developing countries indicate these methods are hardly used and teaching is largely rote, mechanical and expository'.

Critiques of Teacher Education and Training

Absence of a sound, universal model of teaching on which to base teacher training programmes has not inhibited the many complaints and criticisms of teacher training curricula which have been voiced over many years. In particular, conventional college-based training has been attacked (Hawes 1977; Smart 1977; Ezewu 1981). Much of the same criticism may be applied to graduate training in universities.

What are the most widespread criticisms made of college-based initial training?

Overload. The curriculum is often overloaded and overcrowded. In just a few years, trainees are required to cover many syllabuses leading to final examinations. The curriculum traditionally comprises three broad themes, personal education or upgrading, professional education and training in teaching skills (Porter 1977:117-153). Primary teachers must study all the subjects and teaching methods of the primary school, even if they specialise in one or two. Depending on language policy, studies in two or three languages may be required (Prospects 14:1,1985). Professional studies customarily include aspects of Philosophy, Psychology and Sociology as they relate to Education and Child Development. In addition there are theoretical and practical elements to develop understanding and skills in teaching, assessment and classroom management. Extra- and co-curricular studies for character building or political education may be required. Some weeks or months of teaching practice in schools is a standard ingredient.

One actual example of the overloaded syllabuses still only too commonplace is reproduced below. It is for a one-year primary certificate course for trainees with ten or, sometimes twelve, years of education. It is slightly adapted to disguise its origin and, in any event, has recently been revised. This is an ambitious and heavy programme, challenging trainees to prove their abilities in a wide range of different ways. The reasons for overload are not far to seek. Many curricula have expanded by historical accretion. Some topics persist because they are hallowed by tradition even though their usefulness has passed. Much of the material imported from metropolitan countries has been purged but much remains unexamined. Psychological theories based on research in foreign cultures, for instance, is still retained. Furthermore, new areas of study are often added without anything being taken out. Development imperatives, for instance, require Civic Education, Population Education or Community Service to become part of the official timetable.

244

Certificate in Education: Courses of Study

Subjects	Marks Contents	Method	Total
1 Child Psychology & Child Development			100
2 Principles of Education			100
3 National Language	50	50	100
4 Mathematics	15	35	50
5 History & Geography			100
(a) History	20	30	
(b) Geography	20	30	
6 Agriculture & Science			100
(a) Agriculture	60		
(b) Science	20	20	
7 Hygiene, Nutrition & Population Education			50
(a) Hygiene & Nutrition	35		
(b) Population Education	15		
8 Citizenship & Community Development			50
9 Religion			50
10 Physical Education	25	25	50
11 Arts & Crafts	20	30	50
12 Practice Teaching			200
13 Practical activity in all subjects			200
TOTAL			1,200

The overload is accentuated when the programme is divided into short time allocations for each subject, as for a traditional secondary school. Trainees find themselves studying Mathematics, English, Art and Craft and Child Development in the morning, three or four other subjects in the afternoon and Physical Education, Community Service and written assignments in the evening.

To illustrate the fact that this is not a thing of the past, the draft daily time table for a proposed new pre-service, initial training programme in a country which must remain anonymous is reproduced below.

Much of the overload is created by the necessity to cram further general education and professional training into a short time span at the beginning of a teacher's career. The emphasis on education is necessary when poorly qualified people are recruited. Professional training is cramped because,

245

Time Table

Hours	
0500 – 0600	Waking up and getting ready
0600 – 0630	Physical fitness exercises
0630 – 0700	–
0700 – 0730	Breakfast
0730 – 0745	–
0745 – 0800	Morning assembly
0800 – 0900	1st period
0900 – 1000	2nd period
1000 – 1030	Interval
1030 – 1130	3rd period
1130 – 1230	4th period
1230 – 1330	Lunch interval
1330 – 1430	5th period
1430 – 1530	6th period
1530 – 1630	7th period
1630 – 1700	Interval
1700 – 1800	Unscheduled Activities
1800 – 1900	Interval
1900 – 1945	Dinner
1945 – 2000	–
2000 – 2230	Self study
2230	Bed time

for all the rhetoric about recurrent training, the majority of teachers will probably never again have in-service opportunities.

Inappropriate Pedagogical Model. Courses which are atomised by the time table tend to encourage lecture methods and academicism. They do not provide an appropriate model of pedagogy, particularly when the school curriculum has been made more practical, suited to discovery methods and subjects have been integrated. Subject-based examinations likewise encourage atomised learning and hinder the development of an integrated training experience. Lack of a working partnership between training institutions and schools exacerbates gaps between theoretical studies and experience of practical teaching.

A rationale sometimes used to justify full-time residential training is its potential for nurturing positive attitudes in a 'hot house' atmosphere. This may be so. But the fact is that daily life in many training institutions, especially residential, non-graduate ones, is stultifying and strictly regulated

246

with regard to conduct, dress and use of personal time, even for mature adults. This must be detrimental to personal growth and professionalism which places emphasis on autonomy, self-regulation and the exercise of informed judgement and choice.

Irrelevance. Teacher training is a sub-system of the school system. Thus, changes in schools tend to precede those in teacher training. It is not unusual for teacher colleges, especially those in remote areas, to remain unaware of changes in school curricula and textbooks (Turner 1984). Curricula are often developed centrally. They tend to be geared to conditions in city schools and to leave little scope for adaptation to the culture and actual conditions with which teachers have to cope in outlying areas. Different categories of trainees, with different levels of education and experience, may have to follow a uniform course not wholly suited to their needs (Eheazu 1982).

Training institutions are often relatively well-equipped. Demonstration or experimental model schools attached to colleges or universities are also usually well-endowed and serve a privileged group of pupils (often the children of lecturers and teachers). It is rare for trainees to practise their teaching skills in the much poorer conditions of remote rural schools to which they may eventually be assigned. Nor is there much evidence of close coordination between teacher training and the authorities responsible for teacher deployment (Dove 1982a).

The above critique summarises some of the concerns voiced for many years about the quality of teacher training programmes. This has been a general account without specific examples, and for two reasons. First, it is impossible to document good and bad programmes in the absence of comprehensive evaluations of training processes and their outcomes. Second, what appear on paper to be inadequate programmes may be vitalised by energetic and creative management. Conversely, well-conceived curricula can be negated by out-dated and unimaginative management.

In recent years many countries have undertaken serious examination and reform of initial teacher training curricula. Many of the reforms have been implemented in the best training institutions. But much remains to be done in places outside the mainstream of innovation. In particular more resources must be devoted to the training of trainers, a theme to which we return in the Conclusion.

THEORY AND PRACTICE

One criticism mentioned above was the lack of integration and balance between theory and practice in teacher training. To analyse what this really implies the author searched through many teacher training curriculum outlines, syllabuses and training materials from many different countries, from the Solomon Islands to Tanzania and Zambia to Malaysia. There were a number of statements of intention such as the following from a draft document from the Teacher Training Unit of the Ministry of Education in Sri Lanka, Developing Curricula for Colleges of Education (1984:5),

> Foundation Courses in Education
> This area including courses such as psychological, philosophical and sociological foundations of education, educational evaluation and guidance, school and the community etc., is to provide the professional core which teachers need as functioning members of a profession. Traditionally this is an area dominated by theory courses. But in the new curriculum, a concerted effort should be made to relate theory to practice.

Unfortunately, what is universally lacking is a statement of what is meant by 'theory' and how theory and practice should be related. This is an issue which, in the author's view, must be clarified if teacher training is to be based on sound foundations.

What is Theory?
A unique survey of primary teacher training in 20 Latin American countries between 1956 and 1971 estimated that 36 per cent of time went on Theory of Education, 42 per cent on General Education and 35 per cent on Teaching Techniques (Oliveros 1981). However, half the time allotted to Teaching Techniques was devoted to theoretical background and only half for practice teaching and 'other forms of practical training'. These details exemplify the ambiguities which surround the notion of theoretical studies. On the one hand, they are often equated with

disciplines such as Philosophy, Psychology and Sociology from which educational studies are traditionally derived. On the other hand, theory is distinguished from practical activity. However, arguments for the integration of theory and practice claim that theory should be the basis for guiding practice and that practice should support the development of theory (Taylor 1978:117-127; Scheffler 1973).

One type of so-called theory used in teacher training is normative (Moore 1974). Theory in this sense is no more than precepts and exhortation intended to inculcate desirable values and habits in teachers. Many of these values derive from courses on the pre-digested 'Thoughts of Great Educators'. Even today, trainees spend much time memorising the axioms of Plato and Aristotle, Rousseau and Dewey, however inappropriate to their own civilisation and culture. Sometimes curricula are updated to include axioms from the philosophies of great national leaders, such as Gandhi or Nyerere.

Only too frequently the Principles of Education and Philosophy of Education are taught in a similar way, approximating to indoctrination. The only saving feature is that they are often confusing and meaningless to trainees. But this also renders them less than efficient as vehicles for inculcating professional values. It is, moreover, contradictory to the spirit of genuine philosophical enquiry which should expose to trainees the assumptions behind differing sets of values, encourage them to clarify their own thinking and formulate personal philosophies of education (Burns 1982).

Psychology of Education, Child Development and, to a lesser extent, Sociology of Education, are generally justified as major elements in teacher training because they are disciplines which make claim to derive theory from empirical data. Anthropology, cybernetics and communication theories might also justifiably be part of teacher training for similar reasons. The problem is that such 'sciences' have come up with a variety of more or less empirically tested theories about how children learn, how society works and so on. But they have produced few conclusive findings about how to teach. Sometimes trainees are introduced to theories with conflicting implications for teaching. It is very difficult, for instance, for anyone who is not a specialist psychologist to judge between the very different implications for teaching of, for instance, Skinnerian and Piagetian learning theories.

Teacher training curricula are often justifiably criticised as being rag-bags of ill-assorted and unintegrated precepts and theories. Teacher trainers themselves are often specialists in only one area and conduct their teaching in isolation from one another. It is understandable that teachers frequently complain of the irrelevance of theory to practical teaching and fail to follow the curriculum as a coherent and integrated package.

Some of those who deplore this state of affairs press for a continued search for a single, unifying theory of teaching from which a model of training may be derived. The motivation behind this is similar to that of all scientifically-minded people who aspire to discover universal laws of nature. In the opinion of the author, while the pursuit of a natural science of teaching is a worthwhile aim and a universal theory of teaching is in principle a possibility, we are as yet a long way from achieving this goal. Practically-speaking, it will be very difficult to develop an empirically tested theory with guidelines precise enough for teachers to use in every teaching-learning situation. This is because every teaching situation has unique features, bringing together a particular teacher with a particular learner or learners in a particular, unrepeatable set of circumstances.

An alternative approach approximates to 'if it works, use it'. This is a strategy of training which tends to be atheoretical at the same time as empirical. A good example is micro-teaching. This is a training technique often used as a preparation for or supplement to practice teaching in real classrooms (Brown 1975; Perrott 1976). Trainees identify specific skills which they intend to acquire. These may range over a wide variety of areas such as questioning techniques, introducing a lesson, providing feedback or the use of flash-cards. They observe the skills being used, practice them themselves, evaluate their performance and continue to refine their expertise. This may be accomplished with or without a supervisor; and with 'real' schoolchildren, or exclusively amongst trainees who role-play being pupils. Video play-back is a useful but not essential aid for providing feedback.

Micro-teaching is empirical in the sense that there has been much research investigating the conditions under which it works as an effective skills-training technique. It is atheoretical in the sense that no one claims that the technique derives from any one theory of learning or teaching, though it certainly supports, in a commonsensical way, many insights of Psychology, Sociology and communications theory. However, even the most ardent advocate of micro-teaching would agree that it does not provide a theoretical basis for the selection of what skills teachers should acquire. This still remains a matter for the professional judgement of teacher trainers and teachers themselves.

Of course, it may be argued that no human behaviour is atheoretical in the sense that there are always ideas or assumptions, whether explicit or implicit, behind every intentional action. This proposition may be illustrated by the case of Performance-based Teacher Education described briefly in Chapter Nine. This is a training technique which breaks down the process of teaching into discrete, trainable skills. Critics of the approach suggest that there is an implicitly assumed 'theory' of teaching in any choice of particular skills to be emphasised in training and that the theory should be made explicit in order to be scrutinisable (Winter 1982; Taylor 1978:150-4; Alan 1980). They also claim that there is more to successful teaching than the sum of its discrete, observable parts and that skills training alone does not constitute the whole of teacher training.

Teaching Practice and Teaching Theory

The argument here is that the most useful theories are those which trainees formulate for themselves on the basis of practices which they find morally acceptable and conducive to pupil learning. For trainees to evolve personal theories of teaching they need opportunities to practise and test out a repertoire of different teaching skills and styles. Micro-teaching provides a relatively non-threatening way of doing this. Practice teaching in schools should be the opportunity for trainees to develop competence, confidence and habits of self-evaluation.

Unfortunately, though teaching practice is a common feature of teacher training, it is frequently poorly conceived, inadequately organised and under-resourced. It usually comprises, on paper at least, between one quarter and one half of the total training time. It may be arranged for single days over many weeks, with trainees attending college on other days. Or it may be for longer blocks of times during which trainees have little contact with their

251

training institutions. Ideally, it should be an opportunity when trainers and experienced school teachers partner each other in supporting and supervising trainees. There is plenty of evidence that trainees benefit greatly from regular and sustained contact with a skilled supervisor who can encourage them to experiment with various approaches to teaching, provide constructive feedback and reflective interaction (Stones 1984; Cogan 1973). The development of sound systems of school supervision for teacher trainees and for new teachers during their first years of teaching would be one of the most beneficial improvements in teacher training. With the development of 'sandwich' programmes of study-and-work, such as the ZINTEC concept described in Chapter Ten, the potential for intensive school-based supervision is increased.

In fact, teaching practice is often a neglected opportunity. Physical communication between colleges, universities and schools is often difficult and may only be improved through increased resources for transport and housing. But ways of improving the cooperation of principals and teachers in supporting trainees on teaching practice do not require massive resources. Only too often at present, teachers perceive trainees either as unwelcome burdens or as substitute teachers to take over part of their regular teaching load. Similarly, it should not be difficult to reduce misunderstanding between teacher trainers and school teachers. Their relationships are frequently uncomfortable, based as they are on prejudice and myth about their relative competency and status. These misunderstandings come to a head when trainers and teachers fail to agree in their assessments of trainees. There is a great deal of scope for the development of shared, rationally-grounded and operational teaching practice assessment criteria to replace judgements made on impression, prejudice and intuition.

To sum up. Teaching practice, properly carried out, should provide the context for trainee teachers to begin to integrate theory and practice. It should not be merely an apprenticeship whereby they model themselves on experienced teachers without a basis for evaluating sound and unsound practice (Zeichner 1983). Nor should it be a test of endurance, an experience of practical teaching for which theories offered by training institutions prove irrelevant, untestable and useless. Training institutions must develop outreach facilities or extension wings if they are to provide better supervision of trainee teachers in schools.

PLANNING TEACHER TRAINING CURRICULA

It is only too easy to point out weaknesses in contemporary teacher training. Perhaps it is more constructive to set out precise guidelines for planning new curricula. On what basis should the various elements in the curriculum be selected?

Goals and Aims

One source of guidance in planning the training programme are official statements of goals and aims for teacher training from international and national bodies of professional status. The UNESCO International Conference of Education (1975:24) provides one challenging example.

Considered from the point of view of general principles and aims, the programmes of initial teacher education should:
(a) Relate closely to roles and functions expected of the teacher today and prepare the future teacher not only for his instructional role but also for the variety of roles and functions demanded of him by the society and the development of education. Teachers are now more and more involved in various extra-curricular and out-of-school activities and should be prepared so that they will be able to combine teaching and up-bringing into the single process of developing personality.
(b) Prepare future teachers to use effectively and for the benefit of learners all the facilities and resources offered by the social and cultural environment.
(c) Give an opportunity for student teachers to experience these new roles and functions during the training period, by giving them responsibilities in the administration of teacher education institutions, by establishing closer links with various educational institutions and providing practical training so as to develop the students' initiative, responsiveness, resourcefulness and adapt-ability to change, and so enable them in the future to assume such new roles and functions as may appear.
(d) Provide for and ensure the student

253

teachers' personal and professional self-development, so that they will be prepared to continue their education and development in the future either by self-education or by seeking to attend courses of in-service training and also prepare them to develop the same aptitudes in their pupils.

(e) Include adequate provision for general and professional, theoretical and practical preparation. The studies of specialization should be up to date and interdisciplinary in character and cover not only the facts but also the fundamental concepts, principles, structures of subjects so that students acquire an interdisciplinary framework within which they can continue to gain new knowledge independently during their professional life, taking account of the latest developments in the field of their specialization.

(f) Include ample provision for professional development, both theoretical and practical, including introduction to problems of educational research and its application, to elements of experimental technique in education in order to facilitate teacher participation in educational research and strengthen the links between training and research.

(g) Prepare the teacher for the effective use of educational technology, including the media of mass communication.

Trainee Characteristics

An obvious basis for selection is the nature of the clientele. The age, experience, language, culture and educational level of trainees are all important. Such considerations are all the more important when they do not form a homogeneous group. Surprisingly little attention is paid to the different needs of experienced and inexperienced teachers and to styles of training appropriate to adult learners.

Teachers' Roles

Training must relate to the roles which teachers are expected to play. Such role-expectations arise from official policy statements, public pressure and professional opinion. In Chapters Three and Four some of the contemporary roles of teachers were examined in detail. It was argued that their roles in curriculum development, assessment and education-related community involvement are essential to their full development as professionals. Put in another way, the central task of enabling pupils to learn cannot be undertaken fully unless teachers are trained to interpret the curriculum with versatility, to evaluate pupils' progress and learning difficulties and to stimulate community participation in educational efforts.

It is the responsibility of curriculum planners to decide which of all the wide-ranging and challenging roles expected of teachers must take priority in training and what sort of training is appropriate. When adequate provision is available for initial and recurrent training, teacher training can be planned as a developmental process with different elements prioritised and sequenced in a rational way. When initial training is all there is likely to be, care must be taken not to crowd the programme. Basic teaching skills and confidence must be a priority. So must habits and skills in the development of self-evaluation and self-development (Kremer and Ben-Peretz 1984).

Felt Needs
Another important source of guidance in planning the curriculum of teacher training is the opinion of trainees and new teachers themselves. In some respects, who better to judge where the strengths and weaknesses of their training lies or where it could have contributed more? Unfortunately, evaluation by trainees is often neglected or poorly done. True, opinion questionnaires are often used at the end of courses. But their value is doubtful and more penetrating evaluation techniques are rarely carried out systematically for feedback and curriculum revision.

Recently, the Faculty of Education at the University of Malaya carried out a survey of graduates of the Diploma in Education programme on the effectiveness of the course (Boon, Ahmad and Ahmad 1983). The report concludes that more time should be devoted to 'actual classroom practice', more tutorials and discussion groups. More materials and aids should be provided in Bahasa Malaysia and supervisors should liaise more closely with schools and support new teachers in their first year of teaching. The survey thus gives useful feedback for improvements to initial training and 'valuable information to the authorities that plan and organise in-service courses'.

The authors of the Malaysian report recommend an investigation of the competencies of new teachers but acknowledge that this is a time-consuming task requiring direct observation in classrooms. An imaginative approach to identifying teachers' training needs is to have the teachers keep diaries of their everyday teaching experience. One study on these lines, albeit carried out in an industralised European country, yielded some illuminating insights for planners of teacher training curricula (Vonk 1983). The study identified a 'threshold' period in the first year or so of teaching, which most teachers seem to experience. This is characterised by their 'first confrontation with the school and the class'. During training they had developed idealistic conceptions of their roles as teachers with emphasis on the individuality and self-determination of children. In the threshold period they feel lonely, inadequate and unsupported. They begin to undergo 'role re-socialisation', accepting the school reality as teacher dominated and controlled. They experience problems in relationships with fellow teachers, school management and parents, as well as in the classroom.

The study covered a wide range of problems. Here, for brevity, we describe classroom problems only. These relate to the content of learning materials, the organisation of teaching and learning, pupil control, motivation and particip-ation, teachers' feelings about their own performance, school organisation and relations with individual pupils.

Under each of these headings specific issues were explored. Let us take just one area, the problems of the content of learning materials. New teachers reported that they lack skill in presenting subject matter. If pupils fail to understand, teachers find they repeat themselves because they lack a repertoire of strategies. They also lack familiarity with the content of textbooks and cannot judge the relative importance of different areas of the curriculum. They have difficulty judging the level at which they should pitch their teaching. They cannot discern the cognitive skills of pupils nor their existing knowledge of subject matter. Thus, they ask questions which are too simple and set homework tasks which are too difficult.

This brief summary of some of the findings of just one small survey of the problems of new teachers as they perceive them gives an idea of how specific and precise feedback from evaluation studies can be.

Much more work of this type is needed to evaluate the strengths and weaknesses of training and to provide an empirical basis for determining the curriculum of training programmes.

Research

Last but not least, teacher training must continue to search for validity from the findings of empirical research into teaching and learning. Research institutes and universities must take research into education seriously, if only for self interest, for it is from the schools that their future resources must be sought. Certainly, psychologists and sociologists have a part to play in researching education (Desforges and McNamara 1979). But educationists, including teacher trainers and classroom teachers, also need to become more involved from their own perspectives. Without considerable reorganisation of the working arrangements of teachers and much more professional support, it is unrealistic to suppose that every teacher can become a classroom researcher. Nevertheless, appropriate education and training can encourage in teachers a spirit of critical enquiry, habits of reflection and skills in problem-solving and evaluation.

It is a sad fact that much research into learning and teaching originates still in industrialised countries. It is then published in prestigious journals which set international fashions. Indigenous, culturally appropriate research in developing countries needs to be strengthened. Locally produced journals need courageous editors willing to accept material which may challenge accepted findings from industrialised countries (Mazrui 1978; Altbach 1978; Shaeffer and Nkinyangi 1983).

DESIGNING THE CURRICULUM OF TEACHER TRAINING

The principles for selection of the objectives and content of a teacher training curriculum are, then, policy goals and aims, the characteristics and needs of trainees, the roles expected of teachers, and the findings of evaluation and research. What follows is a checklist of questions which should be asked by those designing teacher training programmes.

Scope
- What knowledge and skills (personal, technical and professional) should trainees be able to demonstrate by the end of the programme?
- Which of these accomplishments will enable them to cope as teachers in their first year of work?
- Which will provide a basis for future, largely self-directed, professional development?

Substance
- Which subject matter will best contribute to development of the specified knowledge and skills?
- Which educational and training techniques will best enable trainees to apply their knowledge and skills in appropriate and versatile ways?
- Which methods of assessment will best reinforce and guide learning?
- Which institutional and organisational arrangements, formal and informal, will best provide an environment conducive to personal and professional growth?

Balance
- What weighting is to be allowed to the various elements of the programme?
- What is to be the balance between personal study, trainer contact time, practical activity and supervised teaching practice in and out of school?

Sequence
- How may the various elements be sequenced to provide the best path for development of trainee knowledge and skills?

Linkages
- How may the subject matter and learning experiences be organised so as to make explicit for trainees the links between the various theoretical elements and between theory and practice?
- How may assessment be arranged so as to enable trainees to demonstrate a holistic understanding and the application of appropriate practical skills?

Subject Matter

For pre-service initial training, the subject matter is generally subsumed under personal and professional education and pedagogical training. The following provides a framework for more detailed content.

Personal
- Mastery of the content of the school curriculum to a level more advanced than the level trainees will teach
- Mastery of independent study skills
- Development of skills in enquiry, experimentation, decision-making, problem solving and inter-personal communication.

Professional
Understanding of:
- the role of education in national development
- the organisation and functioning of the education system
- the various roles of the teacher in society
- development of professional values and relationships

Pedagogical
Understanding of:
- child development and the role of language and culture
- selected learning theories and their implications for teaching

Development of competence to:
- select, try out, adapt and apply appropriate teaching methods
- diagnose learning difficulties and apply remedial techniques
- identify the learning needs of individual, gifted and slow learning pupils, as well as average pupils, and apply appropriate materials and techniques
- manage and adapt available teaching-learning time, space and resources in the classroom and the environment
- co-opt the enthusiasm and resources of parents and community to the benefit of pupils.

Syllabuses

Ideally, teacher trainers should be able to design programmes of training adapted to the local context and the needs of trainees. This may be done even when, as is generally the case, the broad guidelines are centrally produced. Unfortunately, the rationales and assumptions behind curriculum plans often remain hidden in the notes of members of the responsible Ministry committees and working parties. Only outline syllabuses are distributed to training institutions. The danger is that teacher trainers will not fully understand the intentions behind the syllabuses and will follow them in a formal and unimaginative way.

Traditionally, curricular prescriptions are translated into syllabuses for discrete courses on school subjects and methods, psychology, and so on. This approach encourages atomised learning and is reinforced by assessment methods which utilise a terminal examination. A multi-disciplinary approach has much more scope for encouraging integrated learning where trainees can perceive the links between theory and practice and the relevance of the training process of their work as teachers. Integration may be encouraged by the development of units of study and practical activity on topics, themes and issues relevant to teaching. The units may be designed to have lateral or sequential coherence. Assessment can be arranged at the completion of each unit and credits built up over time. Importantly too, units lend themselves to the development of specially prepared training materials for group or individual study and practical exercises (APEID 1978). Academic textbooks, often in a foreign language and relevant to a foreign culture, can be relegated to a library.

An example of a syllabus for a multi-disciplinary unit of study is given below. It is intended for the early stages of a non-graduate, initial teacher training programme.

UNIT 1 The Child, the Home and the Teacher
40 Credits

Objectives
To enable trainees to:

i)   identify out-of-school cultural, linguistic and socio-economic factors which may affect children's rate of physical, mental and emotional development
ii)   explore various theories about how children

develop and the implications for teaching
iii) use various techniques for identifying
children's pre-reading and number skills
iv) appraise various techniques which teachers may
use to gain parental cooperation in encouraging young
children to attend school.

Content
(a) Norms for physical and cognitive development in
our country
(b) Nutrition, health and growth and intellectual
development
(c) Parental economic and educational status and
pupil achievement
(d) Links between experience, language and thought
(e) Testing motor skills and cognitive development
(f) Parent-teacher cooperation

Activities
- Self-instructional mini-course on child development and links between experience, language
and thought
- Practical exercises using diagnostic tests with
pupils from local schools
- A community survey and group report
- Simulation and role play (with video playback if
possible) of a meeting with parents to plan
cooperative activities

Study Time
Trainer-trainees contact time (group)   10 hours
Self instructional and written assignments 10 hours
Practical activities and exercises   20 hours

                Total   40 hours

Assessment
- A multiple choice test on all aspects
of the unit   50%
- A report on the home background of one
child and an assessment of motor skills
and cognitive levels   50%

The outline syllabus of an exemplary unit does
not, of course, adequately convey the spirit and
climate of the training environment. It is the
responsibility of the trainers themselves to nurture
a positive environment. But detailed units like the
one described above do encourage trainers to use
methods other than lectures and do encourage
independent learning in trainees.

261

They also involve different working arrangements in training institutions. Specialists have to work in a team to plan and carry through integrated units, teaching activities and assessment. The timetable has to be adapted to cater to practical activities. Special training materials have to be prepared, and in languages with which trainees are familiar (Treffgarne 1981:202).

CONCLUSION

The curriculum and process of teacher education and training are not easy to examine and appraise. Official syllabuses tell us little about the quality of the actual training and few serious evaluative studies in developing countries, based on observation and analysis of what goes on in the training process, have been published. The literature, such as exists, concentrates on organisational and structural matters. However, it is what actually goes on which is crucial to the success or failure of a training programme. For this reason the chapter has pin-pointed a number of issues and problems which should be of general concern to those who plan, manage and administer teacher education and training.

It was noted that efforts must continue to fill in the gaps in our understanding of what constitutes effective teacher training. Weaknesses frequently identified in contemporary training, such as overload and irrelevance, were examined, with particular reference to initial, institution-based training. A critical problem is the nature of educational theory and how teachers may relate it to practice. There was a strong recommendation that more efforts should go into school teaching practice and supervision. Finally, some technical guidelines for planners, designers and implementers of teacher training programmes were put forward with a recommendation that teacher trainers themselves should be very much involved in planning and designing the curriculum.

Research evidence suggests that teacher training in developing countries has tremendous potential for improving the contribution of teachers to educational quality. But it is not enough for additional resources to be put into the building of new teacher colleges or the acquisition of audio-visual equipment. Resources must also be invested in developing the curriculum of teacher training. In the same way as energies in the 1960s and 1970s were concentrated on setting up mechanisms and preparing personnel to reform school curricula, so these efforts must be consolidated in the coming years by improvements in teacher training.

Conclusion

PROPOSALS FOR POLICY AND ACTION

In this final chapter we draw together some of the issues which have been raised in this book for policy on teachers and teacher training. The issues are addressed not merely to policy makers in Ministries of Education but to all those concerned with planning and implementing developmental policy for primary and secondary schools. They are formulated as policy proposals rather than as specific prescriptions because, as has been repeatedly emphasised, the unique context in every country conditions precisely what policy is appropriate.

Five areas are identified as of crucial importance for developmental policy making. These are financial, career structures, administrative support for teachers, professional support and teacher education and training. It cannot be said strongly enough that unless policy makers are willing to confront these issues, the future qualitative development of education systems, from primary right through to tertiary levels, will be limited by the critical constraints of teacher-related factors. All the policy proposals here are framed toward the goal of improving the competence and professionalism of primary and secondary teachers. Very few of the issues or recommendations are new. Indeed, sadly, the files of ministries, teacher associations and the documents of international agencies and foundations concerned with education, are filled with similar words.

The main justification for reiteration is that progress, while existent, is too slow in such a vital area. Much more political will and commitment is necessary to effect substantial results. The second justification is that the time is propitious for serious study of policy, and for action. There are a number of reasons why this is so.

Firstly, there is global concern with the efficiency of education systems in a period of protracted economic depression. Efficiency implies cost containment. It involves making the best use of the resources we have and utilising only those resources which we really need. This means taking a long, hard look at current provision and future needs. It means questioning taken-for-granted assumptions about the appropriate ways of doing things. It means searching out unconventional approaches. The drive for greater efficiency in education has already encouraged governments to confront controversial issues. One major initiative is the improvement of educational management and the development of monitoring and information systems. Another is the issue of teacher utilisation. For example, a number of countries are looking carefully at the possibilities of maximising the time teachers actually spend on instruction or training them to teach at more than one level or in more than one specialisation. Similar examination is needed of the potential for using administrators and paraprofessionals more efficiently.

Secondly, efforts to reform school curricula have brought together people from specialist areas. Curriculum developers, researchers, those involved in examination reform and teacher education and training recognise that improved professional status has to be won from a critical public by improved educational provision and standards. The educational community is thus in a position to work with policy makers, to agree on measures to improve efficiency in return for better working conditions and opportunities for professional development.

The third reason why the time is right for serious policy initiatives is that international and bi-lateral agencies are more easily persuaded nowadays that country programmes and projects which include policy oriented educational research and evaluation are worthwhile sponsoring. Donor agencies are willing to support training alongside investment in infrastructure. Recurrent budget support for textbooks, educational materials and the establishment of needed categories of specialist personnel is more readily available.

TEACHER FINANCING

The reason frequently given for withholding finance to education in preference for other sectors is that

265

returns on educational investment are difficult to attribute and have proved disappointing. The fact that returns on educational investment are not easy to measure is not a valid reason for starving schools of resources. Indeed, it can plausibly be argued that it is just because schools have been under-resourced that investment has not paid off. Moreover, there is no proof that under-financing of education is not detrimental to overall development efforts and, conversely, there are plenty of cogent reasons why neglect must cause harm. The real problem is that efforts in educational development are often terminated before they can begin to show results and careful monitoring and evaluation is not undertaken.

Nevertheless, it has to be admitted that the problem of providing sufficient funds to finance the teaching force is one of the most difficult and contentious for countries which have to find the resources out of beleaguered public exchequers. Yet it is a most important truism that we only get what we pay for. Governments have to face the issue squarely. It is a contradiction to bemoan the low calibre of teachers whilst withholding the salaries and conditions of service which would attract highly motivated and high achieving recruits into the schools. At the same time, policies targetted at increasing the efficiency and stabilising the growth of the teaching force are needed. Governments must have the political will to ensure, through teacher unions, that all teachers are accountable to do a fair day's work.

Imaginative approaches to these twin goals of improving quality and efficiency are important. For countries which have the resources, unified pay scales for primary and secondary teachers would go far towards encouraging well qualified teachers to work at the base of the school system where it is a false economy to post the most humbly qualified teachers. In Chapter Five it was suggested that salary scales and bonuses could be carefully scrutinised for ways of improving merit incentives, on more differentiated scales, without greatly increasing the overall salary burden. In the interests of equity, monetary and non-monetary incentives for teachers prepared to serve in remote and disadvantaged schools, could be provided. There is much scope here for a sharing of experience between countries on deployment policy, the provision of special allowances, housing and so on. Similarly, the potential of community supplements to teachers' salaries, subsistence and accommodation is an area of emerging interest with implications for efficiency, effectiveness and equity.

CAREER STRUCTURES

It is anxieties about the cost implications, again, which often make the authorities reluctant to develop better career opportunities for educational personnel and for teachers in particular. Such anxieties are sometimes behind reluctance to expand provision for in-service upgrading and professional development. Primary teachers, as the most numerous group, are the main victims of career blockages. Well qualified and ambitious males are perceived as the group most easily discouraged from entering a profession which lacks fair prospects in the longer term for promotion and upward mobility.

Official attitudes and policies towards female teachers are similarly ambiguous. In some contexts the recruitment of female teachers is encouraged, as a means of increasing female participation in society in general or and as a means of keeping teacher costs down, on the grounds that females are more likely to accept low salaries and poor career prospects, the assumption being that they are not, and should not aspire to be, the main family income earners. On the other hand, increasing feminisation of the teaching force is simultaneously viewed with trepidation since female teachers are thought to show lower career commitment and are more unwilling to serve in posts away from their families.

Such reasoning is an example of double-think in which society creates the conditions to ensure that only those female teachers prepared to tolerate poor career opportunities are attracted to teaching and then places the blame for the situation on females in general. Again, we have to remind ourselves that we only get what we pay for. There is certainly evidence, as we have seen, of discrimination against females for promotion and leadership positions in education. But, equally, there is no evidence that, if females knew that they had equal chances of promotion, more highly qualified and committed candidates would not come forward. Similarly, if the authorities were to cease perceiving female teachers themselves as the cause of dropout and imbalances in deployment and began to recognise that the problems lie also in the structure of society, employment and family life, more constructive policies could be envisaged.

267

There are signs of progress in both these directions. Promotion policies are being reviewed to encourage female aspirants. Conditions of service are being revised to acknowledge the problems which prevailing social arrangements cause for those female teachers who are career oriented. Increasingly, for instance, maternity leave is granted with pay. Housing for teachers and their families, whether or not the teachers are male or female, is sometimes provided. But more could be done. Positive encouragement to females to enter teaching and apply for promotion posts is one measure. Job sharing for female teachers with family responsibilities is another. Accelerated promotion or other benefits could be available for female teachers willing to teach in remote and disadvantaged schools. Only with much more creative measures will it be possible to enable the teaching profession to benefit from the pool of talent available to be tapped from 50 per cent of the population.

In more general terms, policy makers need to pay attention to two important aspects of the development of career opportunities for teachers, the diversification of promotion posts and the criteria for promotion.

We have already noted the lack of promotion opportunities for teachers who wish to remain in regular classroom teaching, especially at primary level where there are few specialists posts of responsibility in the school itself. It is often the case that promotion is only available by entering administration. Yet there are a number of ways in which promotion prospects are being diversified to create incentives for able and ambitious teachers.

For countries where the qualification levels of primary and secondary teachers are fairly similar, it can only be helpful for promotion to be possible across all the levels of schooling. For example, a primary teacher could be promoted to a post of responsibility in a secondary school or vice versa. Similarly, able teachers with specialist experience gained on the job could be eligible for specially created posts in teacher training, university research and training centres and institutes of education. For such posts, relevant experience and achievements could count for promotion, rather than formal qualifications. Such measures would help to give credence to the oft-repeated notion that the lower levels of the education system deserve just as much recognition as tertiary institutions. Similarly, procedures to enable selection of able teachers for permanent or temporary posts as master teachers, advisers, supervisors and teacher centre leaders could be reviewed to ensure that such opportunities for gaining experience and credits towards promotion are equally accessible to all teachers, however near or far from the ministry they are posted.

But creating opportunities for upward and horizontal mobility are not sufficient in themselves. There has to be also a scrutiny of the selection criteria for the promotion of teachers. In the past, seniority was the main, sometimes the sole, criterion. Today, however, criteria tied to qualifications and performance are more widely accepted. In the opinion of the author, the authorities should encourage the voluntary efforts of teachers to upgrade themselves, so long as this is done without detriment to their daily teaching responsibilities. Some drop out may result as they begin to qualify for other careers, but there is a good chance that many experienced teachers will stay in the profession and contribute more fully to classroom teaching.

But upgrading alone should not normally bring with it the right to automatic salary increment or promotion. Promotion should be tied also to performance. This demands close scrutiny of the procedures used to evaluate teachers' competence and professionalism to ensure rigour and fairness. Also evaluation should not be the sole responsibility of administrative officers but should be shared with professional peers.

In circumstances where it is judged to be important to encourage links between the teaching profession and other occupations, special promotion criteria may be used for teachers with relevant non-teaching qualifications and experience, for instance, in agricultural science or rural extension services, in computer science or technical training in industry and commerce. For all promotion posts, a period of trial or probation before confirmation could be an added guarantee that suitable teachers were in fact being selected.

Recommendations for reform and adjustment of salaries incentives and career structures for teachers are easy to make but not easy to work out and apply. Despite this, many countries are making progress, others continue to avoid the issues because of the possible costs involved and the potential repercussions throughout the public sector. Certainly, policies of this nature cannot be

269

implemented overnight. But until the issues are faced and detailed policies are worked out, their cost implications cannot be known for sure. With imagination, it should be possible to devise selective and diversified means of improving the status and career prospects for teachers without enormous additional expenditure. In some countries determined to improve the quality of the teaching profession, special bodies have been set up, such as a Teaching Service Commission, to plan and administer long term development strategies.

ADMINISTRATIVE AND PROFESSIONAL SUPPORT

Two other important aspects for teacher development policy are dealt with together because they both relate to the everyday conditions in which teachers operate. We have noted previously how important it is to teachers' morale and ability to sustain high standards of work that they should have decent working conditions, materials and equipment. So often highly motivated teachers become discouraged because they do not have the wherewithal to do their work properly. One way in which the authorities may acknowledge these problems is by devolving more financial responsibility to local level and to principals, to purchase items not readily available from central sources.

There are two main challenges here. One is to create flexibility in procedures for the supply and distribution of services, materials and equipment to schools so that local initiative can fill the gaps when routine procedures break down. This has to be done at the same time as applying sufficiently rigorous mechanisms of accountability. The other challenge is to create good channels of communication between administration and teachers. Lengthy bureaucratic procedures which cause delays to schools' requests for action, or even no response at all, create disillusion amongst even the most energetic of teachers.

Serious studies are needed to measure the effects of improved levels of teacher support and supervision at school level. Much more effort needs to be put into strengthening professional supervision and support to teachers in the school. Many inspectorates and advisory services are undermanned. This must be a false economy.

In Chapter Ten it was noted that there is an inherent tension between the advisory and inspectorial and evaluative roles of many field personnel. Where these roles have to be combined because of shortages of personnel, careful training is essential. Reviews of evaluation mechanisms might also be helpful. For instance, selection for promotion should not rest solely on the evaluation of one person. Or such responsibilities should be limited to only a few senior people who do not regularly act in a support role.

Evidence is accumulating that the first line of professional support for teachers lies with school principals. It cannot be emphasised enough that special preparation, training and support for principals would probably be highly cost effective. Similarly, resources invested in training master teachers, leaders in teacher centres and advisory personnel would hardly be wasted, so long as conditions were provided to ensure that they were able and willing to carry out their support roles regularly.

There is also potential for universities and institutes of education to interact much more with schools. It is, after all, in the long term interests of higher education to ensure that its potential clients receive the best possible school education. Policy makers need to examine closely ways in which university personnel, educationalists and other specialists in related fields, could be encouraged to enter into collaboration with schools for action, research and professional training.

TEACHER EDUCATION AND TRAINING

There appears to be global anxiety, not just confined to the developing world, about the low quality of teacher training, particularly its failure to equip teachers with sound pedagogical knowledge and skills. Countries lack basic background information on teachers and their qualifications for the type and level of work they are doing. In addition, few countries monitor what goes on in the process of training and measure whether it achieves its objectives in the longer term.

In Chapter Ten we saw that some countries are experimenting with non-conventional and possibly lower cost strategies and structures of teacher training. Many of them may be perceived as temporary expedients until regular, long, pre-service courses can be reinstated. Yet there may be very positive advantages in some of these innovations. Work-study

271

arrangements, in particular, may offer both
financial and professional benefits. There is a great
paucity of sound research and evaluation into the
cost-effectiveness and cost-benefits of alternative
teacher training strategies. Yet countries looking
for improved teacher training need such research as a
guide to policy.

As we have seen, there is much discussion about
the merits of in-service training for professional
development. Yet we have little comparative
information on the extent, range, let alone impact
and cost, of such provision. Nor are there many
studies which attempt to compare the relative
advantages of different combinations of initial and
recurrent training and which review various methods
of financing them. There is a consensus that
induction training and support to new teachers would
be advantageous but little serious examination of
whether or not it has beneficial effect, nor of how
and by whom it may best be undertaken.

Chapter Eleven emphasised the lack of research
on the process of training teachers. Participant and
non-participant observational studies are needed.
Follow up and tracer studies of trained teachers
would yield valuable insights into the effectiveness
and impact of different types of training. There are
similar, strong arguments for more research into the
utilisation of teacher training materials. Studies
are needed on the level and type of materials
provided, how they are selected, or designed and
developed. Universities, institutes and curriculum
centres have a role to play in ensuring that
materials are culturally relevant and, as far as
possible, based on indigenous rather than imported
research.

This focus on the need for information about the
provision, cost and impact of teacher training must
not obscure the urgent need for practical action to
ensure that teacher training is properly planned and
managed and that there are sufficient resources for
personnel to carry out their responsibilities. In
particular, reviews are needed of planning and
management mechanisms to ensure responsiveness to
local needs.

The recruitment and training of teacher
trainers is an important but neglected area of
policy. Teacher trainers in universities tend to lack
prestige relative to other academics. Those in non-
graduate training are often held to be failed
secondary teachers. 'Lecturers' and 'professors' in
training colleges often lack credibility with

practising school teachers. Those involved in in-
service extension work often have ambiguous status
and poor career mobility. Careers in teacher training
in general tend to lead nowhere else. Career
structures discourage trainers from entering or re-
entering school teaching or advisory work. Many lack
the background and training to extend their work into
much needed developmental research in pedagogy.

Recruitment policies do not always ensure that
the most suitable people are selected to train
teachers. Sometimes the employing authorities switch
secondary teachers into vacant training posts as
vacancies arise. Many career structures ensure that
those who train primary teachers have no experience
or qualifications in primary education. There is a
danger that teacher trainers may stay in the same
type of post until retirement, becoming increasingly
isolated from the real conditions and needs of
teachers in schools.

Little comprehensive information is available
to allow us to ascertain whether or not these
impressions are accurate. Obviously, there will
always be highly competent individuals who belie the
general impression. But policy makers need detailed
surveys of the background, qualifications and
experience of teacher trainers in both graduate and
non-graduate training and in field posts. Without
this information, policy cannot be formulated
soundly.

The training of teacher trainers has to become a
top priority. This includes all those involved in the
preparation and support of teachers, those in
universities and colleges and those in field posts
and advisory positions. Teacher trainers need
initial orientation and systematic opportunities for
professional enrichment, including working contact
with curriculum developers, examination experts and,
above all, classrooms, teachers and children. As we
have seen, there are some small, isolated initiatives
in this direction but it is in general a neglected
aspect of policy. It is quite probable that the
quality of teacher trainers is one of the most
critical factors in improving teacher quality and
that systematic measures to provide for the training
of trainers would have a greatly beneficial
multiplier effect.

CONCLUSION

Some of the policy proposals put forward here require

273

political will and have financial implications. Others, particularly the majority which recommend research and evaluation studies in areas where knowledge is lacking, are neither costly nor controversial. Yet all require determination, vision, good planning and management. There is a great deal to be said for much more regional and international cooperation, across the blurred distinctions between developed and developing worlds, to identify problems and needs, to study unconventional policies and approaches which appear to have promise and, above all, to nourish and sustain the enthusiasm of countries to invest in the development of teacher professionalism for the benefit of youth today and tomorrow.

Aarons, A. (1983) 'Teachers and Health Workers:
    Partners in Primary Health Care: Experiences
    from Papua New Guinea' Community Development
    Journal 18:2, 132-138
Aarons, A. and Hawes, H. (1979) CHILD-to-child
    (Macmillan, London)
Abernethy, D.B. (1969) The Political Dilemma of
    Popular Education: An African Case (Stanford
    University Press, Stanford)
Abu, A. (1975) 'Islam versus Christianity in Sierra
    Leone' in Berman, E.H. (ed.). African Reactions
    to Missionary Education (Teachers College
    Press, New York and London)
Acker, S. (ed.) (1984) Women and Education World
    Yearbook of Education (Kogan Page and Nicholls
    Publishing Company, New York)
Adams, R.S. (1970) 'Analysing the Teacher's Role'
    Educational Research 12:2, 121-127
Adiseshiah, M.S. (1974) 'The Costs of Education and
    the Supply of Teachers' in Commonwealth
    Secretariat, Teacher Education in a Changing
    Society (London) 154-161
Aguilar, P. and Retamal, G. (1982) 'Ideological
    Trends and the Education of Teachers in Latin
    America' in Goodings, R., Byram, M. and
    McPartland, M. (eds.) Changing Priorities in
    Teacher Education (British Comparative Educat-
    ion Society with Croom Helm, London) 140-159
Ahmed, S. (1974) Muslim Community in Bengal 1884-1212
    (Oxford University Press, Dacca)
Akangbou, S.D. (1983) 'Problems and Prospects of
    Implementing Nigeria's Policy on Education'
    Journal of Developing Areas 2, 42-45
Akinpelu, J.A. (1974) 'The Educative Processes in
    Non-literate Societies: An Essay in the
    Anthropological Foundations of Education' West

African Journal of Education 18, 413-442

Akube, A.U. (1983) 'Leadership Performance of Secondary School Principals' Journal of Education in Developing Areas 2, 62-69

Alan, T.R. (1980) 'The Reform of Teacher Education through Research: A Futile Quest' Teachers College Record 82:1, 15-29

al-Attas, S.M. al Naquib (1979) Aims and Objectives of Islamic Education, (Hodder and Stoughton, London with King Abdulaziz University, Jeddah)

Ali, S. (1984) 'Conflict between Religion and Secularism in the Modern World and the Role of Education in preserving, transmitting and promoting Islamic Culture' Muslim Education Quarterly 2:1, 51-57

Altbach, P.G. (1978) 'The Distribution of Knowledge in the Third World: A Case Study in Neocolonialism' in Altbach, P.G. and Kelly, G.P. (eds.) Education and Colonialism (Longman, New York and London) 301-330

Anderson, L.W. (ed.) 1984) Time and School Learning: Theory Research and Practice (Croom Helm, London)

APEID (1978) Developing Instructional Modules for Teacher Education: Selected Exemplar Modules (UNESCO Regional Office for Education in Asia and Oceania, Bangkok)

APEID (1984a) Training Personnel for Distance Education (UNESCO Regional Office for Education in Asia and the Pacific, Bangkok)

APEID (1984b) Training Educational Personnel for Integrated Curriculum (UNESCO Regional Office for Education in Asia and the Pacific, Bangkok)

Arrayed, J.E. (1980) A Critical Analysis of School Science Teaching in Arab Countries (Longman and Libraire du Liban, London)

Asiedu-Akrofi, K. (1983) 'The Ghana National Association of Teachers and Professional Development' in Greenland, J. (ed.) In-Service Training of Primary Teachers in Africa (Macmillan, London)

Avalos, B. (1980) 'Teacher Effectiveness: Research in the Third World - Highlights of a Review' Comparative Education 16: 1, 45-54

Avalos, B. (1985) Teacher Effectiveness and Teacher: Lessons from Research with Reference to Developing Countries (unpublished ms)

Avalos, B. and Haddad, W. (1979) A Review of Teacher Effectiveness Research in Africa, India, Latin America, Middle East, Malaysia, Philippines and Thailand: Synthesis of Results (International

Development Research Centre, Ottawa)

Awori, T. (1975) 'The Revolt against the "Civilizing Mission": Christian Education in Liberia' in Berman, E.H. (ed.) *African Reactions to Missionary Education* (Teachers College Press, New York and London)

Ayot, H. (1983) 'Teacher Advisory Centres in Kenya' in Greenland, J. (ed.) *In-Service Training of Primary Teachers in Africa* (Macmillan, London) 153-172

Bacchus, M.K. (1980) *Education for Development or Underdevelopment?* Guyana's Educational System and its Implications for the Third World (Wilfrid Laurier Press, Ontario)

Bacchus, M.K. (1982) 'Integration of School and Community Learning in Developing Countries' in Barnard, R. (ed.) *The Integration of School and Community Learning in Developing Countries* (University of London Institute of Education, Department of Education in Developing Countries) 1-16

Bacchus, M.K. (1984) *A Review and Analysis of Educational 'Needs' at the Secondary Level in Papua New Guinea* E.R.U. Report 48 (University of Papua New Guinea, Port Moresby) 142

Bagader, A.A. (1984) 'The Kuttab "Quranic School": a Descriptive Essay' *Muslim Education Quarterly* 1:3, 47-56

Bagunywa, A.M.K. (1975) 'The Changing Role of the Teacher in African Renewal', *Prospects* 5:2, 220-226

Balderston, J.B., Wilson, A.B., Freire, M.E. and Simonen, M.S. (1981) *Malnourished Children of the Rural Poor* (Auburn House Publishing Company, Boston, Massachusetts)

Bame, K. (1979) 'Teacher Satisfaction and Salary Issues: Comments for Ghana and Jamaica' in D'Oyley, V. and Murray, R. (eds.) *Development and Disillusion in the Third World Education* Ontario Institute for Studies in Education, Toronto 137-150

Bangladesh, Ministry of Education (1983) *Decentralisation of Powers and Functions relating to Management of Primary Education* (Bangladesh Government Press, Dhaka)

Bartels, F.L. (1975) 'Akan Indigenous Education' in Brown G.N. and Hiskett M. (eds.) *Conflict and Harmony in Education in Tropical Africa* (George Allen and Unwin, London)

Batten, T.R. (1953) 'The Status and Function of Teachers in Tribal Communities' in *The Economic* and Social Status of Teachers World Year Book of Education (Evans, London) 76-94

Beeby, C.E. (1966) The Quality of Education in Developing Countries (Harvard University Press, Massachussetts)

Bennett, N. (1976) Teaching Styles and Pupil Progress (Open Books, London)

Bereday, G.Z.F. and Lauwerys, J.A. (eds.) (1963) The Education and Training of Teachers World Yearbook of Education (Evans Brothers, London)

Bereday, G.Z.F. and Lauwerys, J.A. (eds.) (1966) Church and State in Education World Yearbook of Education (Evans Brothers, London)

Berman, E.H. (ed.) (1975) African Reactions to Missionary Education (Teachers College, New York and London)

Beynon, J., Branch, K., Page, J. and Jack, A.K. el, (1977) The Management of Educational Facilities Programmes - a Focus on Community Participation and Self-reliance, Reports, Studies, S.29, Division of Educational Policy and Planning (UNESCO, Paris)

Birdsall, N. and Fox, M.J. (1985) 'Why Males Earn More: Location and Training of Brazilian Schoolteachers Economic Development and Cultural Change 34:3, 533-556

Bizot, J. (1975) Educational Reform in Peru (UNESCO, Paris)

Blackwell, J. (1977) 'Calcutta Teachers' Centre' in Dove, L. Ankrah (ed.) Teachers Groups and Centres in Developing Countries (Report of a Workshop held jointly by the British Council and the Department of Education in Developing Countries, University of London Institute of Education) 38-42

Blakemore, K. and Cooksey, B. (1980) A Sociology of Education for Africa (George Allen and Unwin, London)

Bloom, B.S. (ed.) (1956) Taxonomy of Educational Objectives: The Classification of Educational Goals (Longman, London)

Blyden, E.W. (1975) quoted in Berman, E.H. (ed.) (1975) African Reactions to Missionary Education (Teachers College, New York and London)

Bolam, R. (1981) Innovations in the In-Service Education and Training of Teachers: final synthesis report on an OECD/CERI project (Organisation for Economic Cooperation and Development, Paris)

Bolam, R. (1984) 'Induction of Beginning Teachers' in

Husen, T. and Postlethwaite, N. (eds.) International Encyclopaedia of Education: Research and Studies, (Pergamon, Oxford)

Boon, K.B., Ahmad, R.H. and Ahmad, K. (1983) Perceptions of Former Bahasa Malaysia Method Students on the Effectiveness of the Diploma in Education Programme, University of Malaya (Faculty of Education, University of Malaya, Kuala Lumpur)

Bowles, S. (1978) 'Capitalist Development and Educational Structure' World Development 6, 783-796

Bray, M. (1981) Universal Primary Education in Nigeria: A Study of Kano State (Routledge and Kegan Paul, London)

Bray, M. (1985) 'High School Selection in Less Developed Countries and the Quest for Equity: Conflicting Objectives and Opposing Pressures' Comparative Education Review 29:2 216-231

Brekelbaum, T. (1984) 'The Use of Paraprofessionals in Rural Development' Community Development Journal 19:4, 232-235

Brooke, N. and Oxenham, J. (1984) 'The Influence of Certification and Selection on Teaching and Learning' in Oxenham, J. (ed.) Education versus Qualification? (George Allen and Unwin, London) 147-175

Brophy, M. and Dudley, B. (1982) 'Patterns of Distance Teaching in Teacher Education' Journal of Education for Teaching 8:2, 156-162

Brown, G. (1975) Micro-teaching: A Programme of Teaching Skills (Methuen, London)

Brown, G.N. and Hiskett, M. (eds.) (1975) Conflict and Harmony in Education in Tropical Africa (George Allen and Unwin, London)

Bruner, J.S. (1972) The Relevance of Education (Penguin Educational Books, Harmondsworth, Middlesex)

Bude, U. (1982) 'Towards a Realistic Definition of the Teachers' Role in Primary Schooling: Experiences and Research Evidence from Cameroon' Compare 12:2, 105-120

Bude, Udo, (1983a) 'The Adaptation Concept in British Colonial Education' Comparative Education 19:3, 341-356

Bude, U. (ed.) (1983b) Curriculum Development in Africa 2nd edn. (German Foundation for International Development, Bonn)

Burns, R. (1982) 'The Need to Problematise Educational Knowledge' in Goodings, R., Byram, M. and McPartland, J. (eds.) Changing

Priorities in Teacher Education (Croom Helm,
London) 85-100
Burroughs, G.E.R. (1974) Education in Venezuela
(Archon Books, London and Connecticut)
Burton, L.M. (1982) 'The Impact of Education on
Political Development' unpublished PhD thesis,
(University of London Institute of Education)
Callaway, A. (1965) 'Continuing Education for
Africa's School Leavers: the Indigenous
Apprenticeship System' Inter-African Labour
Institute Bulletin 2:1, 61-88
Cameron, J. and Dodd, W.A. (1970) Society, Schools
and Progress in Tanzania (Pergamon, Oxford)
Cameron, J. and Hurst, P. (eds.) (1983) International
Handbook of Education Systems 11, Africa and the
Middle East (Wiley, Chichester)
Carnoy, M. (1974) Education as Cultural Imperialism
(Longman, New York and London)
Castle, E.B. (1966) Growing up in East Africa (Oxford
University Press, Oxford)
CERI (Centre for Educational Research and
Innovation) (1972) The Nature of the Curriculum
for the Eighties and Onward (Organisation
Economic Co-operation and Development, Paris)
CERI (Centre for Educational Research and
Innovation) (1975) Handbook on Curriculum
Development (Organisation for Economic Cooper-
ation and Development, Paris)
Chivore, B. (1985) 'The Recruitment and Training of
Non-graduate Secondary Teachers in Zimbabwe
since Independence' (unpublished Ph.D. Thesis,
University of London Institute of Education)
Clarke, P.B. (1978) 'Islam, Education and the
Developmental Process in Nigeria' Comparative
Education 14:2, 133-141
Clift, P., Weiner, G. and Wilson, E. (1981) Record
Keeping in Primary Schools Schools Council
(Macmillan Education, Basingstoke and London)
Cogan, M.L. (1973) Clinical Supervision (Houghton
Mifflin, Boston, Mass.)
Coleman, J.S., et.al. (1966) Equality of Educational
Opportunity (US Government Printing Office,
Washington DC)
Comparative Education Review (1980) 24:2 (special
issue on female education)
Coombe, T. (1985) Secondary Schoolteachers Planning
Unit, Ministry of Education and Culture,
Malawi)
Coombs, P.H. (1985) The World Educational Crisis: the
View from the Eighties (Oxford University
Press, New York)

Bibliography

Cortes, J.R. (1980) 'The Philippines' in Postlewaite
    T.N. and Thomas, R.N. (eds.) Schooling in the
    ASEAN Region: Indonesia, Malaysia, the
    Philippines, Singapore, Thailand (Pergamon,
    Oxford) 1969-172
Cropley, A.J. and Dave, R.H. (1978) Lifelong
    Education and the Training of Teachers
    (Pergamon and UNESCO Institute for Education,
    Oxford)
Cummings, W.K. (1984) The Conceptualization and
    Diffusion of an Experiment in Low-Cost
    Education: A six-nation study (International
    Development Research Centre, Ottawa) unpublish-
    ed ms.
Darras, M. (1985) 'Education in Nutrition at the
    Primary Level in New-Caledonia' in Turner, S.A.
    and Ingle, R.B. (eds.) New Developments in
    Nutrition Education, Nutrition Education
    Series, issue 11, (UNESCO, Paris) 72-75
Davies, L. (1985) 'Women, Educational Management and
    the Third World: A Comparative Framework for
    Analysis' unpublished ms.
Dent, H.C. (1977) The Training of Teachers in England
    and Wales (Hodder and Stoughton, London)
Desforges, C. and McNamara, D. (1979) 'Theory and
    Practice: Methodological Procedures for the
    Objectification of Craft Knowledge' British
    Journal of Teacher Education 5:2, 145-152
Dibona, J. (1983) One Teacher, One School: The Adams
    Reports on Indigenous Education in Nineteenth
    Century India (Biblia Impex Private, New Delhi)
Dillon, B. (1984) 'The Change Agent: A Radical
    Perspective' Community Development Journal
    19:4, 246-251
Dore, R. (1976) The Diploma Disease: Education,
    Qualification and Development (George Allen and
    Unwin, London)
Dove, L. Ankrah (ed.) (1977) Teachers Groups and
    Centres in Developing Countries (British
    Council with Department of Education in
    Developing Countries, University of London
    Institute of Education)
Dove, L.A. (1979) 'Teachers in Politics in Ex-
    Colonial Countries' Journal of Commonwealth and
    Comparative Politics 17:2, 176-191
Dove, L.A. (1980a) 'The Role of the Community School
    in Rural Transformation in Developing
    Countries' Comparative Education 16:1, 67-79
Dove, L.A. (1980b) 'The Teacher and the Rural
    Community in Developing Countries' Compare
    10:1, 17-29

Dove, L.A. (1980c) <u>Curriculum Reforms in Secondary</u>
   <u>Schools</u>: A Commonwealth Survey (Commonwealth
   Secretariat, London)
Dove, L.A. (1981) 'How the World Bank Can Contribute
   to Basic Education Given Formal Schooling Will
   Not Go Away' <u>Comparative Education</u> <u>17</u>:2, 173-
   184
Dove, L.Ankrah-, (1982a) 'The Deployment and
   Training of Teachers for Remote Rural Schools in
   Less-Developed Countries' <u>International Review</u>
   <u>of Education</u> 28, 3-27
Dove, L.A. (1982b) <u>Lifelong Teacher Education and the</u>
   <u>Community School</u> (UNESCO Institute for
   Education, Hamburg)
Dove, L.A. (1982c) 'The Implications for Teacher
   Training of Conflicting Models of Community
   Schooling' in Goodings, R., Byram, M. and
   McPartland, M. (eds.) <u>Changing Priorities in</u>
   <u>Teacher Education</u> (British Comparative Educat-
   ion Society with Croom Helm, London) 101-114
Dove, L.A. (1983a) 'Curriculum Development in the New
   Commonwealth' <u>International Journal of Educat-</u>
   <u>ional Development</u> <u>3</u>:2, 149-157
Dove, L.A. (1983b) 'Teacher Training for Universal
   Primary Education in Bangladesh, 1981-1986'
   <u>International Review of Education</u> <u>29</u>:2, 215-257
Dove, L.A. (1985) 'Mobile Teacher Trainers for UPE:
   An Experimental Programme in Rural Bangladesh'
   <u>Community Development Journal</u> <u>20</u>:1, 41-48
D'Olyley, V. and Murray, R. (eds.) (1979) <u>Development</u>
   <u>and Disillusion in Third World Education</u>: with
   <u>Emphasis</u> on Jamaica (Ontario Institute for
   Studies in Education, Toronto)
Dunkin, M.J. and Biddle, B.J. (1974) <u>The Study of</u>
   <u>Teaching</u> (Holt, Reinehart and Winston, New
   York)
Dzobo, N.K. (1975) 'Values in Indigenous African
   Education' in Brown, G.N. and Hiskett, M. (eds.)
   <u>Conflict and Harmony in Education in Tropical</u>
   <u>Africa</u> (George Allen and Unwin, London)
Eggleston, J.G. (1974) 'Measuring Attainment for
   Curriculum Evaluation' in MacIntosh, H.G. (ed.)
   <u>Techniques and Problems of Assessment</u> (Edward
   Arnold, London) 232-247
Eheazu, B.A. (1982) 'Some Problems and Prospects of
   Operationalising Efficiency in the Pre-Service
   Training of Primary School Teachers in Nigeria'
   <u>Journal of Education in Developing Areas</u>, <u>1</u>:1,
   88-96
Ejiogu, A.M. (1980) 'When Innovations are External to
   the Realities and Needs of an Organisation:

Problems of Educational Innovations in
Developing Countries' Journal of Curriculum
Studies 12:2, 161-166

Ekanayake, S.B. (1982) 'A Survey of the Relationships
between Teachers and Village Communities in Sri
Lanka, 1982' in Dove, L.A., Lifelong Teacher
Education and the Community School (UNESCO
Institute for Education, Hamburg) 136-146

Etzioni, A. (1969) The Semi-Professionals and their
Organizations (Free Press, New York)

Ezeomah, C. (1983) The Education of Nomadic People
(Nafferton Books, Driffield)

Ezewu, E.E. (1981) 'Some Comments on the Curriculum
for Training Teachers for the Primary School
System in Bendel State, Nigeria' Journal of
Education for Teaching 7:1, 164-175

Fafunwa, A.B. (1967) New Perspectives in African
Education (Macmillan, Lagos)

Fafunwa, A.B. (1974) A History of Education in
Nigeria (George Allen and Unwin, London)

Fafunwa, A.B. and Aisiku, J.U. (eds.) (1982)
Education in Africa: a Comparative Study
(George Allen and Unwin, London)

Fagerlind, I. and Saha, L.J. (1983) Education and
National Development: A Comparative Perspective
(Pergamon, Oxford)

Farrant, J.S. (1980) Principles and Practice of
Education, 2nd edn. (Longman, London)

Figueroa, M. (1974) The Basic Secondary School in the
Country (UNESCO, Paris)

Fitzsimmons, S.J. and Freedman, A.J. (1981) Rural
Community Development: A Program, Policy and
Research Model (Abt Books, Cambridge,
Massachusetts)

Flores, P.V. (1981) Educational Innovation in the
Philippines: A Case Study of Project Impact
(International Development Research Centre,
Ottawa)

Forde, T.J.L. (1975) 'Indigenous Education in Sierra
Leone' in Brown, G.N. and Hiskett, M. (eds.)
Conflict and Harmony in Education in Tropical
Africa (George Allen and Unwin, London)

Foster, P. (1965) Education and Social Change in
Ghana (Routledge and Kegan Paul, London)

Fredriksen, B. (1981) 'Progress Towards Regional
Targets for Universal Primary Education: A
Statistical Review' International Journal of
Educational Development 1:1, 1-16

Freire, P. (1974) Education: the Practice of Freedom
(Writers and Readers Publishing Cooperative,
London)

Gagne, R.M. and Briggs, L.J. (1979) <u>Principles of Instructional Design</u>, 2nd edn. (Holt, Rinehart and Winston, New York)

Gall, N. (1974) <u>Peru's Education Reform</u>, Part 1: 'More Schools', West Coast America Series) <u>21</u>:3 (American Universities Field Staff Inc., Hanover, New Hampshire)

Galton, M. and Simon, B. (1980) <u>Progress and Performance in the Primary Classroom</u> (Routledge and Kegan Paul, London)

Gardner, R. (ed.) (1981) <u>Education and Work</u>, Report of a Workshop, (Department of Education, University of London Institute of Education)

Gardner, R. (ed.) (1982) <u>Textbooks in Developing Countries</u> (Department of Education in Developing Countries, University of London Institute of Education)

Gatawa, B.S.M. (1985) 'The Zimbabwe Integrated National Teacher Education Course (ZINTEC) (University of London Institute of Education) unpublished ms.

Gimeno, J.B. (1983) <u>Education in Latin America and the Caribbean:</u> Trends and Prospects 1970-2000 (UNESCO, Paris)

Gimeno, J.B. and Ibanez, R.M. (1981) <u>The Education of Primary and Secondary School Teachers:</u> an International Comparative Study, (UNESCO, Paris)

Goad, L.H. (ed.) (1984) <u>Preparing Teachers for Lifelong Education</u> (UNESCO Institute for Education, Hamburg)

Goble, N.M. and Porter, J.F. (1977) <u>The Changing Role of the Teacher:</u> International Perspectives (UNESCO, Paris and NFER Publishing Company Ltd., Slough)

Greenland, J. (ed.) (1983) <u>In-service Training of Primary Teachers in Africa</u> (Macmillan, London)

Grett, J. (1981) 'Primary Teaching by Television is Abandoned' <u>The Times Educational Supplement</u> (London, 8 May)

Griffin, G.A. (1985) 'Teacher Induction: Research Issues' <u>Journal of Teacher Education</u> 36:1. 42-46

Griffiths, V.L. (1975) <u>Teacher-Centred:</u> Quality in Sudan Primary Education 1930-1970 (Longman, London)

Gross, N., Giacquinta, J. and Bernstein, M. (1971) <u>Implementing Organizational Innovations</u> (Harper & Row, New York)

Guruge, A.W.P. (1984) <u>Learning Potential of School Feeding Programmes</u>, Proceedings and Working

Documents of a Workshop on School Feeding and Education, Coimbarore, Tamil Nadu, India, 14-21 December 1983, (UNESCO, Unit for Cooperation with UNICEF and WFP, Paris)

Guruge, A.W.P. and Ryan, J. (1984) 'Girls and Women's Education: A Discussion Paper' (UNESCO/UNICEF Cooperative Programme, Fifth meeting 19-20 April) unpublished ms.

Guthrie, G. (1982) 'Reviews of Teacher Training and Teacher Performance in Developing Countries: Beeby Revisited (2)' International Review of Education 28, 291-306

Guthrie, G. (1983) 'Policy Issues in Planning Secondary Teacher Training in Papua New Guinea' South Pacific Journal of Teacher Education 11:1, 33-42

Haddad, W.D. (1978) Educational Effects of Class Size Staff Working Paper 280, (World Bank, Washington)

Hammersley, M. (1977) Teacher Perspectives, Educational Studies: A Second Level Course, E202 Schooling and Society, Block II, The Process of Schooling, Units 9 and 10 (Open University Press, London)

Harber, C.R. (1984) 'Development and Political Attitudes: the Role of Schooling in Northern Nigeria' Comparative Education 20:3, 387-403

Harlen, W. (1977) 'A Stronger Teacher Role in Curriculum Development?' Journal of Curriculum Studies 9:1

Harris, A., Lawn, M. and Prescott, W. (1978) Curriculum Innovation (Croom Helm, London and Open University Press)

Havelock, R.G. (1971) Planning for Innovation (Centre for Research on Utilization of Scientific Knowledge, Institute for Social Research, Ann Arbor, Michigan)

Havelock, R.G. and Huberman, (1977) Solving Educational Problems (UNESCO, Paris)

Hawes, H. (1977) 'The Curriculum of Teacher Education' in Gardner, R. (ed.) Teacher Education in Developing Countries: Prospects for the Eighties (Department of Education in Developing Countries, University of London Institute of Education) 52-63

Hawes, H. (1979) Curriculum and Reality in African Primary Schools (Longman, London)

Hawes, H. (1982) 'Professional Support for Teachers in Schools: An Indonesian Case Study' in Treffgarne, C.B.W. (ed.) EDC Occasional Papers No. 3, Department of Education in Developing

285

Countries, University of London Institute of
Education, 1-31.
Hawes, H. and Williams, P. (1974) 'UPE Must Not Fail'
West Africa (23 September-21 October)
Hawkridge, D. Kinyanjui, P, Nkinyangi, J. and Orivel,
F. (1979) 'In-service Teacher Education in
Kenya' in Perraton, H. (ed.) Alternative Routes
to Formal Education: Distance Teaching for
School Equivalency (John Hopkins for World
Bank, Washington) 173-213
Henry, D. (1983) 'Provincial-based In-service Work'
Papua New Guinea Education Gazette (April) 68-
78
Hercik, V. (1976) 'European Models of Teacher
Education in Developing Countries' in Lomax,
D.E. (ed.) European Perspectives in Teacher
Education (John Wiley, London) 179-198
Heyneman, S.P. (1976) 'Influences on Academic
Achievement: A Comparison of Results from
Uganda and More Industrialized Societies'
Sociology of Education 49, 200-211
Heyneman, S.P. (1980) 'Comment on Simmons and
Alexander's "Determinants of School Achieve-
ment"' Economic Development and Cultural Change
28, 403-406
Heyneman, S.P. (1983) 'Improving the Quality of
Education in Developing Countries' Finance and
Development (March) 18-21
Honeybone, R. (1977) 'The Case for a Review' in
Gardner, R. (ed.) Teacher Education in
Developing Countries: Prospects for the
Eighties (Department of Education in Developing
Countries, University of London Institute of
Education), 4-18
Houeto, S.C. (1981) 'Benin: Training Teachers to
Implement the Reform' Prospects 11:2, 193-203
Houghton, H. and Tregear, P. (1969) Community Schools
in Developing Countries (UNESCO, International
Bureau of Education, Hamburg)
Howie, G. (1963) 'The Teacher in Classical Greece and
Rome' in Bereday, G.Z.F. and Lauwerys, J.A.
(eds.) The Education and Training of Teachers
Yearbook of Education (Evans Brothers, London)
41-58
Hoyle, E. (1980) 'Professionalization and Depro-
fessionalization in Education' in Hoyle, E. and
Megarry, J. (eds.) Professional Development of
Teachers, World Year Book of Education (Kogan
Page, London)
Hoyle, E. and Megarry, J. (eds.) (1980) Professional
Development of Teachers, World Year Book of

Education (Kogan Paul, London)

Hubbard, J.P. (1975) 'Government and Islamic Education in Northern Nigeria 1900-1940' in Brown, G.N. and Hiskett, M. (eds.) Conflict and Harmony in Education in Tropical Africa (George Allen and Unwin, London)

Hurst, P. (1978) Implementing Innovatory Projects: a Critical Review of the Literature, World Bank Diversified Secondary Curriculum Study (World Bank, Washington DC)

Husen, T. (1977) 'Pupils, Teachers and Schools in Botswana: A National Evaluative Survey of the Primary and Secondary Education', Annex A of Education for Kagisano, Report of the National Commission on Education in Botswana, (Government Printing Office, Gaborone)

Husen, T. and Kogan, M. (eds.) (1984) Educational Research and Policy: How do they Relate? (Pergamon, Oxford)

Husen, T., Saha, L.J. and Noonan, R. (1978) Teacher Training and School Achievement in Less Developed Countries (World Bank Staff Working Paper no. 310, Washington DC)

Hussain, F. (ed.) (1984) Muslim Women (Croom Helm, London)

Ikramullah, B.S.S. (1963) From Purdah to Parliament (Cresset Press, London)

Illich, I. (1971) Deschooling Society (Calder and Boyars, London)

Illich, I.D. (1977) in Illich, I.D., Zola, K., McKnight, J., Caplan, J. and Sheiken, H. Disabling Professions (Boyars, London) 11-40

ILO (1977) Freedom of Association and Procedures for Determining Conditions of Employment in the Public Service, Report VII (1) and (2), International Labour Conference, 63rd Session, (International Labour Organisation, Geneva)

ILO (1978) Teachers Pay (International Labour Organisation, Geneva)

ILO (1979) Social Security for Teachers (International Labour Organisation, Geneva)

ILO/UNESCO (1983) Joint ILO/UNESCO Committee of Experts on the Application of the Recommendation Concerning the Status of Teachers, 4th Session 1982, Geneva (International Labour Office, Geneva)

Ishumi, A.G.M. (1981) Community Education and Development (Kenya Literature Bureau, Nairobi)

Jackson, J.A. (ed.) (1970) Professions and Professionalization (Cambridge University Press)

Jencks, C. et. al. (1972) Inequality: A Reassessment
of the Effect of Family and Schooling in America
(Basic Books, New York)

Jennings, A. (1983) 'The Recurrent Cost Problem in
the Least Developed Countries' The Journal of
Development Studies 19:4, 505-521

Jennings-Wray, Z. (1984) 'Teacher Involvement in
Curriculum Change in Jamaica' Compare 14, 41-58

Johnson, T. (1972) Professions and Power (Macmillan,
London)

Johnson, T. (1973) 'Imperialism and the Professions'
in Halmos, P. (ed.) Professionalization and
Social Change (University of Keele)

Joyce, B.R., Hersh, R.H. and McKibbin, M. (1983) The
Structure of School Improvement (Longman, New
York)

Joyce, B. and Showers, B. (1981) 'Teacher Training
Research: Working Hypotheses for Program Design
and Directions and Further Study' (American
Educational Research Association, Los Angeles)
unpublished ms.

Kajubi, W.S. (1982) 'Some Comments on the Content and
the Use of Textbooks in Developing Countries' in
Gardner, R. (ed.) Textbooks in Developing
Countries (Department of Education in
Developing Countries, University of London
Institute of Education) 63-90

Kelly, G.P. (1978a) 'Colonial Schools in Vietnam:
Policy and Practice' in Altbach, P.G. and Kelly,
G.P. (eds.) Education and Colonialism (Longman,
New York and London) 96-121

Kelly, G.P. (1978b) 'Schooling and National
Integration: the case of Interwar Vietnam'
Comparative Education 18:2, 175-196

Kelly, G.P. and Elliott, C.M. (eds.) (1982) Women's
Education in the Third World: Comparative
Perspectives (State University of New York
Press, Albany)

Kenya National Examinations Council (1982) C.P.E.
Newsletter 1982 (Nairobi)

Kerr, J.F. (1969) Curriculum Change in Emergent
Countries (University of Leicester School of
Education, England) quoted in Jennings-Wray, Z.
(1984) 'Teacher Involvement in Curriculum
Change in Jamaica' Compare 14:1, 41-58

Khan, M.W. (ed.) (1981) Education and Society in the
Muslim World (Hodder and Stoughton, London with
King Abdulaziz University, Jeddah)

Klitgaard, R.E., Siddiqui, K.Y., Arshad, M., Niaz, N.
and Khan, M.A. (1985) 'The Economics of Teacher
Education in Pakistan' Comparative Education

Review 29:1, 97-110
Kremer, L. and Ben-Peretz M. (1984) 'Teachers' Self-
    evaluation - Concerns and Practices' Journal of
    Education for Teaching 10:1, 53-60
Kurrien, J. (1983) Elementary Education in India:
    Myth, Reality, Alternative (Vikas Publishing
    House, New Delhi)
Lallez, R. (1974) An Experiment in the Ruralization
    of Education: IPAR and the Cameroonian Reform
    (UNESCO, International Bureau of Education,
    Hamburg)
Lansheere, G.de (1980) 'Teacher Selection' Prospects
    10:3, 318-324
Lauglo, J. (1982) 'Rural Primary School Teachers as
    Potential Community Leaders? Contrasting cases
    in Western Countries', Comparative Education
    18:3, 233-256
Lauglo, J. (1985) Practical Subjects in Academic
    Secondary Schools: An Evaluation of Industrial
    Education in Kenya, Final Report from the
    Evaluation of Swedish Assistance to the
    Development of Industrial Education in Kenya,
    unpublished ms.
Lauglo, J. and Gartner, A. (1977) Teacher Tasks in
    Innovative Schools: Utilisation of Teacher
    Aides in some European Countries and the United
    States (Organisation for Economic Co-operation
    and Development, Paris)
Lee, M.N.N. (1982) 'Science Education in Malaysian
    Schools: Some Problems and Suggestions'
    Pendidik Dan Pendidikan 4:1, 58-63
Leiner, M. (1975) 'Cuba: Combining Formal Schooling
    with Practical Experience' in Ahmed, M. and
    Coombs, P.H. (eds) Education for Rural
    Development: Case Studies for Planners
    (Praeger, New York)
Leong, Yin Ching (1982) 'The Objectives and Process
    of Schooling: Perceptions of Secondary School
    Leavers, Teachers, Principals and Parents of
    Kuala Langat District, Selangor in Peninsular
    Malaysia (unpublished Ph D thesis, University
    of London Institute of Education)
Levinger, B. (1984) 'School Feeding Programmes: Myth
    and Potential' Prospects 14:3, 369-376
Lewin, K. and Little. A. (1984) 'Examination Reform
    and Educational Change in Sri Lanka 1972-1982:
    Modernisation or Dependent Underdevelopment?'
    in Watson, K. (ed.) Dependence and Interdepen-
    dence in Education (Croom Helm, London) 47-94
Lewin, K., Little, A. and Colclough C. (1982)
    'Adjusting to the 1980s - Taking Stock of

Educational Expenditure' in Financing Educat-
ional Development (International Development
Research Centre and Canadian International
Development Association, Ottawa)
Lewis, L.J. (ed.) (1962) Phelps-Stokes Report on
Education in Africa abridged version (Oxford
University Press, London)
Lewy, A. (ed.) (1977) Handbook of Curriculum
Evaluation (Longman, New York with UNESCO)
Lillis, K. (1985) 'Processes of Secondary Curriculum
Innovation in Kenya' Comparative Education
Review 29:1, 80-97
Lister, I. (ed.) (1974) Deschooling: a Reader
(Cambridge University Press, London)
Loveridge, A.J. (1978) British Colonial Experience
in Educational Development: a Survey of Non-
formal Education for Rural and Agricultural
Development. (University College Cardiff
Press, Cardiff)
Lynch, J. (1977) Lifelong Education and Preparation
of Educational Personnel (UNESCO Institute for
Education, Hamburg)
Lynch, J. (1979) The Reform of Teacher Education in
the United Kingdom Research into Higher
Education Monographs (Society for Research into
Higher Education, University of Surrey,
Guildford)
Lyons, R.F. (1981) The Organisation of Education in
Remote Rural Areas (UNESCO International
Institute for Educational Planning, Paris)
Magoon, A.J. (1976) 'Teaching and Performance-Based
Teacher Education' in Lomax, D.E. (ed.)
European Perspectives in Teacher Education
(Wiley, London) 235-262
Manalang, P.S. (1977) 'A Philippine Rural School: Its
Cultural Dimension (University of the
Philippines, Quezon City)
Manuel, J.L. (1968) 'The Philippine Community
School' in Community Schools in Developing
Countries (UNESCO, Institute for Education
Hamburg) unpublished ms.
Martin, C.J. (1984) '"Community School" or the
Community's School: Issues in Rural Education
with special reference to South East Asia'
Compare 14:1, 85-106
Mathot,G. (1983) The Lesotho In-service Education
for Teachers (LIET) in Greenland, J. (ed.) In-
service Training of Primary Teachers in Africa
(Macmillan, London) 280-293
Mazrui, A.A. (1978) Political Values and the Educated
Class in Africa (Heinemann, London) 283-379

Bibliography

Mblilinyi, M.J. (1979) 'History of Formal Schooling in Tanzania' in Hinzen, H. and Hundsdorfer, V.H. (eds.) Education for Liberation and Development: The Tanzanian Experience (Institute for Education, Hamburg and Evans Brothers, Ibadan) 76-87

Mexico, Secretaria de la Educacion Publica (1981) Informe del Estudio sobre Algunos Factores que Motivain al Maestro Rural a Querer or No Cambiarse de Escuele (Programa Primaria para Todos los Ninos) unpublished ms.

Molomo, R. (1983) 'The Botswana In-service Team: a Mobile Support Service for Primary Schools' in Greenland, J. (ed.) In-service Training of Primary Teachers in Africa (Macmillan, London) 139-152

Moock, J.L. (1974) 'Pragmatism and the Primary School: the Case of the Non-rural Village' in Court D. and Ghai, D.P. (eds.) Education, Society and Development: New Perspectives from Kenya (Oxford University Press, Nairobi) 105-122

Moore, T.W. (1974) Educational Theory: An Introduction (Routledge and Kegan Paul, London)

Moran, F. (1942) 'El Salvador' in Educational Yearbook of the International Institute of Teachers College (Columbia University Teachers College, New York) quoted in Aguilar, P. and Retamal, G. (1982) 'Ideological Trends and the Education of Teachers in Latin America' in Goodings, R., Byram, M. and McPartland, M. (eds.) (British Comparative Education Society with Croom Helm, London) 148.

Morocco, Ministry of National Education (1981) The Educational Trend in Morocco (Rabat)

Morris, B. (1977) Some Aspects of the Professional Freedom of Teachers: An International Pilot Inquiry (UNESCO, Paris)

Morris, P. (1985) 'Teachers' Perceptions of the Barriers to the Implementation of a Pedagogic Innovation: A South East Asian Case Study' International Review of Education 31:1. 1985 3-18

Morris, I. (1970) Education since 1800 (George Allen and Unwin, London)

Moumoni, A. (1968) Education in Africa (Deutsch, London)

Mrutu, J.A. (1979) 'Teacher Education for Basic Education: the Changing Role' in Mtuu: Basic Education - A Community Enterprise (Ministry of National Education, Dar es Salaam) 55-61.

291

Muelder, W.R. (1962) Schools for a New Nation: The
    Development and Administration of the
    Educational System of Ceylon (K.V.G. de Silva,
    Colombo)
Mukherjee, H. (1982) 'Moral Education in Malaysia' in
    Barnard, R. (ed.) The Integration of School and
    Community Learning in Developing Countries
    (University of London Institute of Education,
    Department of Education in Developing
    Countries) 44-51
Mukherjee, H. and Singh, J.S. (1983) 'The New Primary
    Curriculum Project: Malaysia' International
    Review of Education 29:2, 257-259
Mwanakatwe, J.M. (1968) The Growth of Education in
    Zambia since Independence (Oxford University
    Press, Lusaka)
MacEoin, D. and Al-shahi, A. (eds.) (1983) Islam in
    the Modern World (Croom Helm, London)
MacIntosh, H.G. and Hale, D.E. (1976) Assessment and
    the Secondary School Teacher (Routledge and
    Kegan Paul, London) 108-114
Maclure, S. (1972) Styles of Curriculum Development
    (Organisation for Economic and Co-operation and
    Development, Paris)
Naik, C. (1983) 'India: Extending Primary Education
    through Non-formal Approaches' Prospects 13:1,
    60-72
Nash, M. (1962) 'Education in a New Nation: the
    Village School in Upper Burma' International
    Journal of Comparative Sociology 3, 134-143
Naseef, A.O. (1984) 'Science Education and Religious
    Values: an Islamic Approach' Muslim Education
    Quarterly 1:3, 4-10
Nash, M. (1974) 'Rural Education for Development:
    Burma and Malaysia: a Contrast in Cultural
    Meaning and Structural Relations' in Foster, P.
    and Sheffield, J.R. (eds.) Education for Rural
    Development World Yearbook of Education (Evans
    Brothers, London) 337-349
Ncube A.M. (1983) 'The Zimbabwe Integrated National
    Teacher Education Course (ZINTEC) Programme in
    Zimbabwe' in Bude, U. and Greenland J. (eds.)
    Inservice Education and Training of Primary
    School Teachers in Anglophone Africa (Nomos
    Verlagsgesellschaft, Baden-Baden) 44-56
Nepal, Ministry of Education and Culture (1983) An
    Introduction to the Education of Girls and Women
    in the Nepal Project Women's Education Unit,
    unpublished ms.
Ntumi, R. (1983) 'Trends in Curriculum Development in
    Ghana' in Bude, U. (ed.) Curriculum Development

in Africa, 2nd edn. (German Foundation for International Development, Bonn) 189-201

Nwa-Chil, C.C. (1973) 'The Spread of "Western Education" in Nigeria, Journal of East African Research and Development 3:2, 145-165

Nwagwu, N. (1981) 'The Impact of Changing Conditions of Service on the Recruitment of Teachers in Nigeria Comparative Education 17:1, 81-87

Nyerere, J.K. (1967) Education for Self Reliance (National Printing Company, Dar es Salaam)

Ocho, L.O. (1983) 'Private Proprietary Secondary Schools' Journal of Education in Developing Areas' 2, 129-135

Oliveros, A. (1975) Los Professores Iberoamericanos en Educacion Primaria, (OEI, Promocion Cultural S.A.) quoted in Gimeno, J.B. and Ibanez, R.M. (1981) The Education of Primary and Secondary School Teachers (UNESCO, Paris) 113-114

Ong, Teng Cheong and Moral Education Committee (1979) Report on Moral Education 1979 (Deputy Prime Minister and Minister of Education, Singapore)

Oxenham, J. (ed.) (1984) Education versus Qualification? (George Allen and Urwin, London)

Peil, M. (1977) Consensus and Conflict in African Societies (Longman, London)

Perera, S.M.D. and Wijedasa, R. (1984) 'Sri Lanka' in UNESCO, The Drop-out Problem in Primary Education: some case studies, Regional Office for Education in Asia and the Pacific, 189-232

Perrin, J. (1984) 'The Production of Know-How and Obstacles to its Transfer' Prospects 14:4, 479-488

Perrott, E. (1976) 'Changes in Teaching Behaviour after Participating in a Self-instructional Microteaching Course' Educational Media International no.1, 16-25

Persaud, G. (1976) 'The Hidden Curriculum of Teacher Education and Schooling' in Figueroa, P.M.E. and Persaud, G. (eds.) Sociology of Education: A Caribbean Reader (Oxford University Press) 90-104

Peterson, P.L. (1979) 'Direct Instruction Reconsidered' in Peterson, P.L. and Walberg, H.J. (eds.) Research on Teaching: Concepts, Findings and Implications (McCutchan, Berkeley, California) 57-69

Pollitt, E. (1984) Nutrition and Educational Achievement, Nutrition Education Series, Issue 9, (UNESCO, Paris)

Porter, J.F. (1977) 'Learning to Teach: Priorities for Action' in Goble, N.M. and Porter, J.F. The

Changing Role of the Teacher; International
Perspectives (UNESCO and NFER, Slough, Bucks)
117-153
Postlethwaite, T.N. and Thomas, R.M. (1980)
Schooling in the ASEAN Region (Pergamon Press,
Oxford)
Prawda, J. (1984) Teoria y Praxis de la Planeacion
Educativa en Mexico (Editorial Grijalbo, S.A.,
Miguel Haldo)
Prospects (1984) 'Mother Tongue and Educational
Attainment' (special issue) 14:1
Raggatt, P. (1983) 'One Person's Periphery ...'
Compare 13:1, 1-6
Reimer, E. (1971) School is Dead: An Essay on
Alternatives in Education (Penguin Books,
Harmondsworth, Middlesex)
Rensburg van, P. (1983) The Serowe Experience and
Socially-Equitable Development: some Tentative
Conclusions for Planning' for seminar on 'The
Prospects of Educational Planning related to
Contemporary Development Problems' (UNESCO,
International Institute for Educational Plann-
ing, Paris)
Richardson, T.A. (1963) 'The Classical Chinese
Teacher' in Bereday, G.Z.F. and Lauwerys, J.A.
(eds.) The Education and Training of Teachers
World Yearbook of Education (Evans Brothers,
London), 26-40
RIHED (1983) RIHED Bulletin 10:4 (Regional Institute
of Higher Education and Development, Singapore)
Robinson, A. (1980) Principles and Practice of
Teaching (George Allen and Unwin, London)
Rogers, E.M. and Shoemaker, F.F. (1971) Commun-
ication of Innovations: a Cross-cultural
Approach, 2nd edn, (The Free Press, Collier
Macmillan, London)
Rogers, T.J. (1974) 'Course Work and Continous
Assessment' in Macintosh, H.G. (ed.)
Techniques and Problems of Assessment (Edward
Arnold, London) 157-172
Rosenshine, B.V. and Berliner, D.C. (1978) 'Academic
Engaged Time' British Journal of Teacher
Education 4:1, 3-16
Rosenshine, B.V. (1979) 'Content, Time and Direct
Instruction' in Peterson, P.L. and Walberg,
H.J. (eds.) Research on Teaching: Concepts,
Findings and Implications (McCutchan, Berkeley,
California) 28-56
Roy, A. (1980) 'Schools and Communities: an
Experience in Rural India' International Review
of Education 26:3, 369-378

Roy, A. (ed.) (1984) Education of Out-of School
    Children: Case Studies of Selected Non-Formal
    Learning Programmes in South Asia, (Common-
    wealth Secretariat, London)
Ruberu, T.R. (1962) Education in Colonial Ceylon
    (Kandy Printers, Kandy)
Rutter, M (1979) Fifteen Thousand Hours: Secondary
    Schools and their Effects on Children (Open
    Books, London)
Saha, L.J. (1983) 'Social Structure and Teacher
    Effects on Academic Achievement: A Comparative
    Analysis' Comparative Education Review 27:1,
    69-88
Sanger, C. (1977) Project IMPACT: a Progress Report
    on Innotech Project IMPACT in the Philippines
    and Projek Pamong in Indonesia (International
    Development Research Centre, Ottawa)
Saqueb, G.N. (1983) 'Education in the Eighties in the
    Islamic World' Muslim Education 1:3, 67-80
Sattar, E. (1982) Universal Primary Education in
    Bangladesh (University Press, Dhaka)
Sattar, E. (1985) 'Meher Universal Primary Education
    Project' Roy, A. (ed.) in Education of Out-of-
    School Children: Case studies of Selected Non-
    Formal Learning Programmes in South Asia
    (Commonwealth Secretariat, London) 49-61
Scheffler, I. (1973) Reason and Teaching (Routledge
    and Kegan Paul, London)
Schiefelbein, E. (1983) Educational Financing in
    Developing Countries: Research Findings and
    Contemporary Issues (International Development
    Research Centre, Ottawa)
Schiefelbein, E. Farrelll, J.P. and Sepulveda-
    Stuardo (1983) The Influence of School
    Resources in Chile: Their Effect on Educational
    Achievement and Occupational Attainment, World
    Bank Staff Working Paper no.530, (World Bank,
    Washington)
Schiefelbein, E. and Simmons, J. (1981) The
    Determinants of School Achievement: A Review of
    the Research for Developing Countries
    (International Development Research Centre,
    Ottawa)
Selassie, T.H. (1985) personal communication to
    author
Seng, Ng Tiat (1985) 'Perceptions of Parental Press,
    Academic Motivation and Academic Achievement of
    a Sample of Primary Six Chinese Pupils'
    unpublished M.Ed. thesis (Institute of
    Education, Singapore)
Sestini, E. (1985) 'Professional or Para-

Professional? Factors affecting Pre-school
Policies, Curriculum and Training in Low Income
Countries' Conference on Staff Development for
Education Systems in Low Income Countries,
(Centre for Overseas Studies, Bristol
University) unpublished ms.

Shils, E. (1963) 'Demagogues and Cadres in the
Political Development of New States' in Pye,
L.W. (ed.) Communications and Political
Development (Princeton University Press, New
Jersey) 64-77

Shaeffer, S. and Nkinyangi, J.A. (eds.) (1983)
Educational Research Environments in the
Developing World (International Development
Research Centre, Ottawa)

Shorey, L.L. (1982) 'Report: Focus on Primary
Education: the UWI/USAID Primary Education
Project' Caribbean Journal of Education 9:1,
44-54

Sibanda, D. (1983) 'The Zimbabwe Integrated Teacher
Education Course (ZINTEC)' in Greenland, J.
(ed.) In-service Training of Primary Teachers
in Africa (Macmillan, London) 269-279

Simmons, J. (ed.) (1980) The Education Dilemma:
Policy Issues for Developing Countries in the
late 1980s (Pergamon, Oxford)

Simmons, J. and Alexander, L. (1980) 'Factors which
Promote School Achievement in Developing
Countries: A Review of the Research' in Simmons,
J. (ed.) The Education Dilemma: Policy Issues
for Developing Countries in the 1980s
(Pergamon, Oxford) 77-95

Sinclair, M.E. with Lillis, K. (1980) School and
Community in the Third World (Croom Helm, London
with Institute of Development Studies, Sussex)

Sjostrom, M. and Sjostrom, R. (1983) How do you spell
Development? a Study of a Literacy Campaign in
Ethiopia (Scandinavian Institute of African
Studies, Upsaala)

Smart, N. (1977) 'Teachers, Teacher Education and the
Community' in Gardner, R. (ed.) Teacher
Education in Developing Countries: Prospects
for the Eighties (Department of Education in
Developing Countries, University of London
Institute of Education) 102-119

Smock, A.C. (1981) Women's Education in Developing
Countries (Praeger, New York)

Somerset, H.C.A. (1974) 'Who goes to Secondary
School? Relevance, Reliability and Equity in
Secondary School Selection' in Court, D. and
Ghai, D. (eds.) Education, Society and

Development (Oxford University Press, Nairobi),
149-186
Somerset, H.C.A. (1979) 'Achievement and Aptitude
Testing in the Certificate of Primary Education
Examination, Kenya' in Dove, L.A. and Cameron,
J. (eds.) Selection for Post-Primary Education
in Developing Countries (University of London
Institute of Education) 54-68
Somerset, H.C.A. (1984) The Development of Public
Examinations in Nepal (Ministry of Education
and Culture, Kathmandu)
Spaulding, S. (1975) 'Are Teachers Facing a Crisis of
Identity?' Prospects 5:2, 209-219
Sri Lanka, Ministry of Education (1982) School Census
(Colombo)
Sri Lanka, Ministry of Education (1984) 'Developing
Curricula for Colleges of Education' (Teacher
Training Unit, Colombo) unpublished ms.
Stones, E. (1984) Supervision in Teacher Education: a
Pedagogical Approach (Methuen, London)
Stromquist, N (1982) 'A review of Educational
Innovations to Reduce Costs' in Financing
Educational Developments (International Devel-
opment Research Centre and Canadian Inter-
national Development Association, Ottawa), 69-
94
Tang, J.P. (1985) 'Private Enrollments and
Expenditure on Education: Some Macro Trends'
International Review of Education 31:1, 103-118
Taylor, D.C. (1983) 'Cost Effectiveness of Teacher
Upgrading by Distance Teaching in Southern
Africa' International Journal of Educational
Development 3:1, 19-31
Taylor, W. (1969) Society and the Education of
Teachers (Faber and Faber, London)
Taylor, W. (1978) Research and Reform in Teacher
Education (NFER, Slough, Bucks) 116-127
Thailand, Ministry of Education, (1975) The Changing
Role of the Teacher and the Influence on
Preparation for the Profession and In-service
Training in Thailand Bangkok, 26-7, quoted in
Watson, K. (1980) Educational Development in
Thailand (Heinemann Educational Books (Asia)
Ltd, Hong Kong, Singapore, Kuala Lumpur) 190
Thompson, A.R. (1981) Education and Development in
Africa (Macmillan, London) 201-252
Thompson, A.R. (ed.) (1982) In-service Education of
Teachers in the Commonwealth (Commonwealth
Secretariat, London)
Thompson, A.R. (1983) 'Community Education in the
1980's: What can we Learn from Experience?'

International Journal of Educational Development 3:1, 3-17

Tisher, R. (1980) 'The Induction of Beginning Teachers' in Hoyle E. and Megarry, J. (eds.) World Year Book of Education (Kogan Page, London)

Tjiposasmito, W. and Cummings, W.K. (1981) The Status and Deployment of Teachers in Indonesia (unpublished ms.)

Treffgarne, C. (1981) 'Language Policy in East and West Africa' in Megarry, J., Nisbet, S. and Hoyle, E. (eds.) The Education of Minorities World Yearbook of Education (Kogan Page, London) 198-202

Trevaskis, G. (1969) In-service Teacher Training in English-speaking Africa (Afro-Anglo-American Programme in Teacher Education, New York) unpublished ms.

Turner, J.D. (1984) 'Educational Policy and Teacher Education' International Journal of Educational Development 4:2, 123-127

Un-Din, J. (1974) Jibon Kotha (autobiography) (Firoze Anwar, Palasi Prkashani, Dacca), unpublished translation by T.Timberg

UNESCO (annual) Statistical Year Book (Paris)

UNESCO (1966) Recommendation concerning the Status of Teachers, Special Intergovernmental Conference, 5 October, (UNESCO, Paris)

UNESCO (1974) UNESCO Educational Simulation Model (ESM) Report no. 29 (Methods and Analysis Division, Department of Social Sciences, Paris), Chapter 2

UNESCO (1975) International Conference on Education, Final Report 35th. session (Paris)

UNESCO (1978) Basic Training Programme in Educational Planning and Management, Book III: Quantitative and Financial Aspects of Educational Planning (Regional Office for Education in Asia and Oceania, Bangkok)

UNESCO (1982) Costs and Financing Obstacles to Universal Primary Education in Africa (Educational Financing Division, Paris)

UNESCO (1984) The Drop-out Problem in Primary Education: Some Case Studies (UNESCO Regional Office for Education in Asia and the Pacific, Bangkok)

UNESCO-UNICEF Cooperative Programme, (1978) 'Small Schools Programme: an Attempt to reach the Poor' in Basic Services for Children: a continuing Search for Learning Priorities, Experiments and Innovations in Education no. 36, (UNESCO,

International Bureau of Education, Paris) 63-71
Vonk, J.H.C. (1983) 'Problems of the Beginning
Teacher' European Journal of Teacher Education
6:2, 133-150
Vulliamy, G. (1981) 'Combining a Constructive Rural
Orientation with Academic Quality: High School
Outstations in Papua New Guinea' International
Journal of Educational Development 1:2, 3-19
Wang, B.C. (1982) 'Sex and Ethnic Differences in
Educational Investment in Malaysia: the Effect
of Reward Structures' in Kelly, G. and Elliot,
C. Women's Education in the Third World:
Comparative Perspectives (State University of
New York Press, New York)
Watson, K. (1980) Educational Developments in
Thailand (Heinemann Educational Books Asia,
Hong Kong, Singapore and Kuala Lumpur)
Watson, K. (1983) 'Rural Primary School Teachers as
Change Agents in the Third World' International
Journal of Educational Development 3:1, 19-32
WCTOP (1975) Teachers and the Political Process 24th
Assembly of Delegates, (World Confederation of
Organisations of the Teaching Profession,
Berlin)
Weil, M. and Joyce, B. (1978) Information Processing
Models of Teaching: Expanding Your Teaching
Repertoire (Prentice-Hall, Englewood Cliffs,
New Jersey)
Wellings, P.A. (1983) 'Unaided Education in Kenya
Blessing or Blight?' Research in Education:
(29) 11-28
Welsh, J. (1979) 'Alternative Forms of Teacher
Education in Low-income Countries with
particular reference to Multi-media Approaches'
(unpublished MA dissertation, University of
London Institute of Education)
Westwood. L.J. (1967a) 'The Role of the Teacher - 1'
Educational Research 9, 122-134
Westwood, L.J. (1967b) 'The Role of the Teacher - 2'
Educational Research 10, 21-37.
Wheeler, A.C.R. (1980) The Role of Supervision in
Improving the Teaching/Learning Process in
Nepal, IIEP Research Report No. 38 (UNESCO,
International Institute for Educational Plann-
ing, Paris)
Whitehead, C. (1981) 'Education in British Colonial
Dependencies 1919-39: A Re-appraisal', Compar-
ative Education, 17:1, 71-80
Williams, P. (1977) 'Too many teachers? A Comparative
Study of the Planning of Teacher Supply in
Britain and Ghana' Comparative Education 13:3,

169-180
Williams, P. (1979) Planning Teacher Demand and
    Supply UNESCO, International Institute for
    Educational Planning,
Wilson, B.R. (1962) 'The Teacher's Role: A
    Sociological Analysis' British Journal of
    Sociology 13:1, 15-33
Winter, S.S. (1982) 'The Adoption of Competency-
    based Regulations for Teacher Certification in
    Massachussetts' Compare 12:2, 153-156
Wong, F.K.H. and Chang, P.M.P, (1975) The Changing
    Pattern of Teacher Education in Malaysia
    (Heinemann Educational Books (Asia) Ltd.)
Woods, P. (1983) Sociology of School: An
    Interactionist Viewpoint (Routledge and Kegan
    Paul, London)
World Bank (1974) Education: Sector Working Paper
    (Washington D.C.)
World Bank (1980) Education: Sector Policy Paper
    (Washington D.C.)
World Bank (1984) World Development Report (Oxford
    University Press, New York)
World Bank (1985) World Development Report (Oxford
    University Press, New York)
Yoloye, E.A. (1983) 'Personality, Education and
    Society: a Yoruba perspective' International
    Journal of Educational Development 3:1, 97-104
Young, B.L. (1979) Teaching Primary Science
    (Longman, London)
Zambia, Ministry of Education (1975) Education for
    Development, Educational Reforms, Study Tour
    Reports, Guyana, Jamaica, Cuba, (Lusaka)
Zeichner, K.M. (1983) 'Alternative Paradigms of
    Teacher Education' Journal of Teacher Education
    34:3, 3-9